The Pioneer Journeys of
William "Ranger" Davidson

Patrick K. Bauman

The Pioneer Journeys of
William "Ranger" Davidson

Biography – Local History – Genealogy
Delaware – Pennsylvania – Ohio

© 2017 by Patrick K. Bauman.
Lakeland, Florida USA

Coedited with Philip F. Bauman
Printed by CreateSpace, an Amazon.com company

ISBN: 978-0-9970724-0-2
Library of Congress Control Number: 2018904025

To my wife, Kathryn, who has so
patiently tolerated my years of searching
for "old dead men with beards."

And for Mom and Dad, who inspired
me to become the family historian.

Thanks to Philip F. Bauman for his encouragement,
valuable suggestions, and editorial assistance.

Thanks to Aaron McWilliams at the Pennsylvania
State Archives for his tireless assistance
with the Revolutionary War chapter.

Contents

1. Partial Lineage Chart 1

2. Introduction 3

3. Ancestry 9

4. William's Father 21

5. Delaware 33

6. Pennsylvania 51

7. Revolutionary War 85

8. Other Pennsylvania Records 129

9. Families 159

10. Ohio 205

11. Final Years 231

12. Subsequent Events 249

Appendix 259

Illustrations 282

Bibliography 284

Partial Lineage Chart

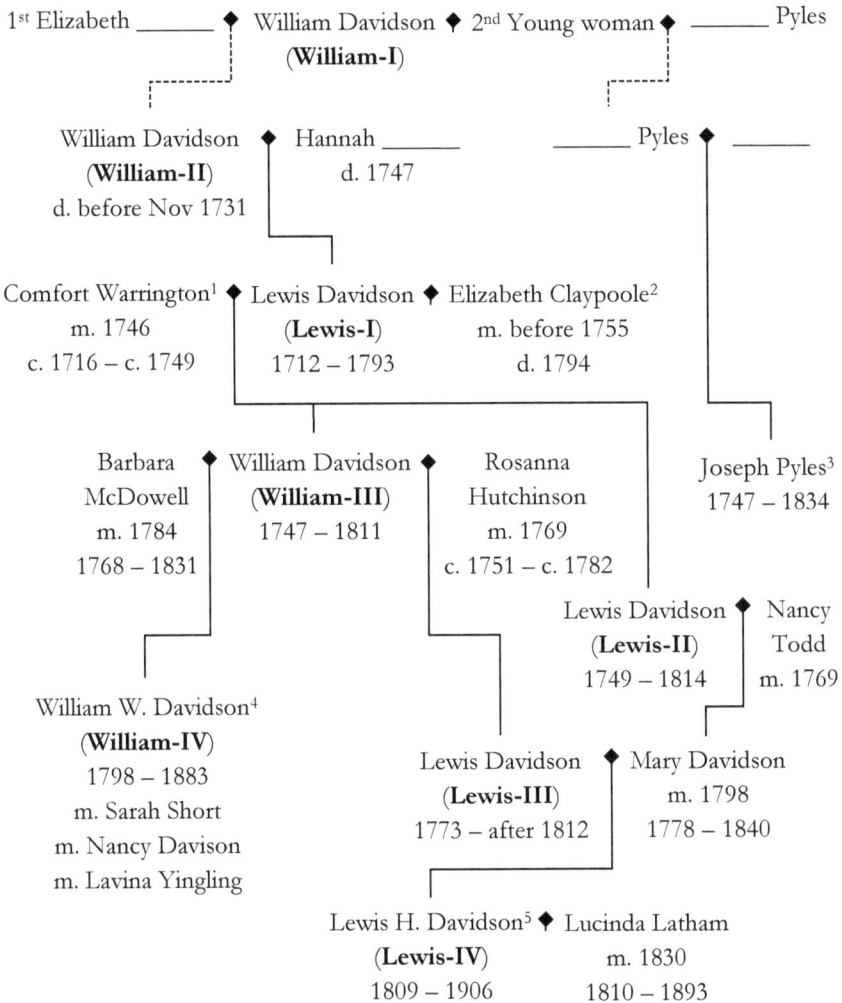

1st Elizabeth _____ ◆ William Davidson ◆ 2nd Young woman ◆ _____ Pyles
(William-I)

William Davidson ◆ Hannah _____   _____ Pyles ◆ _____
(William-II)   d. 1747
d. before Nov 1731

Comfort Warrington[1] ◆ Lewis Davidson ◆ Elizabeth Claypoole[2]
m. 1746   **(Lewis-I)**   m. before 1755
c. 1716 – c. 1749   1712 – 1793   d. 1794

Barbara ◆ William Davidson ◆ Rosanna   Joseph Pyles[3]
McDowell   **(William-III)**   Hutchinson   1747 – 1834
m. 1784   1747 – 1811   m. 1769
1768 – 1831   c. 1751 – c. 1782

Lewis Davidson ◆ Nancy
(Lewis-II)   Todd
1749 – 1814   m. 1769

William W. Davidson[4]
(William-IV)   Lewis Davidson ◆ Mary Davidson
1798 – 1883   **(Lewis-III)**   m. 1798
m. Sarah Short   1773 – after 1812   1778 – 1840
m. Nancy Davison
m. Lavina Yingling

Lewis H. Davidson[5] ◆ Lucinda Latham
(Lewis-IV)   m. 1830
1809 – 1906   1810 – 1893

◆ Marriage.
[1] Lineage traceable to Henry Bagwell, ancient planter of Jamestown (b. 1589).
[2] Lineage traceable to Emperor Charlemagne (742-814).
[3] Preserved tradition about the disappearance of William-I.
[4] Sold remnants of William-III's Ohio tract to create the Village of South Point.
[5] Harbaugh's source of early Davidson family history.
- - Broken lines indicate connections based on tradition.

1

Introduction

With such a common name, it is very possible that our William Davidson could be confused with another and so the subject of this work will here be expeditiously disambiguated from all others.

Our William Davidson was born in Sussex County, Delaware on 20 November 1747. He sojourned to what later became Luzerne Township, Fayette County, Pennsylvania where he lived for over 30 years. While there, he served in the Pennsylvania Militia during the Revolutionary War. He was first married to Rosanna Hutchinson and secondly to Barbara McDowell. In 1799, he migrated to an area now known as South Point, Lawrence County, Ohio where he died on 16 November 1811. This brief synopsis should be adequate for most interested researchers to determine the relevance of this work to their own lineages.

Through the generations, there have been many persons, even within the subject's lineage, named William Davidson. Consequently, to avoid confusion and repetitious clarifications, the central subject of this work will be referenced as William-III. Likewise, the first known Lewis Davidson, who will be shown to be William-III's father, will be called Lewis-I. How these terms were derived is illustrated in the *Partial Lineage Chart* that precedes this chapter. Some of the key family members discussed herein are shown on the chart to help the reader understand their relationships to William-III.

In attempting to provide a well-rounded picture of how William Davidson and his family lived, certain historical information has been included in this work to help the reader appreciate his day-to-day existence. If it may sometimes appear that the activities documented by others were wholly and factually applied to William-III or to his family, this should only be attributed to the limited writing skills of the author, for certain things we can no longer determine. Today we no longer know precisely what food he ate, what books he read, or which roads he traveled. But, we can make educated guesses about the pioneer lifestyle based upon the authentic writings of others who lived during, or at least close to, the same era. The bibliography provides examples of some of these sources.

This work is humbly presented to the reader with apologies offered in advance for any inaccuracies or misstatements that may herein exist. Additionally, a few words must be offered in advance to those grammarians and style hawks who no doubt may be critical of this work on the basis of the English grammar mistakes and questions of style. Admittedly, this author is likely guilty of certain errors of this sort and the bibliography probably does not always precisely follow the rules laid out by Mills' excellent work.[1] But, at least the source citations and bibliographical information is robust and as complete as it could be made, which was considered to be of foremost importance. The quality of this latter aspect certainly surpasses many of the works observed during the completion of this project. As to these topics, no excuse may be offered except to say that the highest quality was attained on the limited skills and budget of the author who was financially unable to acquire an editorial expert to word-smith the manuscript. It is hoped

Introduction

that the readers may overlook these shortcomings in favor of learning new information about their ancestors.

It is all the events that occurred between the birth date and death date, that the story of our subject is hidden, who doubtless never dreamed that a book might someday be written about him. Several vignettes have been written about William Davidson, sketched out by a variety of researchers between the late eighteen hundreds and the 1980's. However, it seems that no one has thoroughly documented what we know of William Davidson's life by actually locating and examining the many available pieces of evidence comprising the puzzle that tell his story. The one work that is perhaps the most thorough would be that of Elizabeth Davidson Harbaugh.[2] Her book, *The Davidson Genealogy* is arguably the single most complete, as well as most often plagiarized work when it comes to William Davidson. A quick search of the internet has shown many entries on web pages using extensive transcripts neatly lifted from Harbaugh's work with no source citation to be found.

One of the motivations for this effort was the frustration that came from the inability to understand how various facts regarding William-III were derived by various authors, including Harbaugh. In many cases, certain historical events in the life of William-III are described by researchers, but no source citation or method of logic was presented to show how these were connected or even associated with the subject. Another motivator came from finding so many inaccuracies on the internet. In many cases, unsupported statements have been seen, contradicting known facts, which indicated that some details were being fabricated and then copied by other researchers virally across the internet.

In this work, every effort has been made during the course of research to verify source information and to carefully document and cite all available sources. Logical explanations as to how some pieces of information were derived or connected to the subject have also been provided.

William "Ranger" Davidson

In no way is any claim being made that every available source document relating to William Davidson has been uncovered. However, extensive efforts were made to acquire copies of the known source documents for first hand evaluation and to also discover additional documents when possible. In certain cases, derivative sources were cited if thought to be substantially reliable, such as the biographical information about Lewis-I's children as well as William-III's children, as provided by Harbaugh.

The name Davidson is not an unusual one, so this places an extra burden on the part of the genealogist. Good practice when researching an individual having such a common name requires the researcher to seek additional evidence for the purpose of substantiating the true identity of the person represented in the source document. Locating such evidence is frequently a difficult task, but fortunately much of the ground-work was laid by Harbaugh, whose book will be frequently cited in the following pages.

All evidence used in the completion of this work will be included in chapter endnotes for the reader's consideration and hopefully will lead the reader to the same conclusions as those of the writer. Admittedly however, some conclusions may seem less certain than others. All too often, the sort of proof one would find most desirable simply no longer exists or perhaps was never created from the beginning.

Surname spelling variations were frequently encountered during research. Perhaps the most common variant is found in *Davison*, but *Davieson*, *Davisson*, and *Daveson* have also been observed. Sometimes the old English long "s" character was used, often mistaken for the letter "f," yielding *Davifon*. During the era under examination, it is not uncommon for the researcher to see the spelling of a name changed, even within the same document, including legal documents such as deeds.

It must be emphasized that since the subject of this work died in 1811, most of the source documents relating to his life were created in the 1700's. The reader should keep in mind that many persons in those days recorded names as they were heard without giving much

Introduction

importance to their correct spelling. A large segment of the population living in that era was not literate and many who could read and write did so with limited skill. In fact, the spelling of many words had not yet been standardized as they are today.

The successful separation of fact from tradition (or downright fiction) and differentiating these is often what lends credibility to works of genealogy. As Hassler points out, "…human memory is very fallible, and tradition is a fragile support for the historian…"[3] However, sometimes tradition is all that is available. Tradition has been included in this work, but it will be made clear to the reader when it seems reliable and when it doesn't and why. The relative believability of tradition is strengthened when multiple sources can be found that relate substantially the same information, when evidence can be found supporting the general possibility of the event, and the provenance of the details can be followed. Such information has also been included when available. In some cases, the general reliability of certain events must be decided by the reader.

---

1.   Elizabeth Shown Mills, *Evidence Explained*, Second Edition (Baltimore, Maryland: Genealogical Publishing Company, Inc., 2012), 885 pages, print.

2.   Elizabeth Davidson Harbaugh, *The Davidson Genealogy* (Ironton, Ohio: self-published, 1948; Ann Arbor, Michigan: Lithoprinted, Edwards Brothers, Inc., 1949), 482 pages, print, Online Computer Library Center number (OCLC): 23167553.

3.   Edgar W. Hassler, *Old Westmoreland: A History of Western Pennsylvania During the Revolution* (Cleveland, Ohio: The Arthur H. Clark Company, 1900), p. 117, digital version, *Google Books* (http//books.google.com : accessed July 2011). The full quote is, "The human memory is very fallible, and tradition is a fragile support for the historian; yet it serves to give life and color to the dull statements of official reports." While it is difficult to disagree, accuracy and full disclosure should not be compromised.

– 3 –

Ancestry

discussion of the earliest roots of the Davidsons is presented
by Harbaugh, taken from a book by Charles Fraser-
MacKintosh that discusses the origin of the name Davidson in
Scotland.[1] The quoted work from Fraser-MacKintosh occurred in the
13th century, but Harbaugh next presents a transcript of a land
transaction in Maryland executed by a man named William Davison in
1663.[2] This sudden leap forward creates a gap in Harbaugh's
documentation spanning more than four hundred years! Although a
colorful story as to the origin of the Davidsons is recounted by
Harbaugh, obviously the branch of the Davidsons from which our
William was descended was not shown to connect genealogically to the
lineage described in the work of Fraser-MacKintosh. While one may
make a reasonable assumption that the name Davidson originated in

9

Scotland, it is in no way sufficient to seek the earliest reference of a name and then claim it as one's own. The name was certainly not unique to a single tribe or clan. Harbaugh may have drawn the idea for her presentation, as well as some of her information, from an earlier work by Callahan.[3]

Without the necessary connections, William-III cannot be tied to Clan Chattan as was supposed by Harbaugh. Therefore, our Davidson pipe music being Tulloch's Salute, their badge being Boxwood, and their home being in Badenoch, are all likewise wishful, but invalid statements. Yet these details have been blindly copied by many persons on the internet as factual.

Unfortunately, little information can be offered here regarding the early Davidson ancestry. The details quickly become murky and source documents are scarce, difficult to find, and generally beyond the scope of this present work. Although it seems somehow less than honorable to be critical of the work of another author without at least improving upon it, at the same time, it is also difficult to ignore exaggerations and errors when they are encountered. However, in spite of whatever criticisms one may find of Harbaugh's work, every descendant of William-III is enormously indebted to Harbaugh whose work is monumental and largely reliable, especially concerning the Revolutionary War figure.[4]

Perhaps one thing that can be provided for consideration on the topic of Davidson ancestry is a summary of the sources examined that point to the possible geographical origin of our Davidson lineage. These are not conclusive, nor derived from evidence, but rather consist of a collection of testimonials of descendants, in other words, family tradition. Which descendants were consulted cannot always be determined with certainty since the authors of the works cited failed to document that information. As already discussed, Harbaugh says our Davidson lineage is of Scotch-Irish origin and this is the prevailing opinion.[5] Callahan, a Daughters of the American Revolution (DAR) record, and Evans, agree with Harbaugh.[6-9] Lewis H. Davidson and

Hanna only mention Ireland.[10-12] So, if the prevailing opinion may be considered reliable, then rest easy that our lineage is Scotch-Irish.

Harbaugh's discussion of the Davidsons prior to emigrating from Scotland to America in Chapter 36 is speculative, disconnected, and difficult to follow. The documents presented from the early American colonial era are not explained and were not shown to be associated with our William-I. Terms and phrases included by Harbaugh such as "it is claimed," "thought to," and "perhaps," are clues to the uncertainty of these connections.

For the benefit of the reader, Harbaugh's portrayal of the early American Davidson lineage is here briefly outlined, using the numbering system from the *Partial Lineage Chart* to distinguish those persons in the lineage having the same names.

William Davidson, also called the emigrant by Harbaugh, and also known as William Davidson-I, was born in Scotland, but lived in Ireland a short time before coming to America in 1649 with his wife, Elizabeth. They settled in Somerset County, Maryland. Harbaugh states that "apparently" Elizabeth was the mother of William, whom Harbaugh calls William Davidson-II. The second William was born in Somerset County and died there before 1732. William-II married Hannah and they became the parents of Lewis (Lewis-I) who was also born in Somerset County in 1712.[13] The widow Hannah and family migrated to Sussex County, Delaware by 1732. According to Harbaugh, Hannah died in 1747. Lewis-I was the father of William Davidson, central to this work, sometimes called "Ranger" and herein called William-III since he was identified as the third William Davidson in the direct lineage. Lewis-I, father of William-III, is discussed in detail in the following pages because the historical events of his life are so closely connected to William-III.

Although the lineage prior to Lewis-I was not extensively examined in the completion of this work, sufficient sources were found to confirm the Davidson lineage in America given by Harbaugh with the only exception of William-I, the emigrant, and his wife.

William "Ranger" Davidson

Harbaugh also includes a brief account as to the fate of William-I stating that, in his old age, he went out one evening to collect firewood, expecting to return within a couple hours, but was never seen again. The following day, a search party "found evidence the Indians had been in the woods" which led to the conclusion that he had been murdered or taken captive. Given our knowledge of the early Davidsons, this event could have occurred in Maryland, probably in the latter half of the 17th century. The family tradition concerning this event was passed down from a grandson (possibly a great-grandson) of William-I's widow. This grandson, Joseph, was descended from William-I's second marriage, to a "young woman," to whom William-I was married when he disappeared. After William-I vanished, his second wife married a man surnamed Pyles. Harbaugh maintains that Joseph sometimes visited Lewis and Mary Davidson, who had settled in Harrison County, Ohio, and through whom this account survived.[14] This Lewis, herein called Lewis-III, was the second son of William-III and first wife Rosanna Hutchinson, who did indeed settle in Harrison County, Ohio.

An even less detailed account was directly given by Lewis H. Davidson (Lewis-IV; a son of Lewis-III and Mary) in a newspaper article in which he simply wrote that William-I, "was captured by the Indians before the Revolutionary War and was lost to all knowledge of his friends."[15] Evans also recorded that William Davidson, the emigrant, was killed by Indians.[16] However, Evans erroneously recorded that William-I was William-III's father, when he was actually William-III's great-grandfather. This same error was recorded in the article published earlier by Lewis-IV thus betraying Evans' likely source for his account. The reader is invited to refer to the *Partial Lineage Chart* shown previously to assist in following the relationships just described.

The Joseph who was the bearer of the information concerning William-I's disappearance was named by Harbaugh, but very little additional information was given about him. Joseph Pyles was born about 1747. While residing in Pennsylvania, he enlisted in the army in August 1776 and was made a sergeant. He was very active and served in several capacities throughout the Revolutionary War. In October 1832, while residing in Hopewell Township, Washington County, Pennsylvania, he applied for a pension. His application was accepted along with his testimony as to his service, which was then checked against the available records, supported by witnesses, and found to be credible by pension authorities. The pension file, claim s. 5169, is available through www.fold3.com. Along with the detailed account of his service, it may be of interest to the descendants of Joseph to know that his pension file bears examples of his handwriting and his original signature. Joseph received a pension benefit for about two years. He died 3 September 1834.[17] Among the documents in Joseph's pension file is a sworn statement by Thomas Davidson of Fayette County, Pennsylvania, identified in the file as a brother of Jeremiah Davidson (both were sons of Lewis-I and half-brothers of William-III). The stated relationships remove all doubt as to the identity of the deponent. In the deposition provided by Thomas, details about Joseph indicate that he and Joseph were well acquainted before and following the war. These details are significant in the sense that they prove the existence of Joseph Pyles and also show that he was well acquainted with the Davidson family.

This bit of family tradition is included because the details regarding how the tradition was preserved are significant. It was found that fragments of the account of William-I survived through three different branches of the family including the Harrison County, Ohio descendants, the Lawrence County, Ohio descendants, and the Pennsylvania descendants. Sworn statements in Joseph Pyle's pension file, which was the only such file found bearing this name, provides a connection between Joseph and the Davidsons. Finally, the account of William-I was later published by Harbaugh. The reader may accept or reject this supposition, but the author would uphold the authenticity of this family tradition, which by definition is an account that cannot be proved, but nevertheless is believed to be authentic.

The only documentation offered by Harbaugh regarding William-I are two transcripts of land records. The first was executed 19

December 1663 and transfers 300 acres of land from William Davison to Thomas Readley, "...for Service done in this Province by myself who came in the year 1649..."[18] The second record says that William Davidson of Somerset County, "...proved 250 acres of land for transporting himself, Elizabeth his wife, Ann, Jane and David Davidson his children into the province..." This record was executed 24 March 1670.[19] Unfortunately, there is no information linking the two records, which could very well relate to two different persons. As intriguing as these documents may be, no actual link is shown connecting William-II to the William-I named by Harbaugh. The absence of further evidence compels us to reduce this connection only to a possibility. This also seems to be the point at which Harbaugh's work on the early Davidson lineage becomes fragmented and uncertain. This isn't to say that more convincing evidence does not exist; however, neither Harbaugh nor this author was able to locate any record offering proof of the relationship.

Clear evidence was found, however, linking William-II and wife Hannah to son Lewis-I. By February 1732, Hannah migrated with her children to Sussex County, Delaware and settled on a 179-acre tract of land that William-II agreed to purchase from Thomas Worington (Warrington) at a cost of £46.[20] The indenture says that Hannah Davidson was then the "widow & relict of Willm Davidson of Somerset [sic] County in the Province of Maryland." Further, a survey associated with the indenture was drawn for "Hanah [sic] Davidson widow," which means that William-II was deceased even before the date of the survey, 16 November 1731.[21] These records thus show that Hannah was married to William-II and that William-II died in Somerset County, Maryland, most likely in 1731.

Another document yields Hannah's occupation. A record for the registered earmark used by Hannah for cattle, sheep, and hogs (crop and split both ears) was located in the Delaware State Archives.[22] Some of the farms of that era were not fenced, so the livestock could wander. The earmark was used as a method of uniquely identifying livestock so the rightful farmer could claim ownership. The earmark was later generally replaced by use of branding, and still later by tagging. Given this information, it is logical to further presume that William-II and Hannah were farmers.

Among the Delaware land records there exists another transaction pertinent to this discussion. In August 1753, the heirs of Hannah, listed as "Lewes," Mary, and Sarah (the latter married to John Arderly) sold the 179-acre parcel, previously owned by Hannah, to Jacob Warrington.[23] Thus, from the Delaware records cited, it was confirmed that William-II was married to Hannah, and that they were the parents of Lewis-I. In still another separate transaction in 1784, the children of Hannah are directly referenced as heirs of Hannah Davidson.[24]

According to the survey conducted in November 1731 for the 179-acre tract of land, later recorded in Hannah's name, we can learn one further small bit of information about William-II. The parcel was "purchased in partnership" with a man named Joshua Stockley. Unfortunately, William-II died before the deed was recorded and the details of the partnership were lost to history; however, this explains the reason the family was moving from Maryland to Delaware.

Joshua Stockley owned an 82-acre tract adjoining Hannah's land and one might speculate that the partnership was an agreement to somehow share in the production efforts or the profits of their combined farms. As to Hannah, Harbaugh presented a transcript of the "acc't of her administration" dated 30 July 1747, thus providing the year of Hannah's demise.[25] Since this record was recorded in the name of "Hannah Davidson," we also know that she didn't remarry after William-II died. Unfortunately, this single record was not found by archivists at the Delaware Archives and therefore could not be personally reviewed.

In summary, we have so far confirmed that William-II, of Somerset County, Maryland was a farmer and had agreed to purchase a 179-acre tract of land in Sussex County, Delaware before he died. The deed to the land was recorded in the name of his widow, Hannah, who continued operation of the family farm along with her children.

Hannah died in 1747, leaving her children, Lewis-I, Mary, and Sarah, as heirs to her property.

The many pieces of evidence showing that the Lewis in Delaware is our Lewis-I, and that Lewis-I was the father of William-III are discussed in detail in the following pages.

1. Charles Fraser-MacKintosh, *Antiquarian Notes a Series of Papers regarding Families and Places in the Highlands* (Inverness, Scotland: printed at the Advertiser Office, 1865), pp. 161-167, *Google Books* (http://books.google.com : accessed April 2011). Harbaugh mentions Fraser-MacKintosh as the source for the very earliest ancestral information of the Davidsons, but her presentation infers a factual connection between the Davidsons referenced in *Antiquarian Notes* and our present day lineage which seems misleading.

2. Elizabeth Davidson Harbaugh, *The Davidson Genealogy* (Ironton, Ohio: self-published, 1948; Ann Arbor, Michigan : Lithoprinted, Edwards Brothers, Inc., 1949), 482 pages, print, OCLC: 23167553.

3. James Morton Callahan, *Genealogical and Personal History of the Upper Monongahela Valley West Virginia*, Volume III (New York: Lewis Historical Publishing Company, 1912), page 1167, digital version, *Google Books* (http://books.google.com : accessed April 2011).

4. The Tilney lineage as shown in Harbaugh's work, which serves as a bridge from William-III to many of the medieval lineages, is incorrect. No source document has been found linking the John Tilney on the Eastern Shore to the John Tilney in England, son of John Tilney and Alice Holland. Furthermore, the Tilney lineage as depicted by Harbaugh contains several inaccuracies when comparing her work to other sources. Harbaugh may have relied, in whole or in part, upon the work of a researcher named Gustave Anjou now known to have created many false lineages including one for the Tilney family. Serious researchers of this lineage should avoid the largely bogus work of Gustave Anjou, but may find more legitimacy in some of the ancient lineages traced to medieval times following the Claypoole line (second wife of Lewis-I). Anjou was paid large fees for creating genealogies for his clients which were passed off as legitimate works to his unwitting victims. For a period of time, Harbaugh was contemporary with Anjou who died in 1942, about the time *The Davidson*

Genealogy was being compiled. If Harbaugh did indeed rely upon Anjou's work she did so as a victim. Anjou's work was not brought under suspicion until long after his death. Although the Tilney component of Harbaugh's book is unreliable, the work Harbaugh presented pertaining to William-III was found to be legitimate and accurate apart from occasional typographical errors commonly found in such works.

5. Although the technical definition may be argued, being Scotch-Irish will here simply refer to one who emigrated from Scotland and settled for some period of time in Ireland before leaving there for some other destination.

6. Callahan, p. 1167.

7. *The Official roster of the soldiers of the American Revolution buried in the state of Ohio*, Vol 1, Daughters of the American Revolution of Ohio (Columbus, Ohio: F. J. Heer Printing Co., 1929), p. 114, entry for "Davidson, William, Lawrence Co.," print, Bartow Genealogical and Historical Library, Bartow, Florida.

8. Nelson W. Evans, *History of Scioto County, Ohio* (Portsmouth, Ohio: Self-published, 1903), reprint (Markham, Virginia: The Apple Manor Press), Part 5, p. 1224.

9. Harbaugh, p. 120.

10. *Commemorative Biographical Record of the Counties of Harrison and Carroll, Ohio* (Chicago: J. H. Beers & Co., 1891), article: "Lewis H. Davidson," pp. 446-453, digital version, *Google Books* (http://books.google.com : accessed April 2013).

11. Charles Augustus Hanna, *Historical Collections of Harrison County in the State of Ohio* (New York: privately printed, 1900), p. 483, digital version, *Internet Archive* (http://www.archive.org : accessed April 2011).

12. These authors may be found in various endnotes throughout this book and also in the bibliography. During examination of their historical works it quickly became apparent that several of the authors, or compilers, whose works are cited herein, freely duplicated the works of the others. Limited effort was expended attempting to determine their true sources. These authors are presented below with the year their works were published and each entry is followed by those thought to be their source(s). This is not to say that each copied in whole the work of the others, but based upon their content, some

portion of the details appeared to be reproduced. This information is somewhat speculative:

Callahan (1912): compare to Ellis.

DAR (1929): DAR member contributed information; compare to Evans.

Davidson (Lewis H., 1890): original.

Ellis (1882): descendants of Jeremiah Davidson in Pennsylvania.

Evans (1903): compare to Hardesty; descendants of William W. Davidson in Lawrence County, Ohio.

Ferguson (1988): compare to Evans, Harbaugh, and Hardesty.

Hanna (1900): descendants of Lewis H. Davidson in Harrison County, Ohio.

Harbaugh (1948): compare to Evans; Hardesty; numerous descendants including Lewis H. Davidson.

Hardesty (1882): descendants of William W. Davidson in Lawrence County, Ohio.

For example, see Ellis, p. 636 and compare to Callahan, p. 1167. The Davidson entry recorded by Ellis and Callahan were likely contributed by descendants of William-III's younger half-brother, Jeremiah. The entry by Callahan (1912) was largely taken from the earlier work of Ellis (1882), but certain events not included by Ellis were added by Callahan.

13.   Harbaugh, pp. 124-125. Hannah's unmarried surname has not been discovered. The surname *Stockley* has been seen on the internet, but no one contacted by email could provide a documented source and many persons questioned about this subject never replied; this is thought to be fabricated.

14.   Harbaugh, pp. 122-123, discusses the disappearance of William-I.

15.   *Commemorative Biographical Record of the Counties of Harrison and Carroll, Ohio*, article: "Lewis H. Davidson," pp. 446-453. The generations listed in this article are confused. Lewis-IV omits Lewis-I, father of William-III and also William-II. This would make William-I the 3rd great-grandfather of Lewis-IV, rather than a single great-grandfather as was presented.

16.   Evans, p. 1224, briefly mentions William-I's disappearance.

17.   "United States Revolutionary War Pension and Bounty Land Warrant Applications, 1800-1900," pension number S. 5169 for Joseph Pyles, Pennsylvania, digital images of penned documents, *FamilySearch* (http://familysearch.org : accessed 7 July 2015), from "Revolutionary War

Ancestry

Pension and Bounty-Land Warrant Application Files," database and images, *Fold3* (http://www.fold3.com : n.d.), citing NARA microfilm publication M804 (Washington, D.C.: National Archives and Records Administration, 1974).

18.   Harbaugh, p. 121, citing "Transfers-1649, Hall of Records, Annapolis, Maryland, Lib. 6, Fol. 118, Transfers – 1649."

19.   Harbaugh, p. 121, citing "Hall of records, Annapolis, Maryland, Lib. 11, Fol. - 298."

20.   Sussex County, Delaware, Deed Book I: 29-30, "Deed of Sale Thom^s Worington to Hann^h Davison," 7 February 1732, recorded 6-9 February 1732, Record Group 4555, Delaware Public Archives, Dover; digital copy of penned document, obtained November 2015.

21.   Sussex County, Delaware, Shankland Survey Book 2: pages 71-72, Survey for "Hanah Davidson," untitled, 16 November 1731, Record Group 4555, Delaware Public Archives, Dover; digital copy of penned document, obtained December 2015.

22.   Sussex County, Delaware, Deed Book Q16: page 298, "Hanah Davison her ear mark for Cattle Sheep and Hoggs," recorded 25 May 1744, Record Group 4555.031, Delaware Public Archives, Dover, digital copy of penned document, obtained December 2015.

23.   Sussex County, Delaware, Deed Book I: page 68, "Jacob Warrington from Lewis Davidson and sisters Deed," 6 August 1753, recorded 7 February 1754, Record Group 4555, Delaware Public Archives, Dover; digital copy of penned document, obtained November 2015.

24.   Elaine Hastings Mason and F. Edward Wright, *Land Records of Sussex County, Delaware 1782-1789, Deed Book N No. 13* (Westminster, Maryland: Willow Bend Books, 2002), p. 4, print.

25.   Harbaugh, p. 125. The reference made by Harbaugh is incomplete and difficult to discern, but appears to be, "Index #1, Record. Liber 1, P. 35. Dover Del. Archives." The record title seems to be, "Hannah Davidson, Dec'd – acc't of her administration 1747 p. 35." The record heading may be, "Hannah Davidson – Estate." It appears that the date her estate was settled was July 30, 1747.

19

4

William's Father

Confusion existed for several decades regarding the identity of William Davidson's parents. This is evidenced by the conflicting statements made in various historical works consulted. Clarity on this point is necessary before certain other important events of William's early life can be established. One author, Hanna, recorded that William-III's father was also named William and that he came from Ireland.[1] But, Hanna's work was undoubtedly drawn from an article penned by Lewis H. Davidson (Lewis-IV), a direct descendant of William-III.[2] Another author, Evans, agrees with Lewis-IV.[3] The entry recorded in the "Roster of Revolutionary Soldiers buried in the State of Ohio" cites Evans.[4] Meanwhile, Ellis infers that Jeremiah (a half-brother of William-III) was a Davidson family immigrant.[5] Callahan concurs with Ellis.[6] However, not one of these statements is correct.[7]

William "Ranger" Davidson

Here we must once again look to Harbaugh who conducted a search of the records at the Register of Wills office at Uniontown, the seat of Fayette County, Pennsylvania government, to uncover a document revealing the true identity of William-III's father.[8] Working in the pre-photocopier days, Harbaugh presents a transcript of the last will of Lewis Davidson (Lewis-I) providing convincing evidence of the true relationship, which also passed the scrutiny of Dorman.[9] For purposes of this present work, a copy of the will was acquired and examined. The transcript presented by Harbaugh, which was found to be materially faithful to the source document, identifies the children of Lewis-I, and names William as a son.[10] The identity of the William named in the will must now be identified with our William-III using some additional facts.[11]

In this case, land records may be used for evidence. The tract of land Lewis-I had purchased on the east side of the Monongahela River in southwestern Pennsylvania is here examined. The significance of this record is not found in the transaction itself, but in the location of Lewis-I whose parcel is in close proximity to several family members. In order to gain the full appreciation of this, a few relationships must first be explained.

Lewis-I's second marriage was to Elizabeth Claypoole.[12,13] Elizabeth's marriage to Lewis-I was also her second marriage. Her previous husband, Thomas Conwell, had died sometime after their second child was born.[14,15] Thomas and Elizabeth had two sons, William and Jehu (reportedly sometimes called John) Conwell. According to Harbaugh and others, William and Jehu were born in Delaware, but later moved to Pennsylvania.[16-19] In fact, there is evidence indicating that William Conwell moved to Pennsylvania at the same time as Lewis-I (more about this in the *Pennsylvania* chapter).

Examination of the "Warrantee Township Map" of Luzerne Township in Fayette County, Pennsylvania reveals that William Conwell owned a tract of land adjoining his stepfather's northern boundary.[20] Thomas Davidson, third son of Lewis-I, is found bordering the eastern edge of Lewis-I's settlement. William-III, oldest son of Lewis-I, was William Conwell's northern neighbor. Jehu Conwell occupied the parcel on his brother's eastern border. After Lewis-I died in 1793, his fourth son, Jeremiah, received the land formerly belonging to Lewis-I, as specified in Lewis-I's last will. At this point, all the sons, as well as stepsons, of Lewis-I are accounted within Luzerne Township, except for Lewis-I's second son, also named Lewis (Lewis-II). According to Harbaugh and Dorman, Lewis-II settled in Fort Cumberland, Maryland which explains his absence from Fayette County.[21]

The close proximity of so many related persons could not have occurred by chance. The "Warrantee Township Map," which was created by the Land Office from land records, confirms the identities of the persons named in the last will of Lewis-I and thereby establishes Lewis-I as William-III's true father. More evidence as to this relationship will be found in the following chapters.

Although the mental image of a pioneer may be one of self-sufficiency and independence, the close proximity of the settlements of these family members produces the picture of a clannish family that maintained close relationships and who carefully orchestrated their relocation to a wild and dangerous frontier environment in a way to assure mutual care and protection. There can be little doubt that the members of this family assisted each other in building homes, clearing fields, planting and harvesting crops, and many other tasks required for their survival.

Although not conclusive by itself, it is notable that in all the documentation examined, no evidence was found indicating the presence of a second person called Lewis Davidson in Fayette County prior to 1793. While perhaps not a remarkable observation, since many persons could have lived and died in Pennsylvania for which there are no extant records, it is at the least encouraging to know that nothing contrary to what is being presented here was found.

It is difficult to continue without making a divergence from the main topic to clarify a point which deserves discussion. Harbaugh says that Lewis-I operated "the first ferry at Red Stone."[22] This reference is to a community originally called Redstone Old Fort which was later called Fort Burd and afterward became Brownsville. Complete records of the early ferries in this region do not exist.[23] However, sufficient evidence does exist to show that not only was Lewis-I not the first ferryman, but Davidson's ferry was not even located at Redstone. Several ferries were in operation on the Monongahela River around the time that Lewis-I assumed the operation of his ferry and this may have produced the confusion. The first ferry claim is a bit of family tradition that must here be dispelled.

The "Warrantee Township Map" of Luzerne Township specifies the partial location of a road labeled "road to Crawford's ferry" leading directly to the land of a pioneer named John Crawford.[24] Thus, this ferry was already in operation in Crawford's name.[25] This tract, called *Fortune*, was warranted by Crawford and later transferred to Lewis-I by patent.[26] Therefore, Lewis-I could not have been the first ferry owner. The *Fortune* tract is located just north of where Muddy Creek spills into the Monongahela River (about a mile south of the small current-day community of Isabella), some eight miles (as the crow flies) south of Brownsville (Redstone Old Fort).[27,28]

Ellis says that Jeremiah Davidson "continued the [operation of the] Ferry established by Crawford" from which one may infer that Jeremiah procured the ferry from the original owner. However, as is shown in the will of Lewis-I, Jeremiah (a half-brother of William-III) received the ferry and the land to which it was attached as an inheritance from his father. So records show that Jeremiah was the third owner of what became known as Davidson's Ferry, not the second owner.[29,30]

As were most ferries of that era, Lewis-I's vessel could be described as a large raft constructed of logs and likely had split boards or puncheons for decking which created a flat surface on which the passengers stood for the short journey. As was common, it was likely a rope ferry wherein one or more heavy ropes, stretched across the river, were anchored on both shores and also attached to the vessel to keep it from drifting downstream. The operator propelled the ferry across the river by pulling a second rope in the desired direction.

Ferry operators charged a toll to their customers, however, a law regulating ferries in Fayette and Westmoreland Counties wasn't passed until the Pennsylvania *Act of March 2, 1827*.[31] Prior to that date it is difficult to discover the tolls charged by the ferry owners because they could set their own rates. Unfortunately, the *Act of March 2, 1827* was passed more than 30 years after Lewis-I died, perhaps rendering the costs set by Pennsylvania invalid for comparison. Instead, we can look to legislation passed earlier by the state of Virginia. Although we don't know how much Lewis-I charged, his fee was likely similar to the Virginia rates established for other ferries operating on the Monongahela River in 1792:

Every man or horse – 4¢
Every coach, wagon, or chariot, including the driver – 24¢
Every four-wheeled chaise or phaeton, including the driver – 16¢
Every two-wheeled riding carriage – 8¢
Every hogshead of tobacco – 4¢
Every head of neat cattle – 4¢
Every sheep, hog, goat, or lamb – 0.8¢[32]

Lewis-I possibly suffered from an illness during the last several years of his life. He recorded in his last will, dated 6 July 1787, that he was then, "…low and weak of body but of perfect mind and memory…"[33] He was then 75 years of age. Lewis-I died in Fayette County and he was buried in Dunlap's Creek Presbyterian Church Cemetery in Redstone Township. We are fortunate that Ellis documented the inscription on the headstones of both Lewis-I and his second wife, Elizabeth Claypoole-Conwell, which have probably since become lost or unreadable. The description made so eloquent by Ellis would be difficult to improve upon:

William "Ranger" Davidson

The Dunlap's Creek graveyard, in the centre of which stood the old Dunlap's Creek log church, contains within its weather-beaten and time-worn old stone-wall inclosure many reminders of the past and of those who were foremost among the pioneers. There are to be found in it many handsome monuments, as well as neglected graves and broken tablets, which tell how apt the living are to forget the dead. Many old tombstone inscriptions are defaced and illegible, others are still easily read. Among the latter are those erected to the memories of...Lewis Davidson, Nov. 16, 1793; "Elizabeth, ye wief of Lewis Davidson," April 24, 1794...[sic].[34]

Ellis recorded that Lewis-I, Jeremiah Davidson, Thomas Davidson, and William Conwell and their wives were members of this Church.[35] As noted, the wife of Lewis-I, Elizabeth, was also buried there, however, as Harbaugh points out, Elizabeth was the second wife of Lewis-I and was not the mother of William-III.[36] To locate evidence as to Lewis-I's first wife we must temporarily leave southwestern Pennsylvania and look to records some three hundred miles southeast.

---

1. Charles Augustus Hanna, *Historical Collections of Harrison County in the State of Ohio* (New York: privately printed, 1900), pp. 8, 483-484, digital version, *Internet Archive* (http://www.archive.org : accessed April 2011).

2. *Commemorative Biographical Record of the Counties of Harrison and Carroll, Ohio* (Chicago: J. H. Beers & Co., 1891), article: "Lewis H. Davidson," pp. 446-453, digital version, *Internet Archive* (http://www.archive.org : accessed April 2013).

3. Nelson W. Evans, *History of Scioto County, Ohio* (Portsmouth, Ohio: Self-published, 1903), reprint (Markham, Virginia: The Apple Manor Press), Part 5, pp. 1224-1226.

4. *The Official roster of the soldiers of the American Revolution buried in the state of Ohio*, Vol 1, Daughters of the American Revolution of Ohio (Columbus, Ohio: F. J. Heer Printing Co., 1929), p. 114, entry for "Davidson, William, Lawrence Co.," print, Bartow Genealogical and Historical Library, Bartow, Florida.

5. Franklin Ellis, *History of Fayette County Pennsylvania with Biographical Sketches of many of its Pioneers and Prominent Men* (Philadelphia: L. H. Everts & Co., 1882), p. 636, digital version, *Internet Archive* (http://www.archive.org : accessed April 2011).

6. James Morton Callahan, *Genealogical and Personal History of the Upper Monongahela Valley West Virginia*, Volume III (New York: Lewis Historical Publishing Company, 1912), p. 1167, digital version, *Google Books* (http://books.google.com : accessed April 2011).

7. In fairness, apart from the Official Roster, these works were compilations of testimonials given by living descendants of early residents. The purpose was to create local histories by preserving the recollections of the contributors that would otherwise have been forever lost. The entries presented in these books provide a valuable and important resource for historians and genealogists alike. However, the reader must keep in mind that the information recorded was frequently based upon memories rather than documentation and sources are rarely, if ever, given.

8. Elizabeth Davidson Harbaugh, *The Davidson Genealogy* (Ironton, Ohio: self-published, 1948; Ann Arbor, Michigan : Lithoprinted, Edwards Brothers, Inc., 1949), p. 128, print, OCLC: 23167553.

9. John Frederick Dorman, FASG, *Adventurers of Purse and Person, Virginia 1607-1624/5*, 4th ed., 4th printing, Volume 1, Families A-F (Baltimore, MD: Genealogical Publishing Company, 2004), pp. 90-116, print. Dorman also cites "Family records provided by Henry Clay Russell, Ashland, KY," whose contributions were not located.

10. Lewis Davidson, Will of Lewis Davidson (Lewis-I), untitled, Register of Wills, Will Book 1, p. 86, photocopy of penned document, dated 6 July 1787, recorded 28 November 1793, proved 4 February 1794, Uniontown, Fayette County, Pennsylvania.

11. Harbaugh presented the transcript of the "Will of Lewis Davidson," but failed to explain how the identities of the persons represented belong to the correct

lineage. Harbaugh further provides the same birthdate and birthplace for Lewis-I as Dorman, but offers no other source apart from the will.

12. Sussex County, Delaware, Court of Chancery, Case File C, number 25, several documents dated between 12 December 1758 and 10 February 1759, Record Group 1225.026, photocopies of penned documents, obtained September 2016, Delaware Public Archives, Dover. Elizabeth Claypoole is named as the wife of Lewis Davison (Lewis-I).

13. Elizabeth is referenced, but not explicitly named in the will of Lewis-I.

14. Harbaugh, pp. 360-362.

15. T. C. Conwell, *The Conwell's of Dyer's Delight*, not published, dated 1984, p. 30, typewritten, 91 pages, digital version, *Ancestry* (http://www.ancestry.com : accessed October 2013).

16. Harbaugh, pp. 360-362.

17. Ellis, p. 634.

18. George Dallas Albert, "The Frontier Forts of Western Pennsylvania," incorporated into *Report of the Commission to Locate the Site of the Frontier Forts of Pennsylvania*, Volume Two (Clarence M. Busch, State Printer of Pennsylvania, 1896), pp. 395-396, digital version, *Google Books* (http://books.google.com : accessed August 2011).

19. The events of William and Jehu (John) Conwell may be found in varying detail in other published historical works as well as those noted. It has been consistently recorded that the Conwell brothers came to southwestern Pennsylvania in June 1767. It is interesting to note that these works refer to William Conwell being a Captain in 1767, more than ten years before he served in the Pennsylvania Militia.

20. John H. Campbell, Chief Draftsman, *Warrantee Township Map: Fayette County, Luzerne Township* (Harrisburg, Pennsylvania: Records of the Land Office, 1920), Record Group 17, Series 17.522, Pennsylvania State Archives, digital version, *Commonwealth of Pennsylvania's Enterprise Portal* (http://www.portal .state.pa.us : accessed March 2011).

21. Harbaugh, p. 336; Dorman, p. 116. Both authors cited the will left by Lewis-II in Maryland.

22. Harbaugh, p. 128.

23. S. B. Nelson, *Nelson's Biographical Dictionary and Historical Reference Book of Fayette County Pennsylvania* (Uniontown, PA: S. B. Nelson Publisher, 1900), p. 358, digital version, *Google Books* (http://google.books.com : accessed May 2011). A public record, such as a license, for Lewis Davidson's ferry was not found, but he left this improvement to his son Jeremiah in his last will in 1793.

24. Campbell, *Warrantee Township Map: Fayette County, Luzerne Township.*

25. Ellis, p. 636. There were many Crawford's in Luzerne Township in the late 18th century and several of them operated ferries, mostly in the northern part of the township. The John Crawford in this discussion was not related to the northern Crawford's who were Quakers.

26. Callahan, p. 1167, also says that Crawford was the original owner of the ferry. However, Callahan incorrectly puts next ownership of the ferry in the hands of Jeremiah, omitting Lewis-I.

27. Boyd Crumrine, *History of Washington County, Pennsylvania* (Philadelphia: L. H. Everts & Co., 1882), p. 636, digital version, *Google Books* (http://books.google.com : accessed April 2011); David Hayfield Conyngham, *Reminiscences of David Hayfield Conyngham* (Wilkes-Barr, PA: Wyoming Historical and Genealogical Society, 1904), p. 94, digital version, *Google Books* (http://books.google.com : accessed April 2011). These books are included because they make brief but direct references to "Davidson's Ferry."

28. Careful examination of current day maps still show roads reaching toward the river's edge thought to be where the ferry was situated. To find the general location, follow the Monongahela River south from Brownsville and look for an easily distinguishable series of bends somewhat akin to "Mickey Mouse ears" which make for a quick reference point on modern-day maps. Continue south and look for the small community of Isabella and then to Muddy Creek and Jacobs Ferry Road.

29. Ellis, pages 249 (1794), 251 (1852), 633 (1882), and 636.

According to Ellis, on page 636 (but not verified), the land and the ferry remained in the hands of Jeremiah Davidson until he died in 1850. These were then purchased by Adam Jacobs in 1862 when it became known as "Jacob's Ferry." Callahan restates this account, but it is likely that Callahan's work was based upon the work of Ellis.

Ellis also recorded that David Davidson established a ferry using a steamboat, but this was later discontinued. Using the map provided by Ellis, it was determined that this ferry was situated on *Dispute Ended*, a portion of which was purchased by William-III's son David in 1807 for $600 (located opposite modern-day Crucible). Although it was called "David Davidson's Ferry" it is uncertain whether this was William-III's son or a later descendent. There is no mention or evidence that William-III ever established a ferry himself.

30.   James Veech, *The Monongahela of Old* (Pittsburg, PA.: 1858-1892), p. 162, digital version, *Google Books* (http://books.google.com : accessed April 2011). Veech mentions Davidson's lower ferry (David's) in reference to some bandits who were said to have a hideout between there and Rice's Landing, about a mile downstream from David Davidson's ferry.

31.   Lewis Clark Walkinshaw, *Annals of Southwestern Pennsylvania*, Volume II (New York: Lewis Historical Publishing Company, Inc, 1939), p. 332, digital version, *Google Books* (http://books.google.com : accessed January 2016). The rates in 1827 were set as follows: 3¢ for each person on foot; 6¼¢ for each person with a horse; 18¾¢ for each one-horse carriage including passengers; 37½¢ for each carriage and two or three horses; 62½¢ for each wagon and four horses; 4½¢ for each horse, mare, or gelding with rider; 2¢ for each cow, bull, or steer; 1¢ for each hog or sheep.

32.   Samuel Shepherd, *The Statutes at Large of Virginia*, Vol. I, from October Session 1792 to December Session 1806 (Richmond: Printed by Samuel Shepherd, 1835), pp. 152-158, digital version, *Google Books* (http://books.google.com : accessed January 2016). Although the rates vary from 3 to 25 cents, most were set at the base rate of 4 cents for each person and a horse. Eight ferries crossing the Monongahela are listed in this source and in all such cases, the toll was consistently set at the same base rate of 4 cents. Some of the laws surrounding the operation of ferries based on Virginia law provide for interesting exemptions. For example, express riders essentially on official military business could ride "ferry free." Those employees of ferrymen considered essential were exempt from militia duty. Some ferry owners who maintained a "necessary" (outhouse) could do so without further incurring an extra fee on their license.

William's Father

33. Lewis Davidson, Will of Lewis Davidson (Lewis-I), untitled, Register of Wills, Will Book 1, p. 86, photocopy of penned document, dated 6 July 1787, recorded 28 November 1793, proved 4 February 1794, Uniontown, Fayette County, Pennsylvania.

34. Ellis, pp. 735-736.

35. Ibid.

36. Harbaugh, p. 128.

5

Delaware

How Harbaugh traced the Davidsons to Delaware is not known, but nevertheless, the records are there.[1] It was previously mentioned that Hannah and her children, Lewis-I, Mary, and Sarah departed from Somerset County, Maryland and travelled about 50 miles (very roughly guessed) northeast to Sussex County, Delaware where William-II had agreed to purchase a tract of land. Unfortunately, he died in Maryland before the survey and the deed were prepared. We also know from these documents that he and a man named Joshua Stockley had formed a partnership in conjunction with the land purchase. But, the nature of this partnership is left to guesswork. A survey was completed in November 1731 for Hannah, widow of William-II, and the deed was recorded in her name in February 1732.[2,3] This 179-acre tract of land was located on the north side of a creek called Bracey Branch on Angola Neck in Indian River Hundred and became the family farm for the next 21 years.[4-6]

It is impossible for us today to fully appreciate the difficulty of this situation for Hannah. Her husband entered into a partnership with another farmer located about two or three days ride on horseback from their established home in Maryland. While the family of five was likely preparing to relocate, William-II apparently died rather unexpectedly. This left Hannah to work out all the details and to accept the fulltime responsibility and hard work of running a farm. In those days, for example, plowing was done using a walk-behind plow pulled by a team of horses or oxen. This, of course, was combined with the additional burden of another fulltime job: setting up house, feeding, and raising her children. All the while, she was in a state of mourning the loss of her husband. It is apparent that she summoned her strength and pressed on, because we know that she continued to run the farm for 15 years, until she died. It is very unfortunate that we are not in possession of more details about Hannah and the nature of William-II's death.

Both Harbaugh and Dorman give the birth year of Lewis-I to be 1712.[7,8] At the age of 19 or 20 in 1732, Lewis-I did not likely yet own the capital needed to purchase his own land when the family came to Delaware. This would explain why he was not found making any land transactions until years later. However, he and his two sisters no doubt played a major role in assisting their mother in running the family farm.

Although unrelated, it may also be of interest to know that the coast of Delaware, including parts of Sussex County, were being assaulted by pirates between 1708 and extending at least through 1717, until Lewis-I was five years of age. Lewistown (today's Lewes, the county seat until 1791) was a frequent target of these raids. Although the attacks had subsided for a time, pirate activity resurged in 1747, the very year that William-III was born! Piracy quickly became rampant and was reported around Lewes, Cape Henlopen, and other points along the coast until the end of 1748. For these two years, both residents and ships near the coast suffered incessant attacks by pirates who sailed their vessels along-side friendly ships and then seized them.

In other cases, they rowed ashore in small boats and raided nearby homes. These attacks were so numerous that the mouth of Delaware Bay was nearly blockaded! The attacks continued until England dispatched two warships, the *Hector* and the *Otter*, which successfully drove off the pirates who apparently moved on to easier prey in the West Indies. This event effectively ended practically all pirate activity in the region around Delaware for decades.[9] Several interesting stories about the pirate activities from this era may be found in the referenced works about Delaware history for the interested readers to discover on their own.

Between 1732 and 1771, Lewis-I can be found in at least nine land related entries in Sussex County, Delaware.[10-18] Counting the initial purchase by Hannah, five of these deal with tracts of land either bought from, or sold to, Jacob and/or Thomas Warrington.[19] These transactions establish that Lewis-I was a farmer who had multiple close business relationships with the Warringtons and brings these two families within arm's length of each other.

This relationship is an important one because Lewis-I's first wife, and William-III's mother, was Comfort Warrington. Comfort's father was William M. Warrington whose last will is the single most significant document linking Lewis-I to his first wife. The will of William M. Warrington states, "…I Give and bequeath to my Daughter Comfort [*sic*] Two Children viz William and Lewis Davidson to Each of them One Shilling Starling [*sic*] to be paid Soon after my Decease."[20] The will of William M. Warrington combined with the Delaware land transactions, discussed earlier, support the conclusion that Comfort, the daughter of William M. Warrington, was the first wife of Lewis-I and the mother of William-III.[21,22]

William M. Warrington died in 1755 and presumably William-III, and his brother, Lewis-II received their shares of the inheritance at eight and six years of age respectively.[23] Lewis-I was not remembered in William M. Warrington's will, probably because Lewis-I had remarried by that time and had started another family.

William "Ranger" Davidson

Additional evidence, that should not be overlooked, associating these two families is found in the fact that William-III named two of his children after his mother. His third child was called Comfort and his eleventh child was named William Warrington Davidson.[24]

As mentioned in the previous chapter, the Conwell family figure prominently in Davidson history. Just as the Davidsons had done, the Conwell family also completed several land transactions in Delaware. One record in particular serves as additional evidence linking the Davidson and the Conwell families and therefore providing further assurance that the persons in Delaware are the same as those in Pennsylvania.

On 16 May 1788, John Stockley, acting as attorney on behalf of Jehu Conwell, sold a tract of land in Sussex County, Delaware to William Perry. This tract of land is described as formerly belonging to Thomas Conwell, deceased, the ownership of which passed to his two sons, Jehu and William. The land abstract further specifies that Jehu was then living in Fayette County, Pennsylvania, precisely where our Davidsons and Conwells had settled![25] This inheritance is important for another reason that will be made clear to the reader a little later in this chapter.

For the benefit of those readers unfamiliar with this part of the country, Delaware still uses the old names for certain boundaries called Hundreds. A Hundred was used centuries ago in England to define a geographical area intended to contain one hundred persons or families. Today, the Hundreds in Delaware are simply geographical subdivisions of the counties, just as civil townships are used in some other states.[26]

All the earlier Delaware tracts of land associated with Lewis-I were located in Indian River Hundred, on or near, Rehoboth Bay, in an area called Angola Neck. Given that William-III's mother and father were located in this area from at least 1732, it is safe to presume this location to be the birthplace of William-III. This is surely how Harbaugh had derived Sussex County to be the location, though no actual record of his birth has been found.[27]

Delaware

Today, Angola Neck is a roughly triangular strip of land nestled between two creeks that usher fresh water into the shallow and salty Rehoboth Bay. The more southerly boundary delineating Angola Neck is Herring Creek which still bears its old-time name. It appears that the northerly waterway was called Burton Creek when Lewis-I and William-III stood on its shores, but today it goes by the name Love Creek. Hannah's land was located on the north side of a small creek called Bracey Branch which ran between the first two waterways mentioned, but for reasons unknown, this creek was not found on modern-day maps.[28]

No record of Lewis-I was found from the time his mother purchased the family's first Delaware tract until 1750, three years after Hannah died. This may indicate that Lewis-I continued to reside on the family farm following his marriage to Comfort, about 1746, and following the births of William-III and his brother, Lewis-II.[29] If so, this rather precisely pinpoints William-III's birthplace. While this remains a possibility, Lewis-I could also have rented a place for himself and Comfort on another nearby farm, which was not uncommon.

All accounts agree that William-III was born in the year 1747.[30-34] Most recently, this date may have come from Evans who had stated that William-III's headstone could be read clearly as late as 1903.[35,36] Harbaugh adds the month and day of November 20th without giving a source, but this information likely came from Lewis H. Davidson's (Lewis-IV) earlier article from 1890, who was apparently the first to provide the full birthdate of William-III in a published form.[37] Family letters authored by Lewis-IV were also Harbaugh's source for many of the details of the early generations of the Davidsons.[38]

Through considerable effort, we have determined that William Davidson was born on Angola Neck, in Indian River Hundred, Sussex County, Delaware, on land adjoining or near Rehoboth Bay. He was the son of Lewis-I, a farmer and later, also a ferryman. William-III was descended from his father's first marriage to Comfort Warrington. The Warrington lineage may be positively traced to an Englishman named Henry Bagwell, Ancient Planter of Jamestown fame.[39] Comfort was born about 1716 and she died about 1749, when William-III was about two years old.[40,41] While no additional account of her death could be found, it seems likely that she did die before 1755 because her father did not include her in his will, yet remembered his grandchildren. William-III was born in 1747 on November 20th. The month and day were recorded by one of William-III's many grandchildren, Lewis-IV.[42]

It is timely here to consider a brief account of the events of Lewis-I since we have reached the period of time in which William-III began his childhood. In 1747, Lewis-I's mother, Hannah, died and his first child, William-III, was born.[43] About two years later, Lewis-II was born and Comfort died. Thus, for Lewis-I, these years were mixed with joy and tragedy. No record as to Comfort's cause of death was found, but complications relating to the birth of Lewis-II might be suspected.

We must next consider some of the transactions made by Lewis-I in terms of real estate. Carefully following the details of the land transactions involving Lewis-I produces some very interesting questions that unfortunately cannot be answered with certainty. These transactions overlap one another and quickly become somewhat difficult to follow. As previously mentioned, Lewis-I was recorded in the deed books making several land transactions in Indian River Hundred. These all occurred following the deaths of his mother, his first wife Comfort, and also Joshua Stockley, the business partner of William-II.

In August 1753, Lewis-I and his sisters, Mary, Sarah and Sarah's husband, John Arderly together sold the old family farm (Hannah's) to Jacob Warrington for £25.[44] This transaction occurred six years after Hannah died though there is evidence that Lewis-I had been prepared to move to another parcel of land three years earlier.

In December 1750, Lewis-I paid £150 to Thomas Warrington and his son Jacob for their 234-acre farm which adjoined Rehoboth Bay.[45] The purchase agreement allowed the Warringtons to continue to reside on the farm until February 1751. However, it wasn't until September 1753 that Lewis-I took possession of the 234-acre farm that was supposed to have been surrendered by the Warringtons more than two and one half years earlier! The transfer of 1753 was made by Elizabeth Titus, executrix of Thomas Warrington, who had since died.[46] We might presume that Lewis-I entered into another agreement with Jacob Warrington (son of Thomas) or with Elizabeth Titus, to extend the Warrington's stay on the farm for more than two years, possibly due to family ties or some other arrangement not recorded.

Interestingly, on the same date Hannah's farm was sold in August 1753, Lewis-I purchased another four acre tract of land from Jacob Warrington for £50.[47] Lewis-I next sold this four acre parcel to Comfort Houston, a widow, in February 1754 for £2.[48] This appears to be the same parcel he purchased for £50 only six months earlier. The great disparity between the purchase and sales price for this parcel remains a mystery.[49]

Additional documents were recorded in which Lewis-I is named as a principal party, however, upon examination it was determined that these documents recorded agreements associated with the land transactions already discussed.

It was important to follow Lewis-I through the transactions because these deals determined where the family was located and what Lewis-I was doing during William-III's early childhood. In the end, all the transactions so far discussed occurred in generally the same neighborhood in Indian River Hundred, adjoining or near Rehoboth Bay. Most, if not all, of the indentures were drawn up and executed in the nearby town of Lewes, using a quill pen and only a few years following frequent acts of piracy in that area.

As might be suspected, it is not now possible to determine exactly where Lewis-I was actually residing as all these transactions transpired. A reasonable guess would be that he continued to reside on Hannah's old farm until it was sold in August 1753. Then in September of that same year, he likely assumed residence on the 234-acre farm he first purchased, but on which he apparently allowed the Warringtons to reside for over two years following its purchase. In any case, at least we know with reasonable precision the area where the family was located.

William "Ranger" Davidson

By September 1753, we now have Lewis-I in possession of his 234-acre farm adjoining Rehoboth Bay. This property included ownership of a small island in Rehoboth Bay called Marsh Island! This island still goes by this name and can easily be found on modern-day maps.[50] By February 1754, Lewis-I's previous real estate holdings nearby had been sold, including his mother's farm.

Since his mother, Comfort, died when he was only about two years old, William-III never knew his real mother and would not even have had any memory of her. Between 1749 and 1754, there is a very good chance that Lewis-I's sisters, Mary and Sarah, assisted in looking after their nephews, William-III and Lewis-II.

It will be remembered that it was in 1754 that Lewis-I married his second wife, Elizabeth Claypoole (Conwell).[51] Elizabeth became William-III's stepmother when he was about seven years of age. Elizabeth joined the Davidson household along with her two children, from her first marriage to Thomas Conwell (deceased), William and Jehu Conwell. William Conwell was about one year older than William-III, and Jehu was about the same age as William-III's younger brother, Lewis-II.[52]

Only about the first eight years of William-III's childhood adventures were spent in Indian River Hundred on the shores of Rehoboth Bay. In March 1755, Lewis-I sold his 234-acre farm after owning it a little over four years and perhaps residing on it for only about a year and a half.[53] In March 1757, we next find Lewis-I residing on a seven acre parcel of land located about 12 miles north in Broadkill Hundred.[54-56] This tract is described as being situated on the north side of Broadkill Creek (also called Broadkiln) near its head waters.

The seven acre parcel purchased by Lewis-I was located in or near the town today known as Milton, but at one time was called Conwell's Landing![57,58] The latter name provides the clue that this was once a center of activity for the many members of the Conwell clan who had settled there.[59] Judging by the land abstracts, Lewis-I's parcel adjoined or at least was very close to the 235-acre Conwell property owned by Elizabeth's first husband, Thomas Conwell, and which ownership was later passed on to sons Jehu and William. This now explains why the family moved from Indian River Hundred and neatly ties into the Conwell land inheritance referenced earlier in this chapter.

It is thought that the family first resided on the Conwell's farm from the time Lewis-I sold his 234-acre farm in Indian River Hundred in March 1755. About two years later, he then expanded their combined real estate holdings by purchasing the seven acre parcel near the Conwell farm in March 1757, when William-III was nine years old. The family resided on this latter parcel for the next ten years.

Broadkill Creek was described by Scharf as "navigable for sloops and schooners to [the town of] Milton about twelve miles from its mouth and flows into the estuary of Lewes' Creek about two miles from the Delaware Bay."[60] This riverway supported trade between the farmers who resided near the river and provided a means of shipping crops to Philadelphia and New York.[61] There can be little doubt that the Davidsons, Conwells, and many others transported their produce to Broadkill Creek for loading onto ships and subsequent transportation to markets elsewhere.

Although there have been some boundary adjustments over the decades, the tracts of land owned by Lewis-I, and where William-III grew up, are still today found within the boundaries of Indian River Hundred and Broadkill Hundred. These two Hundreds together with the two areas called Cedar Creek Hundred and Lewes and Rehoboth Hundred were called "Old Sussex" by early pioneers.[62]

Unfortunately, apart from the will of William M. Warrington, no records directly referencing William-III were found in Delaware. Considering that William-III was relatively young during his entire time there, this is not really very surprising. However, the land records associated with his father do provide us with some scant clues as to what his childhood may have been like.

It is known from the Broadkill Hundred land records that Lewis-I owned an orchard, as did so many other colonists. The orchard may have consisted of a combination of desirable and popular fruit trees, such as peaches, pears, or plums.

The family harvests were likely sold and consigned to merchants located elsewhere, including New York and Philadelphia. Following the harvests, William-III would likely have helped to pack the family produce into kegs, barrels, and other containers which they then loaded onto horse or ox drawn wagons. Their cargo was next hauled to the shores of Broadkill Creek where it would be subsequently loaded onto sloops, schooners, or other sailing vessels and stowed in their holds. The ships sailed or were possibly towed down Broadkill Creek, into Delaware Bay and from there they sailed to other points along the coast.

Being raised on a farm, in the days when all the children did their part and helped in the nurturing and tending of the crops, William-III certainly received a good education in farming and would have assisted in the planting and harvesting of not only fruit, but all the other crops Lewis-I chose to plant. Since most farming tasks were done by hand, the better part of most days was probably spent working in the orchard and tending the fields of the 235-acre Conwell farm nearby. We also know that William-III was educated and could read and write.[63] So at least some of his early time in Delaware was spent in a schoolhouse or he was possibly taught the essentials at home by his stepmother.

Lewis-I didn't sell his orchard parcel in Broadkill Hundred until November 1771. The sale of this parcel serves as one more piece of evidence that this Lewis in Delaware is one and the same with our Lewis-I in Pennsylvania. The language of this indenture refers to Lewis Davison "of Bedford County in the province of Pensylvania [*sic*]" and the "seven acres of land, the House and the orchard where the said Lewis Davison formerly dwelt."[64] This language should provide a good clue as to the topic of the next chapter in William-III's life: his departure from Delaware.

---

1.   Elizabeth Davidson Harbaugh, *The Davidson Genealogy* (Ironton, Ohio: self-published, 1948; Ann Arbor, Michigan : Lithoprinted, Edwards Brothers, Inc., 1949), p. 124, print, OCLC: 23167553. Harbaugh offers no source, but

Delaware

probably learned of the Delaware land records from one or more of the historical works cited herein and possibly from one or more descendants contributing to her work.

2.   Sussex County, Delaware, Shankland Survey Book 2: pages 71-72, Survey for "Hanah Davidson" (untitled), 16 November 1731, Record Group 4555, digital copy of penned document, obtained December 2015, Delaware Public Archives, Dover.

3.   Sussex County, Delaware, Deed Book I: 29-30, "Deed of Sale Thom^s Worington to Hannh Davison," 7 February 1732, recorded 6-9 February 1732, Record Group 4555, digital copy of penned document, obtained November 2015, Delaware Public Archives, Dover.

4.   Henry Clay Conrad, *History of the State of Delaware*, Volume II (Wilmington, Delaware: Henry Clay Conrad, 1908), p. 722, digital version, *Google Books* (http://books.google.com : accessed 2012).

5.   John H. Long, ed., *Atlas of Historical Counties: Delaware* (Chicago, Illinois: The Newberry Library, 2010), digital version, *The Newberry Library* (http://publications.newberry .org/ahcbp/index.html : accessed July 2011).

6.   The location of this parcel being in Indian River Hundred can be confirmed by examining the boundary descriptions of this Hundred as specified by Conrad as well as the map referenced.

7.   Harbaugh, pp. 128 and 360; no source is given by Harbaugh for her information.

8.   John Frederick Dorman, FASG, *Adventurers of Purse and Person, Virginia 1607-1624/5*, 4th ed, 4th printing, Volume 1, Families A-F (Baltimore, MD: Genealogical Publishing Company, 2004), p. 116, print. Dorman cites family records provided by Henry Clay Russell, Ashland, Ky.

9.   John Thomas Scharf, *History of Delaware: 1609 – 1888: General History*, Vol. I (Philadelphia: L. J. Richards & Co., 1888), Chapter X, "Pirates and Privateers," digital version, *Google Books* (http://google.books.com : accessed 2012).

10. Sussex County, Delaware, Deed Book I: 30-31, "Thomas Warrington and Jacob Warrington's Bond to Lewis Davison," dated 17 December 1750, recorded 11 May 1751, Record Group 4555, digital copy of penned document, obtained

November 2015, Delaware Public Archives, Dover. This bond concerned a certain 234-acre tract of land on Angola Neck in Indian River Hundred.

11. Sussex County, Delaware, Deed Book I: page 68, "Jacob Warrington from Lewis Davidson and sisters Deed," dated 6 August 1753, recorded 7 February 1754, Record Group 4555, digital copy of penned document, obtained November 2015, Delaware Public Archives, Dover. Sale by Lewis-I and his sisters of a 179-acre tract of land in Indian River Hundred (Hannah's).

12. Sussex County, Delaware, Deed Book I: 68-69, "Lewis Davison from Jacob Warrington Deed," dated 6 August 1753, recorded 7 February 1754, Record Group 4555, digital copy of penned indenture, obtained November 2015, Delaware Public Archives, Dover. Purchase by Lewis-I of a tract of land in Indian River Hundred, acreage not stated, but thought to be a 4-acre tract.

13. Sussex County, Delaware, Deed Book I: 29-30, "Thomas Warington's Executrix to Lewes Davison," dated 10 September 1753, recorded 8 August 1754, Record Group 4555, digital copy of penned indenture, obtained November 2015, Delaware Public Archives, Dover. Concerns the purchase of a 234-acre tract of land in Indian River Hundred.

14. Sussex County, Delaware, Deed Book I: 69, "Comfort Houston from Lewis Davison Deed of Sale," dated 7 February 1754, recorded 7 February 1754, Record Group 4555, digital copy of penned indenture, obtained November 2015, Delaware Public Archives, Dover. Sale by Lewis-I of a 4-acre tract of land in Indian River Hundred.

15. Sussex County, Delaware, Deed Book I: 93-94, "Lewis Davison to Yates Conwell Deed," dated 12 March 1755, recorded 12 March 1755, Record Group 4555, digital copy of penned indenture, obtained November 2015, Delaware Public Archives, Dover. Sale by Lewis-I of a 234-acre tract of land in Indian River Hundred.

16. Sussex County, Delaware, Deed Book I: 165, "Lewes Davison from Jacob Stafford Bond," dated 12 March 1757, recorded 10 February 1758, Record Group 4555, digital copies of penned document, obtained November 2015, Delaware Public Archives, Dover. This bond concerned a 7-acre tract of land on Angola Neck in Broadkill Hundred.

17. Sussex County, Delaware, Deed Book I: 165, "Lewis Davison from Rosanna Stafford Adm^x," dated 9 February 1758, recorded 10 February 1758, Record

Group 4555, digital copy of penned indenture for a seven acre tract of land, obtained November 2015, Delaware Public Archives, Dover. Purchase by Lewis-I of a 7-acre tract of land on Angola Neck in Broadkill Hundred.

18. Sussex County, Delaware, Deed Book L: 235-236, "Isaac Draper from Lewis Davison," dated 30 November 1771, recorded 6 May 1772, Record Group 4555, digital copies of penned indenture for seven acres, obtained November 2015, Delaware Public Archives, Dover. Sale by Lewis-I of a 7-acre tract of land and house on Angola Neck in Broadkill Hundred, where Lewis Davison formerly dwelt.

19. It is possible that this Thomas Warrington is the half-brother of Lewis-I's first wife, Comfort. Jacob Warrington was the son of Thomas. This was determined from examination of the Delaware land records. However, it was not possible to confirm these relationships due to the numerous branches of this family, many of whom bear the same names.

20. William M. Warrington, Will of William Warrington and Probate Records, untitled, Sussex County Probate, Record Group 4545.009: 1755 – 1796, 11 pages, dated 20 January 1755, proved 27 June 1755, digital copies of typewritten and penned documents, obtained November 2015, Delaware Public Archives, Dover. The will exists today only in the form of a typewritten duplicate according to archivists. Most of the probate records were in their original handwritten form.

21. Harbaugh, p. 128.

22. Dorman, p. 116.

23. Dorman, p. 102. The will was dated 20 January 1755; Dorman adds the date the will was proved as 27 June 1755 providing the death year for William M. Warrington.

24. Harbaugh, pp. 129 and 249. A common traditional naming convention uses the wife's maiden name as the middle name in one or more of the children. This is discussed further in the *Families* chapter.

25. Elaine Hastings Mason and F. Edward Wright, *Land Records of Sussex County, Delaware 1782-1789, Deed Book N No. 13* (Westminster, Maryland: Willow Bend Books, 2002), p. 98, print.

26. J. M. Runk & Co., *Biographical & Genealogical History of the State of Delaware*, Vol. 1 (Chambersburg, PA: J. M. Runk & Co., 1899), p. 56, digital version, *Google Books* (http://books.google.com : accessed April 2016).

27. If a birth record was created for William-III, it would be in the form of a church or bible record since Delaware did not begin keeping state-wide civil records of birth until the 20th century.

28. S. Lewis, *Seventh American Map of Delaware*, engraved by Lawson (Boston: Thomas and Andrews, 1804), Delaware Public Archives, State Map Collection Delaware, Resource Identifier 1325-003-203-0023, digital copy, *State of Delaware, Public Archives* (http://archives.delaware.gov : accessed November 2015). The creek names today were determined by comparing modern-day maps to the one cited herein from 1804.

29. Harbaugh, p. 128. This marriage year of Lewis-I and Comfort was possibly estimated by Harbaugh, based upon the birth year of their first child, William-III in 1747.

30. Harbaugh (1949), p. 129, full birthdate of William-III.

31. Dorman (2004), p. 116, full birthdate of William-III.

32. *Commemorative Biographical Record of the Counties of Harrison and Carroll, Ohio* (Chicago: J. H. Beers & Co., 1891), article: "Lewis H. Davidson," pp. 446-453, digital version, *Google Books* (http://books.google.com : accessed April 2013). Full birthdate of William-III.

33. Nelson W. Evans, *History of Scioto County, Ohio* (Portsmouth, Ohio: Self-published, 1903), reprint (Markham, Virginia: The Apple Manor Press), Part 5, pp. 1224-1226. Birth year of William-III.

34. Charles Augustus Hanna, *Historical Collections of Harrison County in the State of Ohio* (New York: privately printed, 1900), pp. 8 and 483-484, digital version, *Internet Archive* (http://www.archive.org : accessed April 2011). Full birthdate of William-III.

35. Unfortunately, Evans did not provide a transcript of William-III's headstone.

36. *The Official roster of the soldiers of the American Revolution buried in the state of Ohio*, Vol 1, Daughters of the American Revolution (Columbus, Ohio: F. J. Heer Printing

Delaware

Co., 1929), p. 114, entry for "Davidson, William, Lawrence Co.," print, Bartow Genealogical and Historical Library, Bartow, Florida. This entry indicated that Evans read the headstone in 1911. However, his work was published in 1903. Without evidence to the contrary it must be presumed that the headstone was read by Evans no later than 1903.

37. *Commemorative Biographical Record of the Counties of Harrison and Carroll*, pp. 446-453.

38. Harbaugh speaks of the letters of Lewis Hutchinson Davidson in her book on p. 122; the entry for Lewis H. Davidson appears on p. 182, where the letters are referenced again (Lewis-IV). Unfortunately, these were not located during the compilation of this work.

39. Many details of the lineage from William-III to Henry Bagwell (of Jamestown) are presented in the published works of both Harbaugh and Dorman.

40. Harbaugh, p. 128.

41. Dorman, p. 116.

42. See also the later chapter *Final Years* herein, in which William-III's death and burial and also the derivation of his birthdate are discussed in greater detail.

43. Harbaugh, p. 125, provides Hannah's death year in 1747.

44. Sussex County, Delaware, Deed Book I: 68, "Jacob Warrington from Lewis Davidson and sisters Deed," 6 August 1753, recorded 7 February 1754, Record Group 4555, digital copy of penned indenture for 179 acres, obtained November 2015, Delaware Public Archives, Dover.

45. Sussex County, Delaware, Deed Book I: 30-31, "Thomas Warrington and Jacob Warrington's Bond to Lewis Davison," 17 December 1750, recorded 11 May 1751, Record Group 4555, digital copy of penned indenture for 234 acres, obtained November 2015, Delaware Public Archives, Dover.

46. Sussex County, Delaware, Deed Book I: 29-30, "Thomas Warington's Executrix to Lewes Davison," 10 September 1753, recorded 8 August 1754, Record Group 4555, digital copy of penned indenture for 234 acres, obtained November 2015, Delaware Public Archives, Dover.

47. Sussex County, Delaware, Deed Book I: 68-69, "Lewis Davison from Jacob Warrington Deed," 6 August 1753, recorded 7 February 1754, digital copy of penned indenture for 4 acres, obtained November 2015, Delaware Public Archives, Dover.

48. Sussex County, Delaware, Deed Book I: 69, "Comfort Houston from Lewis Davison Deed of Sale," 7 February 1754, recorded 7 February 1754, digital copy of penned indenture for 4 acres, obtained November 2015, Delaware Public Archives, Dover.

49. The purchase from Jacob Warrington on 6 August 1753 does not specify the acreage. It appears that this was the same parcel sold to Comfort Houston in February 1754. This connection was derived by examination of the language common to both deeds in which the abstract of title was recorded. The sale price to Comfort Houston was recorded as only £2 followed by a line which could possibly be interpreted as an unfinished value or alternatively to prevent an unauthorized change to the small value recorded. Unfortunately, the connection between these two deeds cannot be shown with absolute certainty and the great disparity between Lewis-I's purchase price of £50 and his sale price of only £2 remains unexplained.

50. L. W. Heck, A. J. Wraight, D. J. Orth, J. R. Carter, L. G. Van Winkle, and Janet Hazen, *Delaware Place Names*, Geological Survey Bulletin 1245, prepared by the Geological Survey, U.S. Department of the Interior and Geodetic Survey, U.S. Department of Commerce (Washington: United States Government Printing Office, 1966), p. 71, digital version, *USGS Publications Warehouse* (https://pubs.usgs.gov/bul/ 1245/report.pdf : accessed June 2016). Marsh Island was about 0.1 miles across and is located on the west shore of Rehoboth Bay, about four miles southwest of Rehoboth Beach.

51. Harbaugh, p. 360.

52. T. C. Conwell, *The Conwell's of Dyer's Delight*, not published, dated 1984, p. 30, 91 typewritten pages, digital version, *Ancestry* (http://www.ancestry.com : accessed October 2013).

53. Sussex County, Delaware, Deed Book I: 93-94, "Lewis Davison to Yates Conwell Deed," 12 March 1755, recorded same date, digital copy of penned indenture for 234 acres, obtained November 2015, Delaware Public Archives, Dover.

Delaware

54. Broadkill was one of the original hundreds of Delaware established in 1696. The word "kill" comes from the Dutch word for creek. The name was changed in 1833 to BroadKiln.

55. Sussex County, Delaware, Deed Book I: 165, "Lewes Davison from Jacob Stafford Bond," 12 March 1757, recorded same date, Record Group 4555, digital copy of penned indenture for a 7-acre tract of land, obtained November 2015, Delaware Public Archives, Dover.

56. Sussex County, Delaware, Deed Book I: 165, "Lewis Davison from Rosanna Stafford Adm^x," 9 February 1758, recorded 10 February 1758, Record Group 4555, digital copy of penned indenture for a 7-acre tract of land, obtained November 2015, Delaware Public Archives, Dover.

57. Scharf, Vol. II, p. 1263, provides previous names for the town of Milton and also states that the headwaters of Broadkill Creek were found there, serving to pinpoint the location of Lewis-I's tract of land.

58. Heck, Wraight, et. al., p. 75.

59. Scharf, Vol. II, p. 1262.

60. Scharf, Vol. I, p. 3.

61. John Thomas Scharf, *History of Delaware: 1609 – 1888*, Vol. II (Philadelphia: L. J. Richards & Co., 1888), pp. 1256, 1263, digital version, *Google Books* (http://google.books.com : accessed 2012).

62. Heck, Wraight, et. al., pp. 21, 58.

63. The list of possessions from William-III's last will included a collection of 20 books, from which we may safely suppose that he could read. William-III signed his name on his several real estate transactions yielding further assurance as to some level of education.

64. Sussex County, Delaware, Deed Book L: 235-236, "Isaac Draper from Lewis Davison," dated 30 November 1771, recorded 6 May 1772, Record Group 4555, digital copies of penned indenture for seven acres, obtained November 2015, Delaware Public Archives, Dover.

6

Pennsylvania

The next major event in the life of William Davidson, that can be established, is his migration to southwestern Pennsylvania. To gain an appreciation as to the conditions to which early settlers were subjected in this geographical area, a few historical facts are beneficial.

It is not the intent here to recount all the known events in Pennsylvania that preceded the migration of the Davidsons, as this could fill volumes, but merely to paint a broad picture of the struggles and hardships needed to tame this wild geographic region and to expose the reader to the environment to which early settlers were subjected. Readers are much encouraged to use the bibliography of this work to locate and read for themselves the fascinating accounts that can only be outlined here. Both Lewis-I and William-III settled in what is Luzerne Township of Fayette County today, so the following discussion focuses on this general region, although over time the geopolitical boundaries changed several times.

Today we easily travel the paved roads and take for granted the countless modern developments and conveniences that have long since erased what was once a completely untamed land. It is difficult, at best, to imagine all land west of the mountains to be unsettled, completely wild and unbroken frontier. The mountains that figure most prominently in this chapter is the Allegheny Mountains. These are generally described as the western part of the Appalachian Mountain Range and which extend from northern Pennsylvania southwesterly to southwestern Virginia, but also lie in Maryland and West Virginia.

For the early settlers, the allure of the frontier is easily established. The absence of government, boundaries, and taxes was enough for many. There was an abundance of wild game and many fresh water rivers, streams, and creeks watered rich soils. Lush ancient forests of chestnut, pine, cedar, oak, maple, walnut, ash, poplar, beech, and hickory trees stood in pristine beauty.[1,2] Among the more notable game abounded deer, turkeys, and geese and streams bore trout and other freshwater game fish.[3] For the Davidson family, perhaps the greatest motivation to move west was the lack of space. The country east of the mountains was becoming crowded and Lewis-I had four sons and two stepsons who would need arable land upon which to build their lives.

Mountain lions (also known as pumas, panthers, or wildcats), wolves, and bears were perhaps among the earliest frontier residents. Some sources say, contrary to many legends, that no reports of attacks by wolves and mountain lions on humans were ever authenticated. Other sources provide stories of attacks. Whether or not the latter were authenticated is uncertain. In the case of bears, attacks reportedly seldom occurred and those only due to the protective nature of a mother over her cubs. In either case, the ever vigilant settlers frequently feared the possibility of such attacks, though not so much a danger for humans, as a nuisance to the wellbeing of their horses and other livestock. However, one source says the pioneers regularly hunted bears for food, which was said to be preferable to venison.[4] The single most dangerous animal a pioneer could encounter was probably the rattlesnake or copperhead snake. Nevertheless, these dangers were likely considered small obstacles by the pioneers whose larger challenges would come from eastern escapees from justice traveling west to evade capture and from those whom they called Indians.

It is now commonly known, and clearly shown genetically, that the early people who greeted the European explorers in the New World migrated to North America from Asia.[5] We know from their own memories and traditions that the tribe called Lenni Lenape migrated from the western reaches of the North American continent, where they formerly resided, to the Ohio River Valley and the western Pennsylvania region.

During their migration, the Lenni Lenape met another tribe called the Mengwe, who were also migrating into the region. The Lenni Lenape and the Mengwe encountered another large tribe, already established in the area, called the Alligewi. The Alligewi declined to allow the Lenni Lenape and Mengwe to settle in their lands, but gave their permission to allow these newly arrived tribes to pass through their territory. When the Alligewi saw the large numbers of their new visitors, they became alarmed and attacked them. The Lenni Lenape and Mengwe together fought the Alligewi aggressively, showing their enemy no quarter. After many bloody and violent battles the Alligewi, fearing their extinction, escaped from the region. The survivors of the displaced tribe fled south for their lives and their lands were thus forcibly taken by the Lenni Lenape and Mengwe.[6-8]

The conquerors, the Lenni Lenape, were later called the Delaware Indians by the Europeans, who mistakenly thought they had landed on the Asian continent. The Mengwe were a confederacy of at least five major tribes and thus were often referred to as the Five Nations. These included the Mohawks, Oneidas, Onondagoes, Cayugas, and Senecas. In the year 1712, they were joined by the Tuscaroras and afterward were called the Six Nations. But, in addition to the Delaware and

Tuscaroras, they were also joined by some other smaller tribes such as the Shawnee.[9,10] The local tribes were often collectively and generically called Mingo by the British and Iroquois by the French.[11] The settlers also encountered several other independent tribes, however these were not always consistently documented in the sources consulted. Therefore, it was found necessary herein to use the term Six Nations in a generic sense whenever referencing any of the tribes.

From the beginning, the relationship between the settlers and the Six Nations may be described as not always hostile, yet not always friendly. There were many traders on the frontier who were eager to capitalize on the lucrative fur trade in which animal hides were exchanged for various supplies desired by many of the Six Nations. The Six Nations likewise enjoyed this trade which often brought to them prized possessions which enabled them to rise in stature among their own people. But there were divisions among the various tribes, some welcoming the traders and others denouncing the settlers as invaders trespassing on their lands. This friction steadily intensified and mistrust eventually escalated and gave way to aggressions which occurred on both sides in the struggle for land.

Many persons passed through southwestern Pennsylvania in the early 18th century and several expeditions, sent for various reasons, traversed the area that became Fayette County, however, the first attempts at permanent settlement did not likely occur before 1751.[12] Those who moved west of the Allegheny Mountain range did so at their own risk and settlers venturing into the frontier were left to their own devices to protect themselves as they could.

In the early years, pioneers had only game trails and Six Nations paths to follow. These were a maze of unimproved and unmarked routes among the trees and brush, seldom wide enough to allow two persons on horseback to ride abreast, except where the natural widening of the forest occurred.

In 1749, Colonel Thomas Cresap employed Nemacolin, an Indian Chief, to show him the best route for a pack horse from the Potomac River at a place later called Cumberland, Maryland to the confluence of the Allegheny and Monongahela Rivers. This destination, then considered militarily strategic, is now the city of Pittsburgh. This path became known as Nemacolin's Trail even though it had probably been used previously by the Six Nations for many years.[13] George Washington also followed this path in 1753. Washington, then a Major, was ordered by Governor Dinwiddie of Virginia to gather intelligence regarding the activities of the French military who were operating west of the Alleghenies.[14]

In the spring of 1754, Washington returned, as a Lieutenant Colonel, to drive the French from a fort near a trading post established by the Ohio Company. The fort was started by the British under Captain William Trent and was named Fort Prince George, but later was seized and completed by the French and renamed Fort Duquesne.[15,16]

Washington's plan was to first erect a fort at Redstone (Brownsville today), about 40 miles south of Fort Duquesne, and there wait for reinforcements which were needed to supplement his small company. However, before arriving at Redstone, he learned of the approach of a small band of the enemy and elected to attack them. In a subsequent offensive by the enemy, his ill-equipped detachment was attacked by the superior numbers of a combined French and Indian force. Washington retreated to a place then called the Great Meadows (about ten miles southeast of Uniontown). There, his detachment took refuge in a hastily built structure called Fort Necessity. The next day Washington surrendered to the demands of his enemy, but negotiated the release of himself and his men.[17]

Still later, in 1754, a similar attempt was made by the British Major General Edward Braddock who also followed parts of Nemacolin's Trail. Along the way, Braddock ordered his troops to widen the trail and construct a road.

Before reaching his target, Braddock was defeated after marching into an ambush in which he received a mortal wound. George Washington, who had become very sick with a fever, rose to the occasion and at least turned the rout into something closer to an orderly retreat. Washington had two horses shot from beneath him and four bullets passed through his coat in the process.[18,19] Although the retreating troops were not pursued, news of this defeat and the loss of 456 men in the battle spread quickly. Many pioneer families, fearing reprisals, then withdrew from what is now southwestern Pennsylvania.[20] Following Braddock's defeat, much of Nemacolin's Trail became known as Braddock's Road.

The overwhelming fear of attack that largely held back western settlement temporarily turned in 1758. The French set Fort Duquesne ablaze and withdrew from the area after learning of the approach of a large British force led by General John Forbes.[21,22] A new structure, replacing Fort Duquesne and named Fort Pitt, was started in 1759 and was completed two years later. Also, in 1759, British Colonel James Burd led an expedition to open a road to Redstone and he erected Fort Burd there.[23] These events gave the image of at least semi-stabilization and led to a steady trickle of settlers returning west.

The events just outlined were part of the French and Indian War which lasted from 1754 to 1763 and resulted in the withdrawal of the French from those territories claimed by the British.

With the French then out of the way, the British Crown was keen to establish a friendly relationship with the Six Nations in the hopes of acquiring land and other resources for its colonies in an agreeable manner. The colonial authorities then ordered evacuation of the pioneers residing west of the mountains because they were trespassing in the Indian Territories and thereby jeopardizing the diplomatic efforts of the Crown.

However, another seldom discussed reason that King George III was so eager for removal of the settlers was found in the spirit of the pioneers and their demands for the freedoms being continuously eroded in the east. The pioneers represented an armed and independent force that defied the authority of the Crown, ignored the threat of punishment, and they endured the dangers that surrounded them. This measure of fortitude and independence was feared by King George III, who strongly desired submission of the borderers to the colonial system of control, which continuously grew more oppressive. The pioneers represented what authoritarian leaders fear most, a force of citizenry capable of self-defense and resourceful enough to perhaps someday rise up and to fight for their freedom and independence.[24]

While the introduction of more and more settlers in the west surely raised the ire of the Six Nations, they were not the sole trespassers west of the Allegheny Mountains. As the British sought to eject the pioneers, they themselves continued to maintain a string of forts in Indian Territory. Nearly all of these were attacked in what became known as Pontiac's War in 1763. The British subsequently launched several aggressive expeditions against the Six Nations until military pressure leveraged peace negotiations by 1765.[25]

Once peace was again made between the Six Nations and the British, the tide of settlers rebounded and the year 1765 has been called the beginning of the "era of the settlement of Fayette County," which will be shown to be the region in which the Davidsons settled.[26]

To discourage westward expansion, King George III issued a formal proclamation prohibiting settlement west of the mountains. Since no penalty was outlined in this feeble document, it had little effect. Due to the inaction of the pioneers to leave the Indian Territory, Governor John Penn (grandson of Pennsylvania's founder, William Penn), in 1766, sent Captain Alexander Mackay to announce to settlers in the vicinity of Redstone that they were in violation of the law. The settlers were told if they were to persist in their settlements they would no longer be protected. They therefore risked surrendering their possessions to the Six Nations upon whose lands they trespassed and subjected themselves to forcible removal.[27] Several other similar proclamations and warnings followed, each having varying effects on the settlers.

In 1767, it was reported that the proclamations were only partially successful because many families, initially reported as withdrawn, had returned.[28] On February 3, 1768, another proclamation was issued by Governor John Penn requiring the settlers to withdraw or face the penalty of death![29] An envoy led by a Presbyterian clergyman was sent to warn the settlers, but even this plan enjoyed little success.[30]

Finally, in September 1768, representatives of Governor Penn met with the Six Nations and purchased by deed all of southwestern Pennsylvania (as well as much of the middle and northern areas of the state) for £10,000 and thus opened the way to expanded settlement. The treaty was signed at Fort Stanwix (Rome today), New York and was called the New Purchase.[31] This was the last land purchase made by the Penns, which enclosed many bloody battlefields and sites of broken promises from the preceding decades. The Six Nations were not all in agreement to the New Purchase, but temporarily subsided.[32] At this point, the flow of immigrants steadily increased and the Proprietaries' Land Office was opened in April 1769 through which parcels of western land could be legally purchased from the Penns for the first time.[33]

This brings us to an important point in time as this now overlaps the arrival of the Davidsons from Delaware. Following William-III and Lewis-I in the records in this part of the country is not easy. In 1999, the Pennsylvania Archives put together its eleventh edition of a genealogy dedicated solely to the evolving boundaries of the counties in Pennsylvania.[34,35] Locating townships within the counties is even more difficult, but highly important for confirming the identities of the settlers, especially those having common names.[36]

The area in which the Davidsons settled was first known as Cumberland Township in Cumberland County. In 1771, this region became Springhill Township in Bedford County. By 1773, the boundaries had changed again and this same area was found in Menallen Township of Westmoreland County. Beginning in 1783, both Lewis-I and William-III were in Luzerne Township of Fayette County. So the tracts of land on which the Davidsons settled were located in at least four different townships in four different counties depending upon the point in time being examined. A table in the appendix details the various political boundaries that enclosed the Davidson's parcels along with the dates these changes took place.

Pennsylvania

Previously, it has been uncertain as to when William-III migrated to Pennsylvania. It is difficult to separately consider William-III without also taking into account the events of his father since it is known that the entire family eventually settled there. There are few surviving documents that clarify this chapter of their story. The records of the earliest pioneers who settled in southwestern Pennsylvania as early as 1762 are far from complete. Even fewer records survive for those who attempted settlement in the region and later withdrew following the various battles and the proclamations ordering retreat.[37]

Harbaugh says that Lewis-I migrated to Pennsylvania in June 1767 on the basis of a land purchase. However, for William-III, Harbaugh only says that he remained in Delaware "until grown."[38] Given his relatively young age of 19 years in June 1767, it is not unreasonable to suppose that William-III moved west with his family. But, no other source consulted offered any further clues. Consequently, the available records were gathered for examination to narrow down the span of time for his migration and to consider the possible movements of William-III.

An early purchase of land made by William-III places him in southwestern Pennsylvania in March 1779.[39] But, other evidence shows that he was there before this date. Another transaction, from May of 1778, was found in which he agreed to sell a 120-acre tract of land to Thomas Stockley for £54.[40] The description found in the indenture makes it clear that William-III was slicing off a small parcel of a larger tract of land he had already claimed. This larger tract, the one purchased in March 1779, lay on the east side of the Monongahela River and was situated between the tracts of Thomas Stockley and Jonathan Arnold. This description identifies William-III's *Dispute Ended* tract where he resided until 1799 (see the later chapter *Other Pennsylvania Records*). It is interesting to note that William-III sold part of his land claim before he had purchased the land himself!

One other notable piece of evidence confirming William-III's presence in Pennsylvania before 1779 is found in his service in the Westmoreland County Militia in 1778 (as will be shown in the later chapter *Revolutionary War*). Since the militiamen were recruited based upon residence, he would not have been drafted into a Westmoreland County Militia company unless he resided there.[41]

This now brings us to the tax rolls. An early surviving tax list for this region is the 1773 Bedford County Supply Tax in which Lewis-I is found.[42] If William-III had come to Pennsylvania with his father in 1767 and had settled with, or near, Lewis-I then he should appear in this list. This tax roll included all males at least 21 years of age and also renters, who were listed as inmates. So, even if William-III resided with his father at that time or was living elsewhere in the county, but renting, he should have been included, but is not. He may have simply been omitted in error, but for the support of other records to the contrary, this document would compel us to believe William-III was not in southwestern Pennsylvania as late as 1773.[43] In order to be certain, a search for the next earlier available tax record was conducted.

The list of persons on the Bedford County tax roll of 1773 was actually prepared in 1772.[44] Bedford County was created in March 1771, so in order to locate earlier tax records, the search must be resumed in Cumberland County whose borders then included the area where Lewis-I and William-III resided.[45,46]

This effort led to the discovery of both Lewis-I and William-III in tax records created in 1768 and 1769![47,48] The 1768 entry says that Lewis-I had three horses, five cows, nine sheep, fifty acres of land warranted (for the meaning of warranted, see the later chapter *Other Pennsylvania Records*), and ten acres cleared. This indicates that Lewis-I was already rather well settled in this area by that time. It is also clear that the family was intent on establishing and maintaining a permanent settlement. In a separate entry, William-III is merely listed as a Freeman, which meant an unmarried man, at least 21 years of age, and who owned land. Based upon the available land and tax records (see the later chapter *Other Pennsylvania Records* for details), we may conclude that the family remained settled on the same tracts of land, on the east side of the Monongahela River, where they had initially migrated. The 1768 tax record is the earliest record in which William-III would be expected to appear since it was only in November of that year that he would reach the age of majority and the only reason he would not be found in earlier records. The 1768 tax record is the earliest known document placing William-III in southwestern Pennsylvania. Harbaugh probably did not find this record since it is not mentioned in her book.

Given that William-III was residing on the frontier by 1768, it would seem most probable that he came to Pennsylvania with his father no later than June 1767, at the age of 19 years. This date comes from the indenture executed by Lewis-I, previously mentioned and discussed in more detail in the later chapter *Other Pennsylvania Records*. Only eight months following their arrival, the proclamation issued by Governor John Penn to evacuate the region, under penalty of death, was announced. This threat was apparently ignored by the Davidson clan!

The region in which the Davidsons settled was initially Indian Territory. The previous western purchase, dubbed the Albany Purchase of 1754, was more than 50 miles east of the Davidson's claims. Even after the New Purchase was made in November 1768, which included the Davidson's settlements, their land was still on the edge of the frontier. They remained only about 30 miles east of Indian Territory which lay on the west bank of the Ohio River.[49]

Technically, William-III did not legally possess title to the land, so perhaps landholder would be a more accurate term than landowner. As will be shown in the later chapter *Other Pennsylvania Records*, William-III's parcel was actually first owned by his father, who was also a squatter in the eyes of the government. Like so many other squatters, their right to title was shown merely by occupancy which was then loosely termed tomahawk title or tomahawk claim.[50]

Since it has been established that the Davidsons migrated to Pennsylvania from Delaware, we will now presume that they set off from Lewis-I's farm at Conwell's Landing (now Milton) in Broadkill Hundred, Sussex County. The distance from Milton to Brownsville, Pennsylvania is about 350 miles. This distance was measured using modern-day maps and the most direct highways, excluding the bridge across Chesapeake Bay; there wasn't one in 1767! The actual route was likely much less direct than today's roads and therefore quite a bit longer in 1767.

By comparison, one source states that as late as 1789 the journey from Hagerstown, Maryland to Brownsville, a distance of only 144 miles, took about a month for a wagon loaded with more than two thousand pounds of supplies and pulled by four horses.[51] This description refers to the hauling of supplies to the settlers for profit at a much later time when the trails were greatly improved. Another, perhaps more applicable example, indicates that a pack-horse outfit of ten animals, transporting supplies for hire, could travel 15 or 20 miles per day.[52] This would put a 350 mile journey at roughly three weeks.

Obviously, the Davidsons were motivated by personal interest rather than short-term profit, but Lewis-I and Elizabeth had to consider their shared responsibility for the safety and wellbeing of their entire family, including a two year old daughter. When using the example travel distances as a reference, we must also consider the fact that their horse or horses would have been considerably burdened, that their path was very rough, and the terrain was mountainous. It seems reasonable to presume that the Davidson journey took between three and four weeks. Today the same distance can be easily covered in less than a day in the comfort of an automobile.

The migration party probably consisted of at least ten persons. By 1767, Lewis-I and his second wife, Elizabeth, had four children together. In several different passages, Harbaugh specifies that some of the children of Lewis-I migrated to Pennsylvania in 1767 with their parents.[53] However, when considering their ages it is easy to see that none of their children were old enough to be separated from their family at that time. In 1767, their approximate ages would have been: Thomas, 12; Hannah, 10; Elizabeth, 4; and Rachel, 2. Jeremiah was reportedly born after the family migrated to Pennsylvania.[54]

This leaves us to consider the two children from Lewis-I's first marriage to Comfort Warrington. Lewis-II was about 18 years of age in 1767. He was about two years younger than William-III and Harbaugh says that he remained in Delaware until relocating to Fort Cumberland, Maryland.[55] The migration year is not given by Harbaugh.[56]

Also, we must not forget William and Jehu Conwell, Elizabeth's two sons by her first husband, Thomas Conwell. William Conwell would have turned 21 years of age in 1767 and Jehu about 18 years of age.[57]

We know that William Conwell was in Pennsylvania in June 1767 because he witnessed a land conveyance to his step-father, Lewis-I, at that time.[58] William Conwell had reached the age of majority and was the next oldest male in the migration party, which probably form the reasons he was chosen to witness the transaction rather than one of Lewis-I's sons.[59,60]

It is also possible, that there were other persons in the migration party. In addition to the Conwells, the Stockley (Stokely) family is also conspicuous among the records.[61] Land records for the Davidsons, Conwells, and Stockleys are found in Delaware and some of them and their descendants were also neighbors in Pennsylvania.[62,63]

Although the early settlers were surprisingly mobile, a pioneer moving his family in those primitive times was no small undertaking. Their mode of travel was by wagon or pack horses, or some combination of the two, up to the eastern slope of the mountains.[64] But, the trails west of the Alleghenies were in no condition to pull a wagon. One source indicates that none of the streams were bridged and the early trails were ungraded and so narrow and rough that the first supply wagons did not traverse the region until 1789.[65,66] This was twenty-two years after the Davidsons arrived in that area of the wilderness! Up to then, only packhorses could be used.

Many settlers made the journey with only one horse, but if the luxury of two or more was the case, they were tied one in front of another, thus traveling in single file. One of the men would typically lead the way while the family walked alongside the horses with the women and children toward the middle. If there was space, the wife sometimes rode on one of the horses. Another of the men of the party or perhaps the oldest sons brought up the rear of the train, watching to ensure their precious cargo was well secured and not lost along the way. Bells were also said to be important items as they helped to locate the horses after they were freed to graze in the evenings. During the day, grass or leaves were inserted to prevent the clappers from sounding.[67]

The pioneers, for the most part, had to take only essentials with them, and they manufactured many items, such as furniture, themselves. They carried such supplies as "salt, sugar kettles, bar iron, nail rods, dry goods, glass, kegs of rum, gunpowder, lead, etc. A good horse carried two hundred to three hundred pounds besides provisions and feed."[68] Also, at least one bearskin per horse was considered essential to keep the cargo dry and furs were used for beds for the travelers.[69] For years, settlers made pilgrimages back east for additional supplies especially for salt, iron, and other necessities.[70]

The family almost certainly walked from Delaware to Nemacolin's Trail, known to be a good pack-horse trail as early as 1753.[71] By 1767, this trail was called Braddock's Road, discussed previously. Following in the footsteps of Braddock, Washington, Nemacolin, countless fur traders, and the Six Nations, travelers on Braddock's Road leaving from Fort Cumberland (Maryland), would be heading generally west northwest across several ranges of mountains. Just east of Uniontown, Pennsylvania, Braddock's Road led northward to the forks of the Ohio River, where Pittsburgh stands today.[72] Where Braddock's Road continued toward Pittsburgh, the Davidson family would likely have taken a more southerly route, perhaps following the Redstone Trail.[73] This would have taken them some fifteen miles west of Braddock's Road to Redstone, once called Redstone Old Fort (now Brownsville), where a settlement had been established. From Redstone, their course becomes even less certain, perhaps they followed the Monongahela River south until they came to their land or they may have followed any of a number of other old trails from Redstone that have since fallen into obscurity. Their exact route will never be known, however, this just outlined was the general path of many settlers of that time.[74] The

Pennsylvania

Cumberland Narrows was considered the gateway to the west in that era.

Upon arriving at their destinations, settlers, also called borderers, built homes and barns of round logs. The trees were felled by axe or saw and then stripped of small limbs and bark using a hatchet or tomahawk and draw knife. The logs were dragged into position by horses or oxen and then hoisted atop one another. One method used in the erection of walls was to lean split logs against the top log already in place to create ramps called slides. Each successive log used to add height was rolled up the slides to the top tier and then worked into place.[75] The walls of the typical single story cabin were generally between eight and ten feet high.[76] The gaps between the logs were packed or chinked with clay called catan, a mixture of mud and grass or straw.[77] A chimney of split logs was typically constructed on the outside and then well coated with clay to prevent it from catching fire.[78] The fireplace was lined with stone and mortar and was used for cooking as well as for heat and evening light.[79] Often these early cabins had only one or two windows and one door. Sometimes the floor was made of split boards called puncheons and sometimes it was simply compacted earth or clay.[80] The windows were often shuttered and only had glass if it had survived the journey from back east. Sometimes the windows were simply made of greased paper.[81] The doors were hung on wooden hinges and a latch and string was used in place of a modern-day doorknob.[82] When the latch string was pulled inside, the door was locked. When the latch string was hung outside, it was a commonly recognized sign of welcome.[83] Some pioneers included loop holes in the exterior walls to serve as gun ports through which they could shoot their rifles for defense.[84] There were many different styles and construction methods.[85]

Such homemade abodes were usually constructed in a group effort with the assistance of neighbors and the events were called house-raisings or barn-raisings depending upon the structure needed. The overall project was broken into singular tasks and the workers were divided and quickly organized to establish a rhythm which ultimately allowed the bulk of the heavy work to be completed in a day.[86] The term neighbor likely took on a different definition in 1767, perhaps including those other pioneers found within a three or four mile radius. One source estimated there were only about 150 families in the area, today defined as Fayette County, at that time.[87]

We are fortunate to have an authentic description of William-III's cabin. In common fashion, it was constructed of logs which would have been chinked, as described earlier, with catan clay. It was about 22 feet long and about 20 feet wide by one account, but slightly smaller by another. It was a full two story home that had only two windows, each divided into six lights or panes of glass. This information comes from the 1798 Direct Tax, also called the Glass Tax, so this describes the Davidson home about thirty years after William-III first settled in Pennsylvania.[88-92] The cabin would also most likely have had a fireplace. Of course, it is not possible to know whether this was the original structure or a more elaborate abode erected later. Further, the record does not indicate the existence of any additional structures of any kind, not even a barn. The Davidsons probably had an outhouse or "necessary" as they were once called, but even that is not possible to confirm because these were not recorded in the tax records. Interestingly, Jehu Conwell, who lived nearby, built his house of stone, as also recorded in the 1798 Glass Tax.[93]

Once the home was completed, most settlers quickly set about starting a small garden for their own consumption while working toward establishing their farm. Often the women and children tended the family garden, leaving the larger farming tasks to the men. However, the entire family worked on the farm whenever additional hands were needed, especially during planting or harvesting seasons. Before farming could be started, the fields had to be cleared by cutting down the trees and digging out the stumps. Rocks and stones were carried or dragged away. It took Lewis-I, assisted by his family, about a year to clear six to ten acres of land by hand.[94-96]

Plows were home-built of wood, including the teeth and were pulled with horses or oxen. The average plowman could plow one to one and one half acres per day. Each acre required the farmer to walk between eight and twelve miles, depending on the width of the furrows.[97] Grain, carried in satchels through the fields, was sown broadcast by the farmers.[98]

Since Lewis-I had purchased at least two tracts of land from previous owners we might presume that he escaped at least some of the preparatory work that would normally be involved. However, it is not known how much work was still needed to put the farm in working order or whether the house needed to be expanded to accommodate the Davidson family. On the other hand, William-III was the first settler on his parcel, so the development of his tract had to be started from scratch. However, the combined Davidson and Conwell families likely assisted each other in such arduous tasks.

We should here consider the marriage of William-III to his first wife, Rosanna Hutchinson, about 1769.[99,100] This year may be roughly calculated based on the birth date of their first child.[101] However, two other records serve to support the marriage year. In 1768, William-III is listed in the Cumberland County tax record as a Freeman meaning that he was unmarried, at least 21 years of age, and owned land. In the following year of 1769, William-III is no longer listed as a Freeman, but with those who were married.[102]

Rosanna was thought to be born in Pennsylvania, near what later became Gettysburg, nearly 200 miles due east of Redstone. But we don't know how or where they met or where they were married, though Pennsylvania is presumed. Harbaugh says that all the children from William-III's marriage to Rosanna were born in what is now Fayette County, near Redstone, which is consistent with the records already discussed. It is notable that we may not have known about William-III's first marriage without the work of Lewis-IV.[103] Thus, we know that only about three years after settling in Pennsylvania, William-III and his first wife, Rosanna, were married and they began increasing their family the following year with the birth of their first child, John, on 12 December 1770.[104] William-III and Rosanna had five children together (see the later chapter *Families*).

William "Ranger" Davidson

It is worthy of mention that Jehu Conwell built the first grist mill in the county about a year after his arrival to southwestern Pennsylvania. It was said that he had quickly grown tired of the long journey to the nearest mill then in operation. He also built a distillery. Apparently, these combined businesses attracted many local patrons and we may presume that the Davidsons used the close proximity of these operations to their advantage.[105-107]

Many of the settlers along the Monongahela River were of Scotch heritage. They have been described as "bold, stout and industrious men, sharp at bargains, fond of religious and political controversy and not strongly attached to government." In nearly every cabin, it has been said, three things could be found, "a Bible, a rifle, and a whisky jug."[108]

Although neighbors were commonly relied upon for mutual assistance and protection, it has also been noted among some historians that not everyone in the vicinity were necessarily savory characters. In 1770, George Washington visited the growing community near Pittsburgh, about 40 miles north of Redstone, at that time a gathering of some twenty log cabins along the Monongahela River and "inhabited by Indian traders." This village was thought to have tripled in size by 1775 and according to the notes left by George Washington, consisted of "taverns, hard drinking traders, trappers, and mule drivers, its fugitives from eastern justice and its frequent Indian visitors" made Pittsburgh a "rude and boisterous frontier settlement."[109] From these descriptions, it is clear that the Six Nations were not the only potentially hostile human element found in the remote reaches of the frontier.

Several references may be found regarding the blockhouse constructed for defense at the direction of William Conwell, but the story has not been seen put into context with the events of history that motivated the building of the structure.[110]

In early 1774, a series of violent events occurred which was later called Lord Dunmore's War. The details of the events surrounding this chapter of history will be left for the reader to separately discover. However, a summary of the pertinent events follows.[111]

Virginia and Pennsylvania were engaged in a boundary dispute. The region contested by Virginia included today's Fayette, Green, and Washington Counties, Pennsylvania, and beyond (all located in the southwestern part of the state). Fort Pitt was a stronghold in the western region and was militarily strategic, making it a prime target.

John Murray, known as Lord Dunmore, then governor of Virginia, sent a company of men to take possession of Fort Pitt (now Pittsburgh) with the goal of asserting Virginia's claim on the area.[112] For this aggressive land grab, Lord Dunmore selected a man by the name of John Connolly to lead this expedition and Connolly achieved this goal with an armed force. On the journey to Fort Pitt, Connolly's men opened fire upon a group of Indians without provocation, but all escaped unhurt.

After taking possession of Fort Pitt, which had previously been abandoned, Connolly's group seized livestock and other supplies from nearby settlers in a manner essentially described as strong armed robbery.[113] Connolly was captured by Pennsylvania authorities after a short time and was released on bail, only to later return with a larger armed force. At this point, he arrested several magistrates representing the Penn government and disrupted what little governance existed in Southwestern Pennsylvania. Connolly's men resumed their seizure of livestock and other supplies with renewed aggression. At the same time, rumors of an impending Indian war, in part thought to have been inspired by the acts of Connolly, permeated the region.[114]

As one might suppose, such events taking place at a time when the only form of communication was word of mouth, rumors rapidly sprang up and became mixed with facts which led to fear and confusion. The illegal acts upon the settlers by Connolly and the fear of war with the Six Nations spread panic and caused many families to flee back east. It was recorded that in one day more than 1,000 settlers fled east and crossed the Monongahela River at three different ferries.[115]

There is no proof, but one of the ferries could possibly have been Lewis-I's!

Under fear of attack from all sides, many of the settlers that remained on the frontier formed an association at the insistence of Arthur St. Clair (then considered the leader of Westmoreland County). The members of the association agreed to stand together against the aggressions of Connolly and to repel attacks from the Six Nations as necessary. In an effort to protect their possessions and property, members of the association throughout the region agreed to hold their ground, have their weapons ready, and to ride to each other's aid where ever danger arose.[116,117]

In unrelated incidents, several random attacks occurred within the span of a few months by the Six Nations on settlers and settlers against the Six Nations. These events likely contributed to the rumors among the pioneers that war was forthcoming.

One such attack in particular most probably contributed to the escalation of aggressive actions on both sides that ultimately resulted in war. The mother, brother, and sister of a friendly Indian chief named Logan were brutally murdered, along with seven other Indians. Chief Logan was influential and recruited some assistance in carrying out several retaliatory attacks in which settler families, innocent of the attack on Chief Logan's family and friends, were subsequently murdered. It was said that by the time Chief Logan halted the killing, his band had taken 30 victims, counted in both scalps and captives, and that he himself had taken 13 scalps. Although Chief Logan ceased his actions and refused to lead any more war parties, a momentum for war had grown among many of the Six Nations, particularly the Shawnee, who had formed an armed force of supporters. In the meantime, news of these events had spread to Lord Dunmore of Virginia who subsequently dispatched an army of about 3,000 men to the area.[118,119]

The two lines confronted one another in the Battle of Point Pleasant where the Kanawha River empties into the Ohio. The Six Nations were suppressed in this October battle after which peace was again temporarily achieved on the frontier.[120]

Pennsylvania

Connolly was arrested again some months later, but was released and fled from the region. Although some subsequent events occurred, the foregoing provides limited, but sufficient background for the reader to understand the instability on the frontier in 1774 and the concerns impressed upon the settlers.[121]

It was during the time that the association of settlers was formed that many blockhouses were constructed, including the Conwell's. In May 1774, with the help of neighbors, their blockhouse was erected on the Coleman plantation, on the west side of Dunlap's Creek. This location was just a little over a mile northeast of William-III's tract.[122] The spring of fresh water that the blockhouse enclosed was a likely reason that particular site was selected. This safe-house was used by settlers as a gathering place for refuge.

Although no documentation survives as to who was involved in the construction or use of the blockhouse, there is little doubt, given their family ties and the close proximity to each other, that the Conwells were assisted by the Davidsons in building the fort, and that both these families and probably others had sought refuge there. Reportedly at least one child of William Conwell and one child of Jehu Conwell were born there, but there is no record of it ever being attacked.[123]

Of course, blockhouses were built before and after Lord Dunmore's War; this was not an unusual practice. Many communities of pioneers built blockhouses for defense and protection which were effective in achieving the relative safety of the settlers. Several examples of events may be found in which borderers were attacked while working in their fields, many of whom only survived by seeking the safety of nearby blockhouses. Some of these strongholds were later called "stations" by the Militia and were used as rallying points and destinations when frontier patrols were organized during the Revolutionary War.

---

1. John S. Van Voorhis, *The Old and New Monongahela* (Pittsburgh, PA: Nicholson, Printer and Binder, 1893), p. 5, digital version, *Internet Archive* (http://www.archive.org : accessed July 2011).

2. Joseph Henderson Bausman and John Samuel Duss, *The History of Beaver County Pennsylvania*, Volume I (New York: The Knickerbocker Press, 1904), p. 23, digital version, *Google Books* (http://books.google.com : accessed June 2011).

3. Archer Butler Hulbert, *The Ohio River* (New York and London: G. P. Putnam's Sons, The Knickerbocker Press, 1906), pp. 72-74, digital version, *Google Books* (http://books.google .com : accessed June 2011).

4. George Dallas Albert, *History of the County of Westmoreland Pennsylvania* (Philadelphia: L. H. Everts & Co., 1882), p. 163, digital version, *Google Books* (http://books.google.com : accessed August 2011).

5. Michael H. Crawford, *The Origins of Native Americans: Evidence from Anthropological Genetics* (Cambridge, United Kingdom: Cambridge University Press, 1998), print, 311 pages. In addition to Crawford's work, readers on the internet may find a multitude of widely available sources providing DNA evidence as to the origin of the American Indian, including the contemporary study being conducted by National Geographic.

6. Richard C. Adams, *A Brief History of the Delaware Indians* (U. S. Government Printing Office, 1906), pp. 1-4, digital version, *Google Books* (http://books.google.com : accessed March 2010).

7. Bausman and Duss, p. 13.

8. The historical accounts cited herein say the ancestors of the Lenni Lenape "had come from a far country to the westward, where they had dwelt by a great salt sea," perhaps a hundred years or more before the European migration to America.

9. James Veech, *The Monongahela of Old* (Pittsburg, PA.: 1858-1892), p. 17, digital version, *Google Books* (http://books.google.com : accessed April 2011).

10. Bausman and Duss, p. 18. The tribal composure of the Mengwe may be found in many other works in addition to those cited herein.

11. Bausman and Duss, p. 18.

12. Veech, p. 79, discusses the earliest known settlers in the region now called Fayette County, Pennsylvania.

Pennsylvania

13. Franklin Ellis, *History of Fayette County Pennsylvania with Biographical Sketches of many of its Pioneers and Prominent Men* (Philadelphia: L. H. Everts & Co., 1882), p. 21, digital version, *Internet Archive* (http://www.archive.org : accessed April 2011).

14. Veech, p. 40.

15. The Ohio Company was an association initially formed by 20 men, mostly from Virginia and Maryland, for the purpose of establishing trade with the Six Nations and for building a colony west of the Alleghenies.

16. Veech, Chapters IV and V, discusses the succession of expeditions having the goal of building and holding a fort at the forks of the Ohio River.

17. Veech, Chapter IV, describes the movements and events of Lt. Col. George Washington whose orders were to drive the French from Fort Duquesne.

18. Veech, Chapter V, covers the campaign of Major General Braddock.

19. C. Hale Sipe, *The Indian Wars of Pennsylvania* (Harrisburg, PA: The Telegraph Press, 1929), p. 189, digital version, *Internet Archive* (http://www.archive.org : accessed April 2011).

20. Veech, pp. 80, 81.

21. Veech, p. 29.

22. Albert, *History of the County of Westmoreland Pennsylvania*, p. 31.

23. Veech, pp. 29 and 81, credits Colonel James Burd with opening the road to Red Stone Old Fort in 1759.

24. Rufus J. Fears, *A History of Freedom*, Part II, Lecture 20: "The Tyranny of George III," (Chantilly, VA: Teaching Company, 2001), Great Courses, audio compact disc, ISBN 978-1565853553.

25. Veech, p. 83, briefly describes Pontiac's War and the return of settlers to southwestern Pennsylvania following the cessation of that event.

26. Veech, p. 83, declared the year 1765 the "era of the settlement of Fayette County."

27. Veech, beginning on p. 86, outlines the proclamations made by the authorities ordering the settlers to abandon their claims and return to their former homes east of the mountains.

28. Veech, p. 87.

29. Pennsylvania Archives, Series 4, Volume III, p. 358; also Series 1, Volume IV, p. 284, digital version, *Fold3* (http://www.fold3.com : accessed October 2014).

30. Veech, pp. 89-90. The lists of settlers with whom the entourage met starts on p. 92. The Davidsons were not reported in attendance, but Veech points out that no meeting was held with the upper Monongahela settlements on page 92.

31. Veech, pp. 95-96, discusses the first treaty of Fort Stanwix.

32. Sipe, p. 484.

33. Veech, p. 96, begins a detailed discussion as to how the sale of land was conducted by the Penns.

34. *Genealogical Map of the Counties*, Eleventh edition, 1999, (Harrisburg, Pennsylvania: Compiled and prepared in the Land Office, 1933), Pennsylvania State Archives, digital version, *Commonwealth of Pennsylvania's Enterprise Portal* (http://www.portal .state.pa.us/ : accessed January 2011).

35. John H. Long, ed., *Atlas of Historical Counties: Pennsylvania* (Chicago, Illinois: The Newberry Library, 2010), digital version, *The Newberry Library* (http://publications.newberry.org/ahcbp/index.html : accessed July 2011).

36. The term township is used here to mean a civil township; a subdivision of a county having a defined geographical boundary in contrast with a survey township. In some cases, the civil Township has its own administrative government, subordinate to a County.

37. Albert, *History of Westmoreland County Pennsylvania*, p. 40, recognizes the fact that the identities of many early pioneers have been lost. Perhaps most falling into this category included those who did not cluster together to form a rudimentary community, but were scattered across the frontier, at a distance from Braddock's Road.

Pennsylvania

38. Elizabeth Davidson Harbaugh, *The Davidson Genealogy* (Ironton, Ohio: self-published, 1948; Ann Arbor, Michigan : Lithoprinted, Edwards Brothers, Inc., 1949), pp. 128-129, print, OCLC: 23167553.

39. Fayette County, Pennsylvania, Records of the Land Office, Record Group 17, Patent Book, Volume P, Number 15, page 421, patent application, dated 23 December 1784; warrant number 13, dated 8 August 1785; and patent, dated 18 December 1790, for William Davidson, for a 303½-acre tract called *Dispute Ended*, photocopies of penned documents, Pennsylvania State Archives, Harrisburg. The application indicates that William-III had occupied or improved the land in March 1779, from which date interest would accrue, however the date had been changed. For more about this issue, see the chapter *Other Pennsylvania Records*.

40. Westmoreland County, Pennsylvania, Recorder of Deeds, Deed Book A: 209, "William Davidson to Thomas Stockley," 15 May 1778, recorded 23 January 1781, photocopy of penned document, obtained August 2012, Greensburg, Pennsylvania.

41. The lists used for the draft under the 1777 and 1780 militia laws by Westmoreland County are no longer extant, as confirmed by Aaron McWilliams, Archivist, Pennsylvania Archives (email 10-23-2013).

42. *Bedford County, 1773-1775, 16th, 17th, 18th of the 18 Penny TaxSpringhill Township, Continued, 1773*, p. 33, 48th entry for Lewis Davison, unnumbered, digital copy of penned document, Tax and Exoneration Lists, 1762-1794, Series 4.61; Records of the Office of the Comptroller General, Record Group 4, Pennsylvania State Archives, Harrisburg.

43. Archivists at the Pennsylvania Archives, Harrisburg in 2015 conducted a search for William-III in the 1773 Bedford County tax records; Veech, p. 200, reproduced the 1773 Bedford County tax, but William-III was not found in either source.

44. Veech, p. 199.

45. John H. Campbell, Chief Draftsman, *Warrantee Township Map: Fayette County, Luzerne Township* (Harrisburg, Pennsylvania: Records of the Land Office, 1920), Record Group 17, Series 17.522, Pennsylvania State Archives, digital version, *Commonwealth of Pennsylvania's Enterprise Portal* (http://www.portal.state.pa.us : March 2011);

46. Long, *Atlas of Historical Counties: Pennsylvania.* This and the previous citation above were chiefly used for locating the properties owned by Lewis-I and William-III in Pennsylvania.

47. *Tax Rates Book, 1768-1770*, Book 004, "Cumberland Rates 1768," Cumberland County, Cumberland Township, p. 31, 2nd entry for Lewis Davison, p. 33, 4th entry under "Cumberland freemen" for William Davison, digital copy of penned document online, Commissioners Record Series, *Cumberland County Archives* (http://www.ccpa.net/ : accessed January 2016), Carlisle, Pennsylvania.

48. *Tax Rates Book, 1768-1770*, Book 004, "Cumberland Townp 1769," Cumberland County, Cumberland Township, p. 238, entry for Lewis Davison, p. 240, entry for Wm Davison, digital copy of penned document online, Commissioners Record Series, *Cumberland County Archives* (http://www.ccpa.net/ : accessed January 2016); Carlisle, Pennsylvania.

49. Albert, *History of Westmoreland County, Pennsylvania*, p. 40.

50. Albert, *History of Westmoreland County, Pennsylvania*, pp. 40-41.

51. Veech, p. 38.

52. Albert, *History of Westmoreland County, Pennsylvania*, p. 180.

53. The children of Lewis-I can be found on the following pages in Harbaugh's book: William-III, p. 129 & 249; Lewis-II, p. 336; Thomas, p. 368; Hannah, p. 374; Elizabeth, p. 397; Rachel, p. 397; Jeremiah, p. 397.

54. Ibid. Harbaugh offers no source for her information (including the birthdates of the children) which are here assumed to be correct with the only exception of Jeremiah. His birthdate is given by Harbaugh as 1869 which is a typographical error. It is thought that 1769 was intended, which means that he was born after the migration to Pennsylvania.

55. Harbaugh, p. 336, says that Lewis-II settled in Fort Cumberland, Maryland where he died in 1814. Although his place of death is confirmed by the existence of his last will, it seems unlikely that Lewis-II remained behind while the entire rest of the family moved on to Pennsylvania, especially considering his age (about 17 years). Speculatively, it would seem more likely that Lewis-II migrated to Pennsylvania with his family, then later returned east for some

reason and chose to settle in Maryland. No source was found providing further information.

56. John Frederick Dorman, FASG, *Adventurers of Purse and Person, Virginia 1607-1624/5*, 4th ed, 4th printing, Volume I, Families A-F (Baltimore, MD: Genealogical Publishing Company, 2004), print, p. 116.

57. T. C. Conwell, *The Conwell's of Dyer's Delight*, not published, dated 1984, 91 typewritten pages, p. 30, digital version, *Ancestry* (http://www.ancestry.com : accessed October 2013).

58. Westmoreland County, Pennsylvania, Recorder of Deeds, Deed Book A: 239, "Indenture, James Gilmore to Lewis Davidson," 29 June 1767, recorded 22 May 1781, photocopy of penned document, Greensburg, Pennsylvania.

59. The land transaction (James Gilmore to Lewis Davidson) was dated 29 June 1767, but this conveyance was not recorded until 22 May 1781. Since Gilmore put his signature to the document, this indicates that it was prepared in 1767, and therefore witnessed in 1767 by William Conwell. The recording of the indenture was much delayed due to the volume of transactions flooding the land office before and following the Revolutionary War.

60. William Blackstone, *Commentaries on the Laws of England*, Twelfth Edition, Book I of IV (London: A. Strahan and W. Woodfall, 1793), Chapter 17, especially pp. 462-466, *Google Books* (http://books.google.com : accessed June 2016). Blackstone discusses the ages one must have reached in order to legally accomplish various tasks under the law, including the age of majority being 21 years for males.

61. John W. Jordan and James Hadden, *Genealogical and Personal History of Fayette County, Pennsylvania*, Volume II (New York: Lewis Historical Publishing Company, 1912), pp. 603-605, digital version, *Internet Archive* (http://www.archive.org : accessed October 2013). Some of the connections between the Conwell and Stockley families are discussed in this work.

62. F. Edward Wright, *Land Records of Sussex County Delaware 1769-1782, Deed Books L No. 11 & M No. 12* (Westminster, Maryland: Family Line Publications, 1994), print, p. 146. In this transaction, Thomas Stockley of Westmoreland County, sold a 600-acre parcel of land in Angola Hundred, Sussex County, Delaware to Thomas Robinson on 5 February 1778. Thomas Stockley was William-III's western neighbor in Pennsylvania.

63. See Campbell, *Warrantee Township Map: Fayette County, Luzerne Township* as well as the works of Brewer, Mason, Wright, and Malone in the bibliography for Delaware land abstracts.

64. Albert, *History of Westmoreland County, Pennsylvania*, p. 181, gives an excellent description of a packhorse saddle.

65. Veech, p. 38, says pack-horses had to be used west of the mountains until 1789.

66. Albert, *History of Westmoreland County, Pennsylvania*, p. 183, agrees with Veech and provides additional details about pack-horses. Veech personally witnessed the pack-horse trains.

67. Mrs. Ellet, *Pioneer Women of the West* (New York: Charles Scribner, 1856), p. 77, digital version, *Internet Archive* (http://www.archive.org : accessed November 2013).

68. Veech, p. 37; Albert, *History of Westmoreland County, Pennsylvania*, p. 181.

69. Veech, p. 37.

70. Van Voorhis, p. 11.

71. Albert, *History of Westmoreland County, Pennsylvania*, p. 177; Veech, p. 26. Nemacolin was described as a friendly Delaware Indian who owned a cabin on Dunlap's Creek in what later became Fayette County. The southern end of Dunlap's Creek was about a mile north easterly from William-III's *Dispute Ended* parcel. This illustrates that the Davidsons, among others, resided further west on the frontier than did some members of the Six Nations.

72. Albert, *History of Westmoreland County, Pennsylvania*, p. 177. Albert offers a fairly elaborate discussion about the early trails.

73. Veech, pp. 28-29. The Redstone Trail was originally an old Six Nations trail improved into a road by Col. James Burd and was afterward called Burd's Road.

74. Albert, *History of Westmoreland County, Pennsylvania*, p. 38 and p. 179, Footnote 2, the road to Redstone was heavily traveled from 1765.

75. Albert, *History of Westmoreland County, Pennsylvania*, pp. 154-155.

Pennsylvania

76. Ibid.

77. Van Voorhis, p. 7.

78. Ibid.

79. Ibid.

80. Ibid.

81. Albert, *History of Westmoreland County, Pennsylvania*, p. 155.

82. Van Voorhis, p. 7.

83. Ibid.

84. Edgar W. Hassler, *Old Westmoreland: A History of Western Pennsylvania During the Revolution* (Cleveland, Ohio : The Arthur H. Clark Company, 1900), p. 117, digital version, *Google Books* (http//books.google.com : accessed July 2011).

85. Albert, *History of Westmoreland County, Pennsylvania*, Chapter XXX, "The Pioneers-Their Houses, Furniture, etc."

86. Ibid.

87. Veech, p. 99; Albert, *History of Westmoreland County, Pennsylvania*, p. 41; estimate of 150 families in the Fayette and Turkey Foot regions in 1768.

88. *Pennsylvania, U.S. Direct Tax Lists, 1798*, Schedule *A*, penned document, page unnumbered, untitled, line 21, entry for Wm Davidson, Fayette County, Luzerne Township, digital image 29 of 426, *Ancestry* (http://www.ancestry.com : accessed 2011), citing microfilm M372, Tax Lists for the State of Pennsylvania, Records of the Internal Revenue Service, 1791-2006, Record Group 58; National Archives and Records Administration, Washington, D.C.

89. *Pennsylvania, U.S. Direct Tax Lists, 1798*, Schedule *B*, penned document, page unnumbered, untitled, line 51, entry for Wm Davidson, Fayette County, Luzerne Township, digital image 144 of 426, *Ancestry* (http://www.ancestry.com : accessed 2011), citing microfilm M372, Tax Lists for the State of Pennsylvania, Records of the Internal Revenue Service, 1791-

2006, Record Group 58; National Archives and Records Administration, Washington, D.C.

90. *Pennsylvania, U.S. Direct Tax Lists, 1798*, Schedule *D*, penned document, page unnumbered, untitled, line 21, entry for Wm Davidson, Fayette County, Luzerne Township, digital image 281 of 426, *Ancestry* (http://www.ancestry.com : accessed 2011), citing microfilm M372, Tax Lists for the State of Pennsylvania, Records of the Internal Revenue Service, 1791-2006, Record Group 58; National Archives and Records Administration, Washington, D.C.

91. *Pennsylvania, U.S. Direct Tax Lists, 1798*, Schedule *E*, penned document, page unnumbered, untitled, line 51, entry for Wm Davidson, Fayette County, Luzerne Township, digital image 346 of 426, *Ancestry* (http://www.ancestry.com : accessed 2011), citing microfilm M372, Tax Lists for the State of Pennsylvania, Records of the Internal Revenue Service, 1791-2006, Record Group 58; National Archives and Records Administration, Washington, D.C.

92. The *Pennsylvania, U.S. Direct Tax Lists, 1798*, Schedule *B*, specifies this William Davidson (William-III) to be one whose land adjoins William Conwell and Aaron Hackney; this information combined with Campbell's *Warrantee Township Map: Fayette County, Luzerne Township* provides sufficient proof of identity.

93. *Pennsylvania, U.S. Direct Tax Lists, 1798*, Schedule *A*, penned document, page unnumbered, untitled, line 19, entry for Jehu Conwell, Fayette County, Luzerne Township, digital image 28 of 426, *Ancestry* (http://www.ancestry.com : accessed 2011), citing microfilm M372, Tax Lists for the State of Pennsylvania, Records of the Internal Revenue Service, 1791-2006, Record Group 58; National Archives and Records Administration, Washington, D.C.

94. *Tax Rates Book, 1768-1770*, Book 004, "Cumberland Rates 1768," Cumberland County, Cumberland Township, p. 31, 2nd entry for Lewis Davison, assessed eight pounds, eight shillings, four pence province tax and four pounds county tax, digital copy of penned document online, Commissioners Record Series, *Cumberland County Archives* (http://www.ccpa.net/ : accessed January 2016), Carlisle, Pennsylvania.

95. *Tax Rates Book, 1768-1770*, Book 004, "Cumberland Townp 1769," Cumberland County, Cumberland Township, p. 238, entry for Lewis Davison, assessed 19 shillings, four pence, province tax and one pound county tax, digital copy of

penned document online, Commissioners Record Series, *Cumberland County Archives* (http://www.ccpa.net/ : accessed January 2016), Carlisle, Pennsylvania.

96. As previously established, the family was in Pennsylvania by June 1767. Lewis-I had ten acres cleared based on the 1768 tax record; the 1769 tax record says the family had an additional six acres cleared.

97. Bob Powell, *The Walking Plow*, not published, not dated, digital version, 3 pages, illustrated, *ALHFAM.org* (http://www.alhfam.org/pdfs/FARM_PIG_Info_sheet-1.pdf : accessed June 2013).

98. Van Voorhis, p. 12.

99. Harbaugh, p. 129.

100. *Commemorative Biographical Record of the Counties of Harrison and Carroll, Ohio* (Chicago: J. H. Beers & Co., 1891), article: "Lewis H. Davidson," p. 446, *Google Books* (http://books.google.com : accessed April 2013).

101. Harbaugh, p.134; John, first child of William-III and Rosanna, was born 12 December 1770.

102. Merri Lou Scribner Schaumann, *Tax Lists - Cumberland County, Pennsylvania, 1768, 1769, 1770* (Carlisle, Pennsylvania: 1972), pp. 16 (1768), 87 (1769), 168 (1770).

103. *Commemorative Biographical Record...*, p. 446. It appears that Lewis H. Davidson (Lewis-IV) was the first to record this information in widely published form.

104. Harbaugh, p. 134.

105. Ellis, pp. 634-635.

106. Jordan and Hadden, pp. 603-605.

107. *Pennsylvania, U.S. Direct Tax Lists, 1798*, Schedule B, penned document, page unnumbered, untitled, line 41, entry for Jehu Conwell, Fayette County, Luzerne Township, digital image 143 of 426, *Ancestry* (http://www.ancestry.com : accessed 2011), citing microfilm M372, Tax Lists for the State of Pennsylvania, Records of the Internal Revenue Service, 1791-2006, Record Group 58; National Archives and Records Administration, Washington, D.C.

108. Hassler, p. 9.

109. Ibid.

110. George Dallas Albert, "The Frontier Forts of Western Pennsylvania," incorporated into *Report of the Commission to Locate the Site of the Frontier Forts of Pennsylvania*, Volume Two (Clarence M. Busch, State Printer of Pennsylvania, 1896), pp. 395-396, digital version, *Google Books* (http://books.google.com : accessed August 2011).

111. Albert, *History of Westmoreland County, Pennsylvania*, Chapters XIII, XIV, XV.

112. Ibid.

113. Ibid.

114. The reader should be aware that not all accounts agree as to the character of Connolly. According to some, Connolly is described as a Militia Captain protecting the frontier from depredations by the Six Nations; by other accounts he and his men amounted to a group of thugs grossly overstepping their authority. Albert's work, from which this limited account was summarized, included source citations and was thought to be materially credible. Further research into the events of this war, although interesting, are beyond the scope of this work.

115. Sipe, p. 497.

116. Albert, *History of Westmoreland County, Pennsylvania*, p. 67.

117. John N. Boucher, *History of Westmoreland County Pennsylvania*, Volume I (New York: The Lewis Publishing Company, 1906), p. 63, digital version, *Google Books* (http://books. google.com : accessed June 2011).

118. Sipe, pp. 490-492.

119. Sipe, pp. 488-499. Albert provides a quite different account of the events leading up to Lord Dunmore's War, partly due to his focus on local events that occurred in the area around Westmoreland County.

120. Albert, *History of Westmoreland County, Pennsylvania*, Chapters XIII, XIV, XV.

Pennsylvania

121. Ibid.

122. Ellis, p. 634. The distance from the Davidson's and Conwell's to Dunlap's Creek was about one mile. Ellis says the Conwell blockhouse was located about half a mile below Merrittstown, but the Warrantee map shows the Coleman tract and judging by this it seems more likely to have been located just slightly north and west of Merrittstown.

123. Albert, *The Frontier Forts of Western Pennsylvania*, pp. 395-396.

7

Revolutionary War

In 1775, the Revolutionary War officially began with the first shots exchanged between British and American troops at Lexington on April 19th. The Revolutionary War was fought from 1775 to 1783 and during this period many governmental activities were temporarily suspended, including the processing of land purchases in Pennsylvania.

Prior to the Revolution, the colonies were under the jurisdiction of the British Crown and many who later became patriots to America had previous experience loyally serving in the army of King George III, including, for example, George Washington. After the war started, the colonists became the occupying irritant and the displaced British became an ally to many of those in the Six Nations who wanted removal of the settlers.

William "Ranger" Davidson

It is now impossible to determine the full extent of William Davidson's involvement in the Revolution. Many records in general have been lost through neglect, poor record keeping, fires and so forth. It is known that many Westmoreland County records were lost in the burning of Hannastown by the Six Nations and Canadians in July 1782.[1-3] However, the limited extant records still available certainly show that William-III did indeed actively serve in the War as a patriot to America.

It is not known how many persons have searched in vain for a pension file for William-III, including this author.[4] The knowledge gained by researching historical events would have saved many hours of anxiously waiting for a response from the various archives and the many dollars paid for fruitless searches.

The benefit plans enacted by congress prior to 1832 were mostly reserved for disabled veterans or those who were unable to earn a living. Judging by his activities following the war, it is not likely that William-III sustained a disabling wound, nor could he have honestly claimed poverty. He would probably have qualified for a pension based on legislation passed in 1832, and even Barbara would likely have qualified for a widow's pension based on later rules, however neither William-III nor Barbara lived long enough to apply for a pension for which they would qualify.[5] Similar searches for the pension records of others who served in the same company in which William-III served were likewise not found, probably for similar reasons.

It will be remembered that the Davidsons resided in Springhill Township in Bedford County in 1772. In 1773, Springhill Township became part of Westmoreland County.[6,7] As discussed previously, the family settled about six or eight miles southwest of Redstone. This is important to know because the ability to associate individuals with their service records is largely based upon where they resided at the time. Usually the difficult part is locating the patriot's place of residence, but fortunately this task is made easier by examination of the Warrantee Township Maps prepared by the Land Office and which are today held by the Pennsylvania State Archives.[8]

Revolutionary War

Harbaugh had found and cited two Revolutionary War references for William-III in the Pennsylvania Archives, "Rangers on the Frontiers, 1778-1783" and also "Soldiers Who Received Depreciation Pay…" both from Series 5, Volume IV.[9,10] These records confirm that William-III was a Private in the Westmoreland County Militia. It is the reference to Ranger from the former record that gave rise to the posthumous nickname, apparently coined by Harbaugh, for William-III as "Ranger" Davidson to distinguish him from his grandfather and the many descendants who went by the same name. The records cited by Harbaugh are somewhat disappointing, amounting only to a transcribed list of names created by archivists. Nor is any explanation offered by Harbaugh as to how it was assured that the Davidson found in the records was our particular William-III.

Harbaugh also failed to locate, or at least to report, the companies in which William-III served and this information was not found in any other document examined in the preparation of this work. An important document overlooked by (or possibly not yet available to) Harbaugh when her research was conducted was the *Revolutionary War Military Abstract Card*. These cards, prepared by archivists, act as an important index to many of the Pennsylvania soldiers who participated in some way in the Revolutionary War. A card was located for William-III showing that he was assigned to the Westmoreland County Militia, but neither unit nor rank is indicated. The index card includes a reference to *Certificate 7861* issued on 10 December 1785 and bears an amount of £1.0.5. Under the heading *Authorities*, a reference is made to *Vol. A, p 246*.[11] Inquiry was made with the Pennsylvania Archives regarding this information and several important documents were located beyond those described by Harbaugh.

First, the *Certificate Register* was retrieved.[12] This original handwritten source document shows that William-III was compensated one pound, no shillings, and five pence (£1.0.5) for providing either service or supplies to the military.[13] Based on this record, several other documents were located. One of these was a copy of a handwritten *Receipt Roll*, prepared in late 1784 or 1785.[14] This was the earliest document found stating what was owed to each man as recorded by the Company in which they served. The men who were owed payment, listed on the left side of the paper, included (in order):

> Saml McGibbin – 16 [shillings]
> Saml Adams – 2..0..9
> John Adams – 18..1
> Capt. Wm Conwell – 3..14..9
> Wm Davison – 1..0..5

At the right side of the page is written *William Conwell* and beneath his name is *Int paid*. This record is an acknowledgement by Captain William Conwell that he had signed for the certificates and received the interest earned on the pay owed to the men listed. It will be remembered that William Conwell was a stepson of Lewis-I who grew up with William-III, and he also owned a parcel of land adjoining William-III's southern boundary in 1778. The amounts recorded on the *Receipt Roll* represent those amounts not already paid in hand to the soldiers. In other words, William-III may have previously received some of his pay.

The next report is interesting and its importance may be easily missed. The *County Lieutenant Distribution Ledger* lists the men from various companies who were owed money for their service, but most importantly, this report proves that William-III actually served on active duty in Captain William Conwell's company![15]

Next, the *State Ledger* lists the total amount owed to the men who served in Captain Conwell's Company (24 pounds, 1 shilling, 8 pence).[16] There are three important details found in this document: the dates of service, the type or rate of pay, and the reason for compensation.

The dates served were recorded as *24 Sept – 27 Oct 1778*, a period of 34 days. According to the rules, those serving in the Pennsylvania Militia were to serve up to two months on each tour of active duty.

Revolutionary War

The militiamen were generally compensated at the same rate of pay as their counterparts in the Continental Army. Some soldiers also received State pay, which was often indicated when a service was performed by the soldier that merited a bonus or some specific service beyond normal duty. William-III was compensated at the Continental rate as recorded on the State Ledger. In 1778, the approximate monthly salaries for Continental soldiers were: private, 6-2/3 dollars; corporal, 7-1/3 dollars; sergeant, 8 dollars; ensign, 10 dollars; lieutenant, 13-1/3 dollars; and captain, 20 dollars.[17]

The State Ledger includes entries for both active service as well as compensation paid to citizens for the provision of supplies to the military, such as horses, cattle, flour, etc. The fact that the entry for William Conwell's company lists the dates of service and that no supplies or materials are specified, further confirms that the compensation owed to Conwell's company was for actual military service rendered.

The final document, and perhaps the most interesting, is the *Militia Loan Certificate* and the *Certificate Counterpart*.[18,19] Militia Loan Certificates were controlled documents (i.e. numbered) so they could be accounted for. Each soldier owed money was issued a certificate bearing their name (William Davidson), the certificate number (7861), the organization to which they were attached (Westmoreland Co, Militia), the date of issue (10 December 1785) and of course, the amount owed (£1.0.5). These documents were printed on linen paper and completed in duplicate (a left and right-hand side). The *Certificate*, the right-hand side, was torn off and provided to the soldier for redemption at a later time, while the *Counterpart* was retained by the issuing authority. When redeemed, the certificate was authenticated by matching its jagged edge to its counterpart, similar to an indenture or early deed. Once redeemed, the counterpart was marked paid, "Now settled," and the certificate was collected from the soldiers and pasted into ledgers for archiving. The brief discussion on the Pennsylvania State Archives web site regarding pay states:

William "Ranger" Davidson

Pay for military service was often long delayed. Thousands of militiamen returned from tours of active duty unpaid, bearing only a slip signed by a commanding officer. General financial confusion and the collapse of wartime currencies made prompt payment impossible, but eventually, under an act of April 1, 1784, Pennsylvania compensated such [debts owed to soldiers in] payment for their active service and settled accounts with certain other public creditors by passing to them interest bearing Certificates of the funded or Militia Debt. These certificates (bonds in the modern sense) were ultimately redeemed at face value. Unfortunately, when redemption came many of the original holders had long since sold their certificates at heavy discounts.[20]

The Militia Loan Certificates were bearer instruments. Whoever had possession of the certificate also held title to the principal value as well as any unpaid interest. It was common practice for the soldiers to "assign" or sell their certificates to another person in exchange for some form of currency or to barter for supplies. Such trades came with a degree of risk because it was uncertain at that time when, or whether, the government would have the financial capability of actually repaying these debts. Due to the risk involved, the purchaser of the certificate typically required a discounted purchase price or an amount below the face value shown on the certificate. Such deals were not regulated, but privately negotiated.

The certificates earned interest at the rate of 6% beginning 1 July 1783, so William-III was already owed the value of his certificate plus nearly one and a half year's back interest by the time it was issued to him on 10 December 1785, for service he performed in 1778! The interest at that time was typically calculated and paid annually. Beginning in 1786, interest was paid twice per year, but could be collected at various times.[21]

William-III may have appeared in person when his certificate was torn off and handed out by an agent from the Comptroller General's Office, however, there is also a chance that he never saw his certificate. As noted previously, Captain William Conwell accepted the interest payment in place of William-III and the other three men shown on the Receipt Roll which could indicate that William-III's certificate had been assigned to Conwell. Unfortunately, it is not possible today to determine the exact arrangement between the two men. Captain Conwell may have only been authorized to collect the interest payment on William-III's behalf.

Two other persons may have subsequently taken ownership of William-III's certificate or at least accepted interest payments for him and later delivered those amounts to the actual owner. By November 1787, a man named Nathaniel Breading (a neighbor of both Davidson and Conwell) was receiving payments. The last known bearer of William-III's certificate was a man named Theophilus Philips who began receiving interest payments by March 1788.[22] William-III's certificate was held for five years and ultimately redeemed about 1790.[23] As previously stated, we don't know whether William-III collected the interest for five years and redeemed his certificate or whether he had long since sold it.

The search for other entries among the war records pertaining to William-III (or anyone else), is possible by visiting the internet website http://www.fold3.com (formerly www.footnote.com) where many of the Pennsylvania State Archives records have been scanned and are available at no cost as of this writing. One of these documents was the Muster of Captain Conwell's Company in which William-III is found again, included under the heading, "List of Soldiers Who Served as Rangers on the Frontiers. 1778 – 1783." This record is significant because it puts William-III into context with a Company in which he served.[24]

In another search, Captain William Conwell was found in "A Return of the Officers of the Fourth Battalion of Westmoreland County Militia With the No. of the Company." Listed in the 2nd

Company is Captain William Conwell along with Jesse Rude, 1st Lieutenant; John Armstrong, 2nd Lieutenant; and Saml. Adams, Ensign.[25] These men were officers to whom Private William Davidson may have reported sometime during his service.

Yet another transcribed list of miscellaneous soldiers who served in the Militia included the following entry, here reproduced in its entirety, "Wm. Conwell, Capt. of Ranging co., Westmoreland co., 1778."[26]

The reader should keep in mind that the previous references to William-III's Revolutionary War involvement so far discussed relate to the same period of service. A second record of Captain Conwell, recorded in 1791 was located, but William-III was not listed in this record.[27]

To summarize the records that survive, William-III, a private, served a 34-day period of active duty (24 September through 27 October 1778) in Captain William Conwell's Company in Westmoreland County, a component of the Pennsylvania Militia, as organized in 1778.

In January 1778, William Conwell was elected Captain of 2nd Company, 4th Battalion.[28] However, the service system required the men to serve on a rotation when called to active duty. This caused the men to serve in a different company number when called up. The rotation was based upon the class to which each soldier was designated. Unfortunately, we don't know with certainty to which class William Conwell or William-III were assigned. Nor do we know whether this battalion even adhered to the rotation rules (discussed in more detail later in this chapter). For these reasons, the name of the company captain is generally considered a more important distinction than the company or battalion number when attempting to associate a soldier with either his permanent or his active duty unit.[29]

The records thus show that William-III actively participated in the Revolutionary War. Given his age (31 years in November 1778), he was subject to call to report for active duty throughout the war, but the records evidencing his further service were not found and may in fact no longer exist.

Revolutionary War

Although the purpose of William-III's service in 1778 remains hidden from the record, it is quite possible that he was part of a detail operating in support of Continental troops. In May 1778, Brigadier General Lachlan McIntosh was put in charge of the Western Department by General Washington. His predecessor, Brigadier General Edward Hand, had requested reassignment following several failed attempts to gain control of the frontier. McIntosh subsequently assumed command at Fort Pitt along with the men of the Eighth Pennsylvania and Thirteenth Virginia Regiments of the Continental Line.[30]

McIntosh devised an aggressive plan to march west from Fort Pitt with the aim of attacking Detroit, some 350 miles northwest through hostile territory. Following several delays for a variety of reasons, McIntosh began his campaign in mid-September, later than originally intended. He ordered Fort McIntosh to be built near the mouth of the Beaver River where it emptied into the Ohio River (where the town of Beaver, Pennsylvania stands today). This was the furthest point west that supplies could be more easily transported by water and McIntosh planned to use this defensive position as an advance supply depot.[31]

Due largely to slow progress in moving two regiments on primitive trails through the harsh wilderness and difficulties obtaining needed supplies, little was accomplished during this campaign apart from erecting Fort McIntosh, only about 35 miles from Fort Pitt. Fort Laurens was also erected on a site located about a half mile south of where the town of Bolivar, Ohio stands today. This fort was placed there to satisfy an agreement with the Six Nations. By the time the small stockade of Fort Laurens was built, winter was setting in and a small garrison of men was left to defend the two distant forts while the disappointed McIntosh retired to Fort Pitt. By February, McIntosh concluded his frustrations by requesting his own recall from the frontier, in similar fashion as his predecessor.[32]

The point of this discussion is that the period of service of William-III coincides with the campaign of McIntosh. It will be recalled that William-III served from 24 September until 27 October in 1778. This is approximately when McIntosh began his campaign and extends until the completion of Fort McIntosh, which reportedly took four weeks.[33]

At certain times, federal troops operating in the Western Department (essentially the frontier counties) requested assistance and support from the Pennsylvania Militia. Such activities were typically coordinated through the Supreme Executive Council and the County Lieutenants, generally for a specific operation or period of time.

All of this information combines to form a good chance that Captain Conwell's Company (along with Private William Davidson) served in support of McIntosh's expedition, possibly operating under the agreement to provide additional support until a structure could be erected to protect and garrison the main force, in other words, until Fort McIntosh was completed.[34-36]

While a good chance exists that William-III did serve in the manner just described, unfortunately no documentary evidence was found that would show proof for this conclusion.[37]

One additional authentic military record was found in searching the Pennsylvania Archives, but it has been added last in this discussion because only one document exists. Examination of Pennsylvania Archives Series 6, Volume II, page 314, revealed a transcript listing *William Daveson* elected ensign in the Return of Westmoreland County's 4th Battalion, 4th Company dated 24 September 1783.[38,39]

It is significant that the record transcript created by archivists specifies *Daveson* but the spelling in the actual handwritten source document could also be *Davison*, which is a more common spelling variant of *Davidson*. The only other person on this return for this company was a man whose name was spelled *Reason Virgin* in the transcript.[40] Again, the source document reveals the actual spelling of *Rezon* which may be taken as a spelling variant of *Rezin*.[41] Rezin Virgin was elected captain of this company.

For the reasons just described, additional attention was given to this record to determine whether this William Davidson was in fact our William-III. The fact that Rezin Virgin was drafted into a Westmoreland County battalion is proof enough that he was then residing in that place since only residents were included in the draft. Next, it was necessary to show that Rezin resided near William-III.

In October 1785, Rezin warranted a 330-acre tract of land called *Virgin's Delight*, about two miles northwest of William-III's *Dispute Ended* tract, putting these two men within the same general neighborhood.[42-44]

Additional research resulted in the discovery of several sources placing Rezin Virgin in Westmoreland County before the war and also evidencing his service as a captain in the Militia. Among these, is a brief biography by Leckey describing Rezin's residence on the Fayette County side of the Monongahela River during the war and his active participation as a captain.[45]

Rezin was also named in at least two court hearings held at Fort Pitt (also then known as Fort Dunmore). The jurisdiction of this court was then in dispute, but was held nevertheless by a Virginia magistrate in territory simultaneously claimed by Pennsylvania as Westmoreland County. In May 1775, Rezin himself petitioned the court to consider building a road from "the foot of Laurel Hill…to the Mouth of Wheeling." Rezin was appointed as a "viewer" to advise the court as to the conveniences and inconveniences surrounding such a project. If the proposed road was reasonably straight, it would run through Westmoreland County from east to west and possibly not far from Rezin's property. The road was ordered to be constructed in September the same year.[46]

In another hearing, the court appointed Samuel McBride a Constable "in the room of Razon Virgin." This is here interpreted as meaning that a new Constable was appointed by the court to replace Rezin who had recently held that office. This second hearing occurred in January 1775.[47] Both court records are strong statements as to Rezin's long-term interest in his Westmoreland County settlement.

Perhaps even more compelling evidence is found in the pension records for soldiers from Westmoreland County who testified under oath in court that they served under Captain Rezin Virgin. In one file, William Alexander testified that he served under the Captain in May and September 1777. In a second file, the deponent, James Huston, states that he was captured while on a "spy" mission on the frontier in March 1782 while under the command of Captain Rezin Virgin. James was released in 1783 and returned to his home in what had by then become Washington County, but was formerly a part of Westmoreland County.[48]

In 1783, Fayette County was formed and the settlements of both Rezin and William-III were then found in Luzerne Township. It may also be shown that Rezin continued his settlement in Fayette County by the tax record of 1785 and by the completion of his land patent in August 1787.[49,50] In fact, it can be shown that he was still there at least until 1800 when both the U.S. Federal Census and Pennsylvania's Septennial Census were taken.[51,52]

Although more sources were found than those referenced here, those just discussed were deemed sufficient for the purpose at hand. Thus, by showing that Rezin Virgin was a neighbor of William-III, that he resided in Westmoreland County before his election to Captain in 1783, and that he continued to reside there throughout his commission (3-years), we may conclude that the two persons in the Return of 1783 are our William-III and his neighbor Rezin Virgin. It is notable that an archivist at the Pennsylvania State Archives agreed that this was a reasonable conclusion.[53]

This second record is therefore attributed to William-III, who was elected on 24 September 1783, by the 4th Company of the 4th Battalion, to serve as the lowest ranking commissioned officer, an ensign, in the Westmoreland County branch of the Pennsylvania Militia. The election of Captain Rezin Virgin's Company took place just 21 days after the Revolutionary War ended. In this case, the 4th Company of the 4th Battalion describes the permanent unit to which William-III was attached rather than the corresponding active duty unit.[54]

In the Continental Army, infantry ensigns were given the duty of carrying the colors or flag of the regiment and they had the responsibility of ensuring the appropriate dress and cleanliness of the men comprising the company. The Militia ensigns likely had identical or at least similar duties as their Continental Army counterparts and frontier ensigns may have taken on some of the duties normally assigned to company lieutenants. A company lieutenant was responsible for ensuring that the lower ranking soldiers performed their duties, inspected their weapons, and monitored provisions. They may also have set guards while on active duty. The U. S. Army abolished the rank of ensign in 1800.[55,56]

Fayette County was formed only two days after the election of Rezin and William-III. Following this boundary change both men then resided in Luzerne Township. They would have retained their commissions, but it is unlikely they retained their assignments to the same battalion or company once the Fayette County authorities took administrative control.

Officers at that time were not required to be land owners, but they did agree to serve a minimum of three years, the duration of their commission, which extends the known service record of William-III considerably, even though the details of this service do not exist.[57]

Next, it is necessary to address two other sources describing William-III's Revolutionary War service including Harbaugh who states, "Tradition claims he transported food and other supplies from Baltimore, Md., during and after the Revolutionary War, by trains of pack-horses to Western Pa. and Eastern Ohio."[58] No source is supplied for this information, which was possibly slightly altered and paraphrased by Harbaugh from a DAR record published in 1929. The quote from this latter source reads, "Our tradition is that he had charge of a pack horse outfit transporting food from Philadelphia to Valley Forge."[59] While not impossible, it is unlikely that a private on the western frontier would be given charge of a supply mission over the distant mountains back east. A private was the lowest rank a soldier could hold and supplying General Washington's army has long been a popular exaggeration of an ancestor's war-time service. Both Harbaugh and the DAR record cited, correctly reduce this claim to tradition since there are certainly no extant records to support it and no mention of any descendent testimony was offered by these sources.

William "Ranger" Davidson

Certain terms must now be clarified briefly for the reader as these may cause confusion in the ensuing discussions. The Continental Army or Continental Line refers to troops commanded by General George Washington. The Pennsylvania Line refers to regiments, initially comprised of men from Pennsylvania, which were part of the Continental Army. The Continental Army could be ordered to serve in any geographic location as the needs of the military were determined. In today's terms, the Continental Army essentially meant federal troops, components of which were the forerunner of today's U.S. Army.

The Pennsylvania Militia was generally limited to operation within state boundaries and was a distinctly different organization having separate lines of authority from Washington's Army. These troops were organized, managed, and commanded by Pennsylvania's governing arm, the Supreme Executive Council, which directed the actions of the Militia through County Lieutenants.

During research, an important distinction came to light which must be clarified and explained, probably to the great disappointment of many readers. The capacity in which William-III actually served is vague and can no longer be positively determined from the records that survive. Although William-III was definitely in the Pennsylvania Militia, there is no proof that he ever served in the capacity of a ranger.

Technically, to be called a "ranger," means that the soldier was specifically recruited into a Company of Rangers, also called a Ranger Company.[60] These companies were composed of volunteers, established by Pennsylvania's Supreme Executive Council and directed by the County Lieutenants. As such, the rangers were not organizationally attached to a battalion and therefore did not have a battalion commander. Ranger Companies typically served an active duty tour of six months or longer and generally acted with more operational freedom than their Militia counterparts. There were fewer than a dozen Ranger Companies formed over the course of the entire war as evidenced by examination of the Council's minutes and correspondence.[61]

Revolutionary War

For clarification and convenience only, the phrase Regular Militia or Militia Regulars will be used herein to refer to those men in the Pennsylvania Militia not serving in a Ranger Company; but, keep in mind that these specific terms carry no meaning outside of this book.

The Pennsylvania Militia was under the command of the Supreme Executive Council, but unlike the Ranger Companies, a much longer chain of command was established which flowed from the Council to the County Lieutenants, then to the battalion commanders, and finally through the ranks to the company captains. Unlike Ranger Companies, service in the Regular Militia was compulsory and the militiamen were subject to serve several tours of duty, on a rotational basis, each lasting a period of two months or less. Captain Conwell's company was not known to have been organized as a Ranger Company and in fact was a Regular Militia company, at one point, attached to the 4th Battalion as the documentation shows. Captain Virgin's company was also attached to the 4th Battalion when William-III was elected ensign in 1783 and was also a Regular Militia company.

So, from where did the idea come that William-III was a frontier ranger? This misunderstanding undoubtedly stemmed from a few documents published by the Pennsylvania Archives in the early 1900's. Many military records were compiled and organized under the guidance of archivist Dr. William H. Egle for the purpose of assisting researchers in finding Revolutionary War participants. The works applicable to this discussion were mostly drawn from the militia loan account records, including the registers, distribution ledgers, and payrolls.[62] These records mostly relate to Militia units from the frontier counties (Westmoreland, Washington, Northampton, Bedford, Northumberland). Unfortunately, certain aspects of Egle's work are misleading if not incorrect. Among Egle's works were transcripts which list William-III among "Rangers on the Frontiers," and as a "Continental Line" soldier. While it is true that some of the men in Egle's lists did in fact serve as the document titles infer, many did not; they were simply grouped together under certain headings. These publications at best mislead researchers to believe, as did Harbaugh, that William-III served in a Ranger Company in the Continental Army. However, as has been discussed, Conwell's and Virgin's companies were not actually Ranger Companies, but it is easy to see how a casual researcher would place reliance on such records and could easily reach a mistaken conclusion. It was likely Egle's work that prompted Harbaugh to dub William-III, *William "Ranger" Davidson*, a nickname that has gained much recognition among descendants and a reason for this book's title.

Those serving in a Regular Militia company on the frontier, as did William-III, very likely did patrol or range the frontier as a part of their regular service.[63] In fact, several examples exist among the records of various companies for which the stated purpose of the tour of duty was to range the frontier.[64] The Militia Regulars rode over the same ground and essentially had the same objectives and duties as the Ranger Companies.

This now brings us to an important question. William-III resided on the frontier and his service was there, which allows us to say it is very likely he did range the frontier sometime during his service in the Pennsylvania Militia. As mentioned previously, Captain Conwell's unit is even described as a "ranging company" (as opposed to a Ranger Company). If you consider these circumstances and are accepting of probabilities, then the nickname "Ranger" remains. However, if convincing documentary evidence is required that would serve to prove service in a Ranger Company, then "Ranger" Davidson he is not. So, now the reader must decide whether or not William-III should continue to bear the nickname that has made him so well recognized.

Now that it has been established that William-III took an active part in the Revolutionary War and his factual service has been separated from tradition, a historical background into the framework and role of the Militia is needed.

Readers are directed to the work of Hanna Benner Roach whose extensive research into the actual role of the Militia should not be ignored by any serious researcher having a Revolutionary War era interest in Pennsylvania. Roach draws on the available records at the

Revolutionary War

Pennsylvania State Archives to paint a true picture of the activities of the Pennsylvania Militia, in which our William-III served. It is largely from Roach's work that the following details are summarized.[65]

The Militia was organized under an act by the Pennsylvania Commonwealth dated 17 March 1777 and provided for a mandatory draft applicable to all able bodied men between the ages of 18 and 53. It has been estimated that about 60,000 men were enlisted under the act.[66]

The lists of men prepared for the draft were derived from the tax rolls and battalion districts were delineated geographically. Thus, it was normal for the men in any given company to reside in the same neighborhood. Each battalion was composed of eight companies with each company to number 80 to 100 men.[67] But, this could vary greatly for a variety of reasons, particularly on the frontier. In William Conwell's Company, in which William-III is listed, only 25 men are included.[68] In a return prepared in May 1778 by Colonel Edward Cook, Conwell's 2nd Company, 4th Battalion, included only 34 men.[69]

Unlike the modern military practice of today in which men who rise slowly through the ranks with increasing experience and potential are eventually promoted to higher positions, the men in each Revolutionary War era battalion elected their own field officers. This was largely because officers were needed immediately; there was no time for extended periods of training or assessment. These men were expected to serve a term of three years and officers during the earlier years were required to be freeholders (landowners).

When the ranks were initially formed, the men were assigned to a "permanent" battalion and company. The men of the eight companies comprising each battalion were further divided into eight classes by drawing lots. The pool of men from all companies comprising each class was subject to being called to service on a rotational basis, generally in numeric sequence from the first through the eighth class.[70]

When called to active duty by class, all men from all companies having the designated class were formed into new companies and new battalion(s), if full battalion(s) were needed. This rotation caused each man to be assigned to an active duty company and battalion different from his permanent company and battalion. Thus, each man was generally assigned to two different Militia units. Each class normally served a two month tour with their active duty company and then returned to their permanent company until their class was called to active duty again.[71]

The western battalions frequently operated outside these rules due to the instability on the frontier and the nature of frontier warfare.[72] The records associated with William-III do not specify the class to which he was assigned nor even whether his battalion was made subject to the rotation rules. These issues further make it impossible to identify his active duty field officers.

To further obscure the ability to trace a soldier to his particular units, the Militia was reorganized about every three years (1777, 1780, 1783). This frequently renders any previous company and battalion reference for a given individual obsolete for subsequent service periods. If called to active duty in 1777 and also in 1780, the recruit could have been attached to a different battalion and company during each period.[73] This makes the period of organization an important component when citing a soldier's service.

Hopefully this explanation is sufficient for the reader to gain a rudimentary understanding of the service system. To delve deeper into such administrative matters is beyond the scope of this work, but those who are interested are here again referred to the work of Roach.

Locally, a County Lieutenant, holding the rank of Colonel, who was actually a civilian appointee, acted as local administrator of Militia business. In Westmoreland County, in 1778, Archibald Lochry was the Colonel and under him Edward Cook served as one of the Sub-Lieutenants (holding a civilian rank of Lieutenant Colonel). It was Edward Cook, who also served as a Colonel when he later replaced Lochry, and whose name appears on some of the documentation relating to William-III's war service.[74]

It was the job of the County Lieutenant, and those who assisted him, to provide the Militia arms, ammunition, and other supplies, and to locate substitutes and collect fines. The County Lieutenants were commanded by Pennsylvania's Supreme Executive Council. When the various classes of men were called up for duty, the County Lieutenant would notify the Captains who in turn were required to notify every man in their respective companies to report for active duty. The Captains physically rode to each man's home or place of business and left a written notice.[75] So Edward Cook, on orders from Lochry, contacted Captain William Conwell, who in turn rode to the home of William-III (as well as the other men in the company) and left a written notice on his door as to when and where to report for duty.

Roach cautions that locating an ancestor who was subject to the Pennsylvania draft is not enough to establish the role of that ancestor as a patriot. Under the Militia rules, if a man was called up, he could evade service by hiring a substitute to take his place. If a substitute was not provided, then a fine was paid. The fine was to be used by the County Lieutenant to hire a substitute.[76]

The recruits, organized in their permanent battalions, were required to attend training or drill only twelve times per year, but in many cases the prescribed schedule was not strictly followed.[77]

As shown by Roach, many of the Militia soldiers who did serve active duty spent much of their time marching from one location to another, frequently never seeing action. Sometimes by the time the men arrived at their destination, their two month tour of duty had nearly expired. Frequently, the battalions were so ill-equipped there was little they could achieve if actually engaged by the enemy. Perhaps drawing on the work of Roach, the Pennsylvania Archives goes on in even plainer language:

> Only in extreme cases was any individual militia man required to drill with his neighbors as many as twelve times each year, and at most he was called upon to perform during the entire course of the war, two or possibly three, short tours of active duty. Many men listed on company rosters never drilled, and tens of

thousands enrolled in the militia never experienced a single day of active duty. Avoiding militia calls was not difficult. A man who failed to report for drill merely paid an Exercise Fine. A militiaman called for active duty who found such duty inconvenient was permitted to hire a Substitute to march and fight in his stead. Frequently no substitute was furnished, but instead a Substitute Fine was paid. Militia fines became an important source of revenue.[78]

While many writers tend to romanticize Revolutionary War service, the facts exposed by Roach and the Pennsylvania Archives, paint a much less iconic image of the Pennsylvania Militiamen. Roach stresses that the records of the Pennsylvania Militia are far from complete and her study largely omitted battalions serving the frontier, probably due to lack of records.

In spite of the foregoing discussion, the danger that daily surrounded the pioneers should not be trivialized. Life on the frontier brought additional hardships not experienced by those residing east of the mountains. It was difficult to keep the frontier battalions fully staffed by the Militia due to the frequent acts of violence occurring all around the settlers, many of whom were preoccupied with their own personal defense.

In our case, we are fortunate to know that William-III served at least a short period of active duty, however, no company or regimental histories exist for the Revolutionary War as they do for the Civil War. We will likely never know the extent to which Captain Conwell's company and Captain Virgin's company were actively engaged in battle, if at all. While no battle records were found relating specifically to William-III, there are many documented cases of encounters with the Six Nations and Tory sympathizers among the Westmoreland County records.

The Pennsylvania Archives, Series 6, Volume II, contains many records documenting the capture and loss of men sustained by the

Militia on the frontier during the Revolution. Unfortunately, the records do not recount the details of most of these events, but rather the outcomes of the expeditions are reduced to lists of men who served along with brief descriptions of their fate. From the many examples that may be found only a few are reproduced here:

> Hugh Steer, taken prisoner
> Brownlee, killed by the Indians, July 13, 1782
> Lt. Anderson, captured, taken to Canada, returned 1782.

The need for increased protection for the frontier was exemplified in the letter dated 25 April 1778, written by Lieutenant Colonel Archibald Lochry, Westmoreland County, to Thomas Wharton of the Supreme Executive Council. In this letter, Lochry explains why difficulties were encountered in finding enough men to fill vacancies in the 4[th] Battalion:

> ...I am sorry to have reason to inform you that the Enemy [is] driving Captivating and killing so many of our Frontiers[men] [it] is the Only Cause [of] our Comp[an]y. Returns is reduced so low as they now stand...[79,80]

The effectiveness of the attacks on the frontier may be largely attributed to the British lieutenant governor, Colonel Henry Hamilton, who was then based in Detroit. By May 1776, he began to run interference between the colonists and the Six Nations.[81] His efforts intensified the division among the Six Nations, some of whom desired peace. Hamilton provided supplies and weapons to the Six Nations and Tory supporters for the purpose of launching raids into the frontier lands. Hamilton worked toward keeping the Six Nations and others convinced that the Colonies would lose the war under the superior numbers, organization, and wealth of the British Empire.

William "Ranger" Davidson

Inciting many of the Six Nations to war was not a difficult task given that borderers in settlements west of the New Purchase had already trespassed in the Indian Territories. At various times the Six Nations, assisted by British agents and also the Canadians, took part in many bloody raids including the burning of Hannastown in Westmoreland County.[82]

In response to the attacks and harassment of the frontiersmen, the Regular Militia from the western-most areas, which included Northumberland, Northampton, Bedford, Washington, and Westmoreland Counties, began ranging the frontier. As discussed previously, some volunteers also formed Ranger Companies to help support the defensive efforts.[83] The borderers were accustomed to the hardships of survival on the frontier and many had experience in dealing with the Six Nations in terms of barter and trade, but they also knew the country better than those troops east of the Allegheny's.

Generally, the mission of the Militia on the frontier was to reduce attacks on the settlers by their enemies, including Canadian and other mercenaries hired by the British. But, there were also attacks by roving bands from the Six Nations operating independently.

In the return of Captain Conwell's Company, when William-III served on active duty in 1778, the company consisted of 25 men. In a payroll abstract created in 1791, from a unit under the command of Captain Conwell, there were 60 men listed.[84] In contrast, the Six Nations typically operated in small bands numbering from four or five to perhaps something more than twenty.[85] They traveled light, often leaving their horses or canoes at a safe distance. The unsuspecting target was approached on foot for stealth, attacked quickly, and afterward the perpetrators promptly left the vicinity.[86]

Apart from their scalped victims and devastated livestock, the enemy also left behind proclamations authored by Hamilton urging the settlers to defect and to align themselves with King George in exchange for protection and rewards.[87] This combined guerilla warfare and propaganda campaign was effective at spreading both doubt and terror among the "buckskins," as some in the Six Nations referred to them, and also proved exceedingly difficult to combat. In 1779, Colonel Brodhead, then in command of the Western Department, reported that Westmoreland County was being attacked daily.[88]

The militia companies at least brought a military presence to the affected areas and may have initially produced a minimal deterrent by imposing the threat of reprisal. They made general patrols, for example, to "run the Pennsylvania and Virginia line" engaging the enemy whenever encountered and in some cases to track down the perpetrators of attacks.[89] There is little doubt that this was rather ineffective over the long haul considering the vast distance to be guarded. The Six Nations, who were skilled at quick and quiet movement, easily evaded the relatively noisy patrols of a company of Militiamen on horseback. The low effectiveness was especially felt in the first few years of the 1780's. In desperation, the Supreme Executive Counsel began offering rewards for the return of prisoners ($1,500) and for scalps ($1,000).[90]

Generally speaking, a common complaint of the colonial supporters during the Revolutionary War was the seemingly incessant lack of supplies.[91] The Militia companies assigned to the frontier experienced the same troubles as their counterparts east of the mountains. By reading some of the correspondence of the Westmoreland County officers it can be shown that the frontier was in need of everything from firearms, black powder, ball ammunition, and clothing, to paper on which to write their reports. To make matters worse, during their attacks, the enemy also killed the domestic animals of the settlers and burned their crops. This was quite a devastating tactic, especially in 1780 when food supplies became dangerously low and many soldiers were threatened with starvation.[92] The winters between 1778 and 1780 were especially severe. Although the saying that the "land yields well when the winter has been hard," may have been accepted at the time, it was in the summer of 1780 that several western forts were evacuated due to the lack of food.[93]

Transporting supplies west over the mountains was expensive, slow, and had many difficulties including attack, robbery, and desertion.[94] This lack of food led to fears of desertion and defection. The combined enemy forces continued their attacks killing settlers within sight of the garrison at Fort Pitt that could not function due to lack of supplies.[95]

At the time, Westmoreland County represented all of the southwestern part of the state. As a testament to the continued difficulties regularly encountered on the frontier, several citizens gathered and passed resolutions in 1780 petitioning the government to reoccupy the western forts. The intended effect was to provide protection of the settlers from the confederacy of British and Six Nations that continued to roam the frontier.[96] In a letter from the pen of Colonel Daniel Broadhead, writing from Fort Pitt in 1780 he stated, "For heaven's sake hurry up the companies voted by the honable [sic] assembly or Westmoreland County will soon be a wilderness."[97]

In some cases, great pains were expended to supply the frontier with needed supplies. In July 1776, when it was perceived that the frontier was not adequately supplied with gunpowder to provide an adequate defense for war, a mission was carefully planned and led by Captain George Gibson and Lieutenant William Linn acting on orders from the Governor of Virginia.

A flatboat was constructed at Pittsburgh and fifteen supporters floated down the Ohio and Mississippi Rivers to New Orleans where they were to purchase supplies from the Spanish government. The true purpose of their mission was kept secret and they disguised themselves as traders. The mission was very dangerous on several levels, as the Six Nations were at war with the Kentucky borderers and were known to frequently attack boats on the Ohio River. Tory spies were known to circulate in the area around Fort Pitt and there were British outposts along the way.

Although the Spanish were then at peace with the British, they agreed to assist the colonists who were at odds with their traditional enemy. The mission was endangered when British agents in New Orleans learned of the presence of Gibson which led to his pretended arrest by the Spanish government. Gibson was later set free under the guise of escape and he and 3,000 pounds of black powder were successfully smuggled aboard a sailing ship bound for Philadelphia. Under the command of Linn, another 9,000 pounds was hauled aboard barges and taken in a slow and tedious ascent up the Mississippi and Ohio Rivers and was delivered in safety to Fort Pitt, arriving ten months after the mission had started.[98]

In June 1778, the mission of Gibson and Linn was ordered to be repeated under the command of Captain David Rodgers of Redstone. Just as the previous mission had gone, the journey was made, the powder was secured and the flatboats were loaded successfully.

On the return voyage, the party of 40 men was lured ashore and into an ambush by the enemy. Outnumbered two to one, many of Rodgers' men fell in the first volley. Ultimately only 13 survived and these owed their survival to the thick density of the underbrush and the darkness of the night that quickly fell on them after the shooting started.

Robert Benham, one of the wounded, had been shot through both legs, yet managed to conceal himself in the top of a fallen tree. He remained hidden there for two days until hunger convinced him to shoot a raccoon that wandered into range. Soon after, he heard the call of another man whom he at first thought was the enemy, but in reality was a patriot from their mission named Basil Brown. Brown had been shot through the right arm and the left shoulder and could not use either arm, but had evaded the enemy in a similar manner as Benham. So these two wounded comrades found themselves in the hostile wilderness, one unable to use his legs and the other unable to use his arms.[99]

To survive, Brown flushed out game so Benham could bring it down with his rifle. Brown then kicked the game to Benham who dressed it and cooked it. Brown also carried water to Benham in his hat by holding it between his teeth and dipping it into the river. So together they survived by each doing the work that could not be accomplished by the other. This went on for 19 long and desperate days when Brown managed to hail a passing flatboat and they were rescued. After a recovery period, they were able to return to their homes at Redstone.[100]

In 1779, Colonel Daniel Broadhead in command at Fort Pitt, had started a systematic method of scouting and patrolling the frontier.[101] The first extant record found reflecting this sort of organization in Westmoreland County was recorded in 1782 when the records hint that the Militia became somewhat more organized in their approach. References are made to the "stations" which were a string of known positions scattered through the frontier that served as reference points from which the Militia companies would gather and then begin their patrols, sometimes in a looping fashion and ending where they started. They also patrolled between stations along the edge of the frontier. Some of these stations were block houses while others were little more than fortified barns. Some of the names of these stations survive in the records, but most do not. Myers Blockhouse, Carnahan's blockhouse, Barn Fort, Brushy Run, Rayburn's Station, and Vance's Fort are a few examples found among the Westmoreland County documents.[102]

It was not typical for the frontiersmen to be allotted many supplies, but they did receive rations, lead balls, and black powder when such supplies were available. In 1791, the value of each food ration was not to exceed a cost of 8¢.[103] The borderers tended to be self-sufficient and often carried their own personal firearms, usually long rifles and hatchets.[104] At least one Continental Line regiment, the Eighth Pennsylvania, received uniforms described as "hunting shirts, with broad-brimmed hats looped up and long leggings..."[105] However, most frontier recruits wore the clothes on their backs as their uniforms and many did indeed don buckskins and moccasins, and some of those not supplied a blanket slept on bear skins while on the trail.

In 1778, it was recommended by Col. Hartley in Northampton County, that those patrolling the frontier should be mounted on horses and armed with a sword, two pistols, and a short rifle. Hartley goes on to request clothing in the form of hunting shirts and "woolen overhalls" or "Leggins," but it is not known whether his requests were fulfilled.[106]

Revolutionary War

The firearm perhaps most commonly in use then was the flintlock. To load, black powder was poured into the barrel from the muzzle, then a lead ball was pushed down to the breech using a ramrod designed for that purpose. The weapon was then primed by pouring black powder into a small cup, mounted adjacent to the hammer called the pan.

To shoot, the operator pulled back a large spring loaded hammer which, when pulled far enough back, would lock in the cocked position. When ready, the shooter pulled the trigger after which the hammer would spring forward. The hammer held a piece of flint rock which would strike the frizzen, a small steel projection on the barrel, causing a spark. The spark flooded the pan igniting the black powder placed there when the weapon was primed. The burning primer powder in turn sent sparks through the flash hole, a small opening leading into the breech of the barrel, there igniting the main charge. When the main charge ignited, it would essentially explode inside the breech, driving the lead ball down the barrel and hopefully toward the intended target. An experienced user could reload and fire three to four times per minute.

The flintlock was unreliable since the least dampness could cause ignition failure. The sulfur in the black powder caused the barrel and the mechanism to corrode. This resulted in making the flintlock increasingly difficult to load and dangerous to fire. Although some members of the Six Nations carried and used flintlocks, contrary to some modern stories, many favored their bows and arrows to the musket or rifle. The bow did not fail in wet weather, and since they fired without report, the position of the shooter was less precisely betrayed. Within a certain range, the bow, in the hands of a skilled archer was no less accurate than the smooth bore muskets.

Mostly only hints of different objectives of the Militia assigned to the frontier survive in the records. Examples include "…in order for running ye line," or "to range the Frontiers," and "ordered to guard the line." They also performed escort duty as found in the example, "…escort provisions to Fort Hand." Some companies manned forts,

"...stationed at Fort Wallis." In one case, the Militia was called on by Colonel John Perry to provide "...one boats crew," for an expedition on a river (neither the river nor the purpose of the mission were stated). Some were even more generic, such as "...ordered to randivouse."[107] The Pennsylvania Archives also lists three essential types of duty assigned to the Militia Regulars:

> The militia did provide a significant defensive force patrolling the south side of the Schuylkill River and engaged in occasional clashes with British outposts and scouting parties including heavy skirmishes at Whitemarsh on December 7. Due to the sixty-day turnover, however, none of the men who were at Brandywine in September would have been present at Whitemarsh in December. It is known that no Pennsylvania militia served at Valley Forge, Monmouth, or Yorktown. The second type of service was duty on the frontier in Northumberland, Northampton, Bedford and Westmoreland counties. Occasionally, militia reinforcements from Cumberland, Lancaster, and York counties would be brought in to reinforce these frontiers as occurred in the summer of 1778. A third type of militia duty was in providing guards for supply depots located in Lancaster, Lebanon and Reading and at various prisoner of war camps.[108]

Unlike many of the Pennsylvania Line, who were frequently marched many miles to their place of service, those who served in frontier companies and their families were in a more precarious location. On the edge of the frontier, they found themselves essentially living in a battle zone. In learning of the numerous accounts that occurred on the frontier, it seems doubtful that William-III could reside in that region throughout the war, serve in the war, and not have been engaged in some action.[109]

Revolutionary War

Finally, in 1783, peace was made with Great Britain, but the Indian attacks continued because their many separate and scattered tribes and villages had not yet been informed. This activity caused those serving on the frontier to be called into active service to repel Six Nations excursions long after those east of the mountains had disbursed.[108] In April, congress was notified by Pennsylvania's Supreme Executive Council that 40 persons had been killed and captured on the frontier since spring.[111]

Major Ephraim Douglass was sent to meet with the Six Nations to apprise them of the peace talks between the United States and Great Britain and to attempt to achieve peace with the Six Nations as well. Douglass held a meeting in a great council with the British and eleven tribes. He was successful and the attacks on the Pennsylvania frontier effectively ceased.[112]

---

1. Pennsylvania Archives, Series 6, Volume II, p. 262, digital version, *Fold3* (http://www.fold3.com : accessed October 2012).

2. Edgar W. Hassler, *Old Westmoreland: A History of Western Pennsylvania During the Revolution* (Cleveland, Ohio : The Arthur H. Clark Company, 1900), Chapter XXVI, p. 176, digital version, *Google Books* (http//books.google.com : accessed July 2011).

3. George Dallas Albert, *History of the County of Westmoreland Pennsylvania* (Philadelphia: L. H. Everts & Co., 1882), Chapter XXVIII, p. 138, digital version, *Google Books* (http://books.google.com : accessed August 2011).

4. Two separate requests sent to NARA failed to locate a Revolutionary War Pension record for William Davidson. During research, evidence was found that Harbaugh had also conducted a similar search at NARA in the 1940's. Requests for similar information from the Pennsylvania Archives were equally disappointing.

5. Howard H. Wehmann, "Revolutionary War Pension and Bounty – Land – Warrant Application Files: National Archives Microfilm Publications Pamphlet

William "Ranger" Davidson

Describing M804" (National Archives and Records Service, General Services Administration, Washington: 1974), digital version, *National Archives* (http://www.archives.gov/ : accessed 2011), p. 4.

6. John H. Long, ed., *Atlas of Historical Counties: Pennsylvania* (Chicago, Illinois: The Newberry Library, 2010), digital version, *The Newberry Library* (http://publications. newberry .org/ahcbp/index.html : accessed July 2011).

7. *Atlas of the County of Fayette and the State of Pennsylvania* (Philadelphia: G.M. Hopkins & Co., 1872), digital image, page 37, *USGenWeb Archives* (http://usgwarchives.net/ maps/pa/county/fayett/1872/luzerne.jpg : accessed May 2011).

8. John H. Campbell, Chief Draftsman, *Warrantee Township Map: Fayette County, Luzerne Township* (Harrisburg, Pennsylvania: Records of the Land Office, 1920), Record Group 17, Series 17.522, Pennsylvania State Archives, digital version, *Commonwealth of Pennsylvania's Enterprise Portal* (http://www.portal.state.pa.us : accessed March 2011).

9. Pennsylvania Archives, Series 5, Volume IV, "List of 'Soldiers of the Revolution who received pay for their services,' Taken from Manuscript Record, having neither date nor title, but under 'Rangers on the Frontiers, 1778-1783' was published in Vol. XXIII, Penna. Archives, Third Series, by the Former Editor. (c)," beginning on p. 597, "Westmoreland County" and "Continental Line," beginning on p. 734, entry for William Davidson, a private, p. 739, digital version, *footnote* (http://www.footnote.com : accessed October 2008).

10. Pennsylvania Archives, Series 5, Volume IV, "Soldiers Who Received Depreciation Pay as Per Cancelled Certificates on File in the Division of Public Records, Pennsylvania State Library. (c)," beginning on p. 105, "Westmoreland County Militia," beginning on p. 427, entry for William Davidson, a Private, Continental Line, p. 434, digital version, *footnote* (http://www.footnote.com : accessed October 2008).

11. William Davidson, *Revolutionary War Military Abstract Card*, number 2569, citing Westmoreland, Militia, Certificate 6871, issued 10 December 1785, Register Vol. A, p. 246; Revolutionary War Military Abstract Card File, 1785-1893, series 13.50, Record Group 13, Pennsylvania State Archives, Harrisburg, digital version, *Fold3* (http://www.fold3.com : accessed 2008). The card was selected for examination because it fit with Harbaugh's description of William-III's

service record. Once it was learned, from subsequent documents linked to this entry, that William Conwell was his Company Captain, this confirmed the record as correct since it was known that William Conwell was a neighbor of William-III. All the subsequent Revolutionary War records obtained were retrieved from the Pennsylvania State Archives.

12. William Davidson, *Certificate Register*, Registers, Volume A, 1784 – 1785, p. 246, entry numbered 7861 for William Davidson; Westmoreland County, Militia Loan Accounts, Records of the Office of the Comptroller General, Record Group 4, Pennsylvania State Archives, Harrisburg.

13. The British Parliament passed Currency Acts in 1751, 1764, and 1773 that regulated colonial paper money. Colonial America frequently used the British denominations of pounds, shillings, and pence as its money before, during, and following the Revolutionary War. These are frequently designated as £ for pounds, *s* for shillings, *d* for pence (from the Roman denarius); the abbreviated form doesn't use the letters but separates the denominations by one or two decimal points such as: £ 1..0..5. It wasn't until the *Coinage Act of 1792* was passed that the U.S. began using its own currency denominations.

14. Westmoreland County, Receipt Roll, page untitled and undated, Wm Davison (interest received by Capt Wm Conwell), prepared in 1784 or 1785, Certificate Counterparts, 1785-1786 (No. 6291-10381; box 3), Series 4.37; Militia Loan Accounts, 1781-1792; Records of the Office of the Comptroller General, Record Group 4; Pennsylvania State Archives, Harrisburg.

15. William Davidson (William Conwell's compy), *County Lieutenant Ledger*, page untitled and undated, Westmoreland County, "Distribution Ledger B, 1784-1785 (One Volume)," pp. 38-39; Militia Loan Accounts, 1781-1792; Records of the Office of the Comptroller General, Record Group 4; Pennsylvania State Archives, Harrisburg.

16. Capt. Wm Conwell's Co., *State Ledger*, page untitled and undated, No. CXII, p. 472, entry 27, United States Account Ledger, B, Nos. CII – DCLXXXVII, Miscellaneous Accounts, including records of transactions involving the Commonwealth and the United States, 1782-1809; Records of the Office of the Comptroller General, Record Group 4, Pennsylvania State Archives, Harrisburg.

17. Aaron McWilliams, Archivist, email dated 29 April 2016, Pennsylvania State Archives, Harrisburg.

18. Westmoreland County, Militia Loan Certificate Book 5, Certificate 7861, untitled, 10 December 1785, issued to William Davidson, 1785-1786, Nos. 7711-9630 (1 Volume), Records of the Office of the Comptroller General, Record Group 4; Pennsylvania State Archives, Harrisburg.

19. Westmoreland County, Certificate Book 5, Certificate Counterpart, untitled, number 7861, 10 December 1785, issued to William Davidson, Certificate Counterparts, 1785-1786 (No. 6291-10381; box 3), Series 4.37; Militia Loan Accounts, 1781-1792; Records of the Office of the Comptroller General, Record Group 4; Pennsylvania State Archives, Harrisburg.

20. "Revolutionary War Records Overview," *Pennsylvania Historical & Museum Commission* (http://www.phmc.pa.gov/Archives/Research-Online/Pages/Revolutionary-War.aspx : accessed February 2014), Pennsylvania State Archives, Harrisburg.

21. Aaron McWilliams, Archivist, email June 2017, Pennsylvania State Archives, Harrisburg.

22. This was probably the same Theophilus Phillips who served as a Lieutenant Colonel, fifth battalion, 1782, Westmoreland County. See Pennsylvania Archives, Series 6, Volume II, p. 295. Tax records also show that Phillips resided in Fayette County in 1785, see Pennsylvania Archives, Series 3, Volume XXII, p. 567.

23. Aaron McWilliams, Archivist, email June 2017, Pennsylvania State Archives, Harrisburg.

24. Pennsylvania Archives, Series 3, Volume XXIII, p. 284, "Westmoreland County, Rangers on the Frontiers – 1778 – 1783," also, p. 316, Westmoreland County, digital version, *Fold3* (http://www.fold3.com : accessed November 2012). William Conwell's Company of 25 men, including William-III, are listed. These records are transcripts prepared by archivists, not original handwritten documents.

25. Pennsylvania Archives, Series 6, Volume II, p. 285, "A Return of the Officers of the 4th Battlion of Westmoreland County Militia with the No. of the Company," digital version, *Fold3* (http://www.fold3.com : accessed November 2012), probably recorded about March 1778.

26. Pennsylvania Archives, Series 3, Volume XXIII, p. 819, "Miscellaneous Lists of Soldiers of the Revolution," digital version, *Fold3* (http://www.fold3.com : accessed November 2012).

27. Pennsylvania Archives, Series 6, Volume V, p. 314, "A Pay Abstract for Part of the Third & Part of the Fourth Battalion of Fayette County Militia Called into Actual Service Under the Continental Establishment From the 4th of September Until the 11th of September 1791, Both Days Included Under the Command of Capt. William Conwell," digital version, *Fold3* (http://www.fold3.com : accessed October 2012). William-III is not listed among the 60 men that were included.

28. Pennsylvania Archives, Series 6, Volume II, p. 306, Fourth Battalion officer elections, dated 3 January 1778, Captain William Conwell, 2nd Company. See also, Pennsylvania Archives, Series 6, Volume II, p. 285, "A Return of the Officers of the 4th Battlion of Westmoreland County Militia with the No. of the Company," digital version, *Fold3* (http://www.fold3.com : accessed October 2012), dated 2 April 1778.

29. The 2nd Company, 4th Battalion was Conwell's permanent unit. If the rotation rules were being followed, Captain Conwell's active duty unit would have been comprised of 2nd class men from the 4th Battalion (their permanent units). His active duty unit would be 4th Company in the newly formed battalion, if an entire battalion was needed. From this information it is possible to derive William-III's permanent assignment in 1778, as 2nd Class, 4th Battalion (company unknown) and his active duty unit would have been 4th Company (battalion unknown). However, many active duty units included multiple substitutes and men assigned from other classes when needed to fill vacancies. Captain Conwell himself may have been serving as a substitute for another captain over the active duty unit, which could mean that his company did not consist of men of the 2nd class. These factors render the assumptions made herein possible, but uncertain.

30. Hassler, pp. 60-86.

31. Ibid.

32. Ibid.

33. Hassler, p. 80.

34. Hassler, p. 80. Hassler states, "Westmoreland County failed to contribute [men to McIntosh's Campaign], as her own borders were almost daily harried by savage bands." However, he does go on to say that Virginia "furnished nearly 800 men." Hassler's statements on this point are somewhat misleading. At the time of McIntosh's Campaign, much of southwestern Westmoreland County, Pennsylvania was simultaneously claimed by Virginia as the District of West Augusta, later called Monongalia. Consequently, many Westmoreland men enrolled in Virginia's Militia and did serve in conjunction with McIntosh's Campaign as documented in their pension files. The files cited include the soldiers' sworn testimonials as recorded by Courts of Common Pleas. In such cases, witnesses who could attest to the applicant's service record were also required to supply their statements under oath. Two of the files cited include service under Captain Rezin Virgin, who had been serving in that capacity years before William-III served with him in 1783. These files therefore support the fact that Westmoreland County men did serve in McIntosh's Campaign, only enrolled in Virginia's Militia. By the time these soldiers applied for their pensions, Virginia's territorial claims were settled and southwestern Westmoreland had been divided into Washington, Green, Fayette and other counties, Pennsylvania.

35. *U.S., Revolutionary War Pension and Bounty-Land Warrant Application Files, 1800-1900*, pension file for James Huston number W. 2803, deposition dated 12 October 1832 in Washington County, Pennsylvania, pension certificate 18930 issued 6 December 1832, penned documents, unpaged and unnumbered, digital images 658-715, *Ancestry* (http://www.ancestry.com : accessed November 2016), citing Revolutionary War Pension and Bounty-Land Warrant Application Files (NARA microfilm publication M804, 2,670 rolls), records of the Department of Veterans Affairs, Record Group 15, National Archives, Washington, D.C. James Huston was drafted into Captain Rezin Virgin's company, Virginia Militia, but was assigned to Captain Joseph Ogle on active duty and assisted in building Fort McIntosh and Fort Laurens on General McIntosh's Campaign. He states that the work was the "most severe and trying labor" as they were "compelled" to carry the logs for Fort McIntosh on their backs! In March 1782, he and only four other men served in Captain Rezin Virgin's company, "...acting as Indian spies on the frontiers" when they were surprised by a party of Indians. He alone was captured, taken to Detroit and held prisoner at various locations until the war ended in 1783. He was then released and returned home to Washington County in Pennsylvania. His pension was $23.33 per year.

Revolutionary War

36. *U.S., Revolutionary War Pension and Bounty-Land Warrant Application Files, 1800-1900*, pension file for Captain John Minter number S. 9027, deposition dated 21 November 1832 in Delaware County, Ohio, pension certificate 20135, penned documents, unpaged and unnumbered, digital images 32-61 of 967, *Ancestry* (http://www.ancestry.com : accessed November 2016), citing Revolutionary War Pension and Bounty-Land Warrant Application Files (NARA microfilm publication M804, 2,670 rolls), records of the Department of Veterans Affairs, Record Group 15, National Archives, Washington, D.C. Captain John Minter deposed that he resided in Westmoreland County when he marched west with McIntosh's campaign and assisted in building Fort McIntosh and Fort Laurens while serving in the Virginia Militia.

37. Aaron McWilliams, Archivist, email June 2017, Pennsylvania State Archives, Harrisburg.

38. Pennsylvania Archives, Series 6, Volume II, pp. 313-315, digital version, *Fold3* (http://www.fold3.com : accessed November 2012). This transcribed record revealed William-III's service as an Ensign.

39. Westmoreland County Militia, *Return of elections of officers*, penned, 24 September 1783, page unnumbered, entry in 4th Battalion, 4th Company for William Davison, received July 2011, Records of Pennsylvania's Revolutionary Governments, Record Group 27, Series 27.33, Pennsylvania State Archives, Harrisburg.

40. Rezin Virgin was born in 1750 in Frederick County, Maryland (today Montgomery County), son of Jeremiah Virgin and wife Lucy Dickinson or Dickerson. Rezin married Jemima Arnold about 1770 or 1771 in Bedford County (today's Fayette County), Pennsylvania. Rezin owned land on both sides of the Monongahela River, but reportedly moved east of the river when hostilities escalated. See Campbell's Warrantee Township Maps of North Franklin Township, Washington County (*Virgin's Dove*) and Luzerne Township, Fayette County (*Virgin's Delight*). Rezin removed to Kentucky after 1801, ultimately settling in Greenup County where he owned several parcels of land. He died and was buried there by 1828.

41. The variations in the spelling of "Rezin" and "Davidson" provide two good reasons for researchers to obtain copies of source documents whenever possible, rather than relying upon derivative transcripts.

William "Ranger" Davidson

42. Fayette County, Pennsylvania, Records of the Land Office, Record Group 17; Patent Book, Volume P, Number 11, page 42, patent application, dated 27 October 1785; warrant number 2, dated 27 October 1785; and patent, dated 8 August 1787, for Rezin Virgin, parcel called *Virgin's Delight*, photocopies of penned documents, Pennsylvania State Archives, Harrisburg.

43. Rezin owned a parcel of land west of the Monongahela River which fell into the region under a jurisdiction dispute between Pennsylvania and Virginia. This parcel called *Virgin Dove* was "Surveyed November 13th 1785 in pursuance of an Entry of the Virginia Commissioners Certificate made with the principle Surveyor of Ohio County Virginia." Even if Rezin was residing on *Virgin Dove* before 1783, that parcel also fell within Westmoreland County; however, other records show that he had taken up long-term settlement on his *Virgin's Delight* tract east of the Monongahela in what later became Luzerne Township in Fayette County.

44. Campbell, *Warrantee Township Map:* Fayette County, Luzerne Township (*Virgin's Delight*) and Washington County, North Franklin Township (*Virgin's Dove*).

45. Howard L. Leckey, *Tenmile Country and its Pioneer Families* (Baltimore, Maryland: Genealogical Publishing, Inc., 2001), pp. 16 and 45. The following is found on p. 16, "Brice Virgin, sergeant under Cresap, was one of the four brothers, sons of Jeremiah Virgin. Rezin, John, Thomas, and Brice Virgin lived on the Fayette side of the Monongahela River opposite the mouth of Tenmile Creek. All of them took an active part in the frontier defense." Also, on p. 45, "Rachel Teagarden, married Kinsey Virgin, son of Captain Rezin Virgin, who lived across the Monongahela from the Teagardens." Kinsey Virgin's tract called *Virgin's Wish* is located just south of Rezin's *Virgin's Delight* in Luzerne Township, Fayette County, on the east side of the Monongahela River.

46. W. J. Holland, Editor, *Annals of the Carnegie Museum*, Volume I, 1901 – 1902 (Published by the authority of the Board of Trustees of the Carnegie Institute: September 1902), p. 539, digital version, *Internet Archive* (http://www.archive.org : accessed April 2011). From the minutes of the court held at Fort Dunmore (Fort Pitt), May 1775, Rezin Virgin petitioned to "veiw [sic] a road" from the foot of Laurel Hill...to the Mouth of Wheeling.

47. Holland, p. 559 (ms. 69). In January 1776, "Samuel Mcbride is app[ointed] a Constable in the room of Razon Virgin, and It is Ord[ered] that he [be] Summoned [sic]."

Revolutionary War

48. *Revolutionary War Pension and Bounty-Land Warrant Application File, 1800-1900*, Pennsylvania pension file for William Alexander, deposition dated 25 December 1832 in Mercer County, Pennsylvania, number W. 4623, pension certificate 18513 issued 9 September 1833, penned documents, unpaged and unnumbered, digital images 470-528, *Ancestry* (http://www.ancestry.com : accessed November 2016), citing Revolutionary War Pension and Bounty-Land Warrant Application Files (NARA microfilm publication M804), records of the Department of Veterans Affairs, Record Group 15, National Archives, Washington, D.C. William Alexander served under Captain Rezin Virgin in May and September 1777 in the Virginia Militia for the purpose of defending Fort Shepherd on Big Wheeling Creek in Ohio County, Virginia. Although he served in a Virginia unit, Rezin resided in the area that ultimately became Westmoreland County, Pennsylvania. See also, notes 35, 40, 43, and 45 in this chapter.

49. *Pennsylvania, Tax and Exoneration, 1768-1801*, Fayette County, Luzerne Township, penned document, untitled, p. 50, entry for Reason Virgin, assessed one pound, eight shillings, nine pence in 1785, digital image 1 of 25, *Ancestry* (http://www.ancestry.com : accessed 2011), citing *Tax & Exoneration Lists, 1762–1794*, Series No. 4.61; Records of the Office of the Comptroller General, Record Group 4; Pennsylvania State Archives, Harrisburg.

50. Fayette County, Pennsylvania, Records of the Land Office, Record Group 17; Patent Book, Volume P, Number 11, page 42, patent application, dated 27 October 1785; warrant number 2, dated 27 October 1785; and patent, dated 8 August 1787, for Rezin Virgin, parcel called *Virgin's Delight*, photocopies of penned documents, Pennsylvania State Archives, Harrisburg.

51. 1800 United States Census, population schedule, penned, Luzerne Township, Fayette County, Pennsylvania, p. 564, unpaged, line 11, unnumbered, entry for Rezin Vergin, digital image 5 of 5, *FamilySearch* (https://familysearch.org/ : accessed June 2014), citing NARA microfilm publication M32 (Washington D.C.: National Archives and Records Administration, n.d.), roll 38; FHL microfilm 363,341.

52. *Pennsylvania, Septennial Census, 1779-1863*, Fayette County, Luzerne Township, penned document, untitled, p. 31, 30th entry for Rezin Virgin in 1800, digital image 17 of 25, *Ancestry* (http://www.ancestry.com : accessed 2011), citing *Septennial Census Returns, 1779–1863*, Box 1026, Records of the House of Representatives, Records of the General Assembly, Record Group 7; Pennsylvania State Archives, Harrisburg.

53. The agreement on the part of the archivist (Aaron McWilliams) was qualified since he did not have all the evidence for first hand examination that would substantiate the entire case. Accepting on face value that the author was in possession of such documents, the archivist was in agreement with the conclusions presented herein.

54. If called to active duty and the rotation rules were then being followed, Captain Virgin would command the 4th Company in a newly formed battalion (if a battalion was needed). The new unit would be comprised of 4th class men from the 4th Battalion of Fayette County, their permanent units (companies unknown). This also supposes no substitutes were required.

55. Aaron McWilliams, Archivist, email January 2018, Pennsylvania State Archives, Harrisburg, citing Robert K. Wright, Jr., *The Continental Army*.

56. Spencer C. Tucker, *The Encyclopedia of the North American Indian Wars, 1607-1890*, Volume One (Denver, Colorado: ABC-CLIO, 2011), p. 663.

57. William-III should have a Militia Officer's Index Card prepared and added in the Pennsylvania Archives, but this request was denied.

58. Elizabeth Davidson Harbaugh, *The Davidson Genealogy* (Ironton, Ohio: self-published, 1948; Ann Arbor, Michigan : Lithoprinted, Edwards Brothers, Inc., 1949), p. 129, print, OCLC: 23167553.

59. *The Official roster of the soldiers of the American Revolution buried in the state of Ohio*, Vol 1, Daughters of the American Revolution of Ohio (Columbus, Ohio: F. J. Heer Printing Co., 1929), p. 114, entry for "Davidson, William, Lawrence Co.," print, Bartow Genealogical and Historical Library, Bartow, Florida.

60. Aaron McWilliams, Archivist, email August 2017, Pennsylvania State Archives, Harrisburg.

61. The approximate number of Ranger Companies formed during the Revolutionary War was affirmed by archivist Aaron McWilliams, but was not personally confirmed by the author.

62. The subtle fact that some of the transcribed records frequently contain persons whose experiences do not fit the titles of the documents in which they appear, and which mislead the readers of such documents, was only discovered through numerous discussions with archivist Aaron McWilliams at the Pennsylvania

Archives. This information does not appear to be common knowledge nor does this appear to be elsewhere documented.

63. The Regular Militia companies in the western-most regions so commonly ranged the frontier they are sometimes called "ranging companies." In one source, Conwell's unit is described as a ranging company which is technically accurate (Pennsylvania Archives, Series 3, Volume XXIII, p. 819). However, as pointed out, the Regular Militia ranging companies were distinct and separate from volunteer Ranger Companies.

64. Pennsylvania Archives, Series 6, Volume II, digital version, *Fold3* (http://www.fold3.com : accessed October 2014).

65. Hanna Benner Roach, FGSP, FASG, *The Pennsylvania Militia in 1777*, reprinted from "The Pennsylvania Genealogical Magazine," Volume XXIII, Number 3, 1964, 70 pages, print. The reprint retains the page numbers as they originally appeared, pp. 161-230.

66. Roach, p. 162.

67. Ibid.

68. William Henry Egle, M.D., ed., *Rangers on The Frontiers - 1778-1783*, Pennsylvania State Archives (Harrisburg, Pennsylvania: State Printer, 1897), Series 3, Volume XXIII, Westmoreland County, p. 316, entry for Captain Conwell's Company, 25 men listed, digital version, *footnote* (http://www.footnote.com).

69. Pennsylvania Archives, Series 6, Volume II, p. 311, "A Return of the 4th Battalion of Militia with Rank and Number in Westmoreland County." William Conwell, 2nd Company, 34 men. Prepared by Colonel Edward Cook, dated 23 May 1778.

70. Roach, p. 164.

71. Roach, pp. 164-165.

72. Aaron McWilliams, Archivist, emails June 2016, Pennsylvania State Archives, Harrisburg.

73. Roach, p. 163.

74.	For entries regarding the County Lieutenants, see the Pennsylvania Archives, Series 2, Volume XIV, p. 672; Series 3, Volume VII, p. 122; Series 2, Volume III, p. 682.

75.	Roach, p. 165.

76.	Roach, pp. 162, 166.

77.	Roach, p. 167. Drill was to take place twice in April, three times in May, twice in August and September, and once in October. Battalion parade days were to be held in May and October.

78.	"Revolutionary War Records Overview," *Pennsylvania Historical & Museum Commission* (http://www.phmc.pa.gov/Archives/Research-Online/Pages/Revolutionary-War.aspx : accessed February 2014), Pennsylvania State Archives, Harrisburg.

79.	Pennsylvania Archives, Series 6, Volume II, p. 310, digital version, *Fold3* (http://www.fold3.com : accessed October 2014). Letter from Archibald Lochry.

80.	Pennsylvania Archives, Series 6, Volume II, p. 404, digital version, *Fold3* (http://www.fold3.com : accessed October 2014). Lieutenant Colonel Archibald Lochry was appointed County Lieutenant of Westmoreland County by the Supreme Executive Council on 21 March 1777. For more on Lochry, see Hassler's Chapter XXI, dedicated to his fatal campaign in 1781; see also, p. 146 for concerns regarding Lochry's command and his successor, Edward Cook.

81.	Hassler, p. 22. Hamilton's interference with the Six Nations; see also, Chapter VII beginning on p. 44.

82.	Hassler, Chapter XXVI, p. 176, Tories, Canadians, and Six Nations burned Hannastown; also see p. 184, describing further Canadian assistance against the colonists.

83.	Hassler, p.31. The formation of ranger companies.

84.	1) Pennsylvania Archives, Series 3, Volume XXIII, page 316, Westmoreland County, September 1778, 25 men are listed in Captain William Conwell's 2nd Company, 4th Battalion; 2) Pennsylvania Archives, Series 6, Volume II, page

311, Westmoreland County, probably recorded in May 1778, 34 men are listed in a Return of Captain William Conwell's 2nd Company, 4th Battalion; 3) Pennsylvania Archives, Series 6, Volume V, page 314, Fayette County, September 1791, 60 men are listed in a pay abstract for part of the 3rd and part of the 4th Battalions under command of Captain William Conwell (Company number(s) not recorded).

85.   Hassler, p. 38. Description of the war parties of the Six Nations.

86.   Hassler, p. 89. The Six Nations left their canoes at a distance for quiet approach to their targets.

87.   Hassler, pp. 39, 44, 118. Hamilton's tactics are described, encouraging defection of the settlers to the Tory cause.

88.   Hassler, p. 90. Colonel Brodhead reported that attacks were occurring in Westmoreland County daily.

89.   Hassler, in Chapter XIV, provides examples of the Militia tracking down perpetrators of attacks.

90.   Hassler, p. 106.

91.   Hassler, pp. 105; 109 – 115. The incessant lack of supplies on the frontier.

92.   Ibid.

93.   Ibid.

94.   Ibid.

95.   Ibid.

96.   Consul Willshire Butterfield, *An Historical Account of the Expedition Against the Sandusky* (Cincinnati : Robert Clarke & Co, 1873), p. 8, digital version, *Internet Archive* (http://www.archive.org : accessed March 2011). Butterfield discusses the resolution by the settlers requesting the reoccupation of western forts in early 1780, several of which had been abandoned due to the lack of supplies.

97.   Pennsylvania Archives Series 1, Volume VIII, p. 246, digital version, *Fold3* (http://www.fold3.com : accessed October 2014). Letter from Colonel

Broadhead to Joseph Reed, president of the Supreme Executive Council pleading for the support of additional companies.

98. Hassler dedicated Chapter V to Gibson's mission for black powder.

99. Hassler dedicated Chapter IX beginning on p. 54, to Rodger's unsuccessful mission for black powder.

100. Ibid.

101. Hassler, p. 89.

102. Pennsylvania Archives, Series 6, Volume II, digital version, *Fold3* (http://www.fold3.com : accessed December 2015); the first mention of stations used by soldiers in Westmoreland County in 1782.

103. Pennsylvania Archives, Series 2, Volume IV, p. 647, digital version, *Fold3* (http://www.fold3.com : accessed December 2015). The cost of rations for the rangers.

104. Hassler, p. 67. Description of uniforms and weaponry.

105. Ibid. The 8th Pennsylvania was a Pennsylvania Continental Line Regiment, not a militia unit, but most of its companies were recruited from Westmoreland County.

106. Pennsylvania Archives, Series 1, Volume VI, 1778, p. 730, digital version, *Fold3* (http://www.fold3.com : accessed October 2014). Recommended wear and weaponry for frontier soldiers.

107. Pennsylvania Archives, Series 6, Volume II, digital version, *Fold3* (http://www.fold3.com : accessed October 2014). The various duties of the militia are described throughout the returns.

108. "Revolutionary War Militia Battalions and Companies," *Pennsylvania Historical & Museum Commission* (http://www.phmc.pa.gov/Archives/Research-Online/ Pages/Revolutionary-War-Militia-Overview.aspx : accessed November 2016), Pennsylvania State Archives, Harrisburg.

Revolutionary War

109. Hale C. Sipe, *The Indian Wars of Pennsylvania* (Harrisburg, PA: The Telegraph Press, 1929), pp. 505-684, digital version, *Internet Archive* (http://www.archive.org : accessed April 2011).

110. Hassler, p. 188-190. Continued attacks by the Indians following the end of the Revolution; also, Roach, p. 229.

111. Hassler, Chapter XXVIII, covers the events at the end of the Revolution.

112. Ibid. Some of the tribes participating in the counsel included the Chippewa, Ottawa, Wyandot, Shawnee, Delaware, Kickapoo, Wea, Miami, Pottawattamie, Piankeshaw, and Seneca. Douglass also met separately with the Mohawk and Iroquois.

8

Other Pennsylvania Records

LAND **RECORDS**. Prior to 1768, all the land west of the Alleghenies in Pennsylvania still belonged to the Six Nations and there was no legal method for purchasing land. Some settlers made personal contracts with the Six Nations by barter or trade. Although not legally binding, they did possibly purchase their relative safety.[1,2]

In September 1768, Governor John Penn purchased much of the middle and northern parts of Pennsylvania as well as all of the south western part of the state from the Six Nations by deed specified in the treaty of Fort Stanwix.[3] This transaction, called the New Purchase, enabled the opening of the *Proprietaries' Land Office* in April 1769

William "Ranger" Davidson

through which parcels of western land could be legally purchased from the Penns for the first time.[4]

In the first few months, a lottery was performed for some of the earliest claims in southwestern Pennsylvania. Essentially, settlers whose entries were drawn for particular parcels were deemed winners. In cases of duplicate claims, settlers who could show that they had made improvements to their land won out. The winners were allowed to keep their claims.[5]

The lottery was replaced within a few months by the four step warrant process. Under this system, an application was initially prepared which was used to establish first claim on the property. After examination and approval of the application by the land office, a warrant was issued. The warrant signified acceptance of the application, stated the terms to which the settler agreed for payment, and was an official request for a survey. The survey was a scale drawing depicting the relative size and shape of the tract under the claim. Once "returned," the survey also confirmed the number of acres contained in the parcel. Provided the purchaser met all the terms of the purchase, a patent was issued. The patent transferred legal title from the government to the purchaser and completed the process. This just described was the process by which the ownership of land was transferred from the proprietary owners (and later the U.S. government) to private interests. So, if title to real estate was transferred by patent, then the purchaser generally became the first owner of record.

Transactions between existing land owners were documented using an early form of a deed called an indenture.[6] The indenture contained the legal details of the transaction, handwritten with quill pen and ink, usually in duplicate on a single sheet of paper. The two originals were then cut apart leaving a jagged edge common to both. One copy was retained by the issuing authority and the other was given to the land owner. When subsequent transactions occurred, the owner's indenture could be authenticated by matching the indentured edges of the two documents. If three originals were made, it was called a tripartite indenture and the third copy was provided to the court. At some later time, an official facsimile of each indenture was made by manually copying the exact language from the original indenture into large bound ledger books for filing purposes. Ideally, a second person would compare the two documents to ensure accuracy and then words similar to "recorded and compared" were added at the end of the recorded copy to show that the entry was completed and verified as correct. In most cases, only the recorded versions of the indentures are available today. Unfortunately, the persons transacting the business signed the original indenture, and not the recorded copy, so examples of the ancestor's signature from this source do not exist.

Even after the land office opened, settlers frequently took possession of their land before making application. This was done out of concern that another settler, finding the land unoccupied, might seize control and steal the claim. By taking possession without having filed the appropriate documents, the settler was technically a squatter who had no legal right to the property. However, when duplicate claims were made, the Land Office generally favored the claimant who had made improvements to the land, the very action that was later discouraged by legal authorities.[7] In the early days, rather than being punished, the squatter was rewarded. In most cases, the improvements included a dwelling because the settlers had already occupied the land and had taken up residence on the parcels they claimed.

These claims were sometimes called tomahawk claims because the pioneers marked the boundaries of their parcels by making distinctive hash marks on trees using a tomahawk or hatchet. This was commonly the case when trees were designated as the boundary markers in surveys. William-III marked his Pennsylvania claim by making hash marks on trees and by making large piles of stones.[8] As time went on, the boundary markers would sometimes disappear. In those cases, adjoining landholders would agree on a new marker. This process of remarking the boundaries was called processioning.

It will be remembered that the Davidsons took up residence in Cumberland County, nearly two years before the Proprietaries' Land

William "Ranger" Davidson

Office opened, and marked out their tomahawk claim in June 1767. In September 1768, the New Purchase was made, bringing southwestern Pennsylvania into the colonies. But, as previously mentioned, the Proprietaries' Land Office wasn't established until April 1769.

The warrant system was a relatively new development on the frontier and settlers were rapidly pouring into the area. As a result, the Land Office was overburdened with requests and many of the applications were not processed for several years. When the Revolutionary War began in April 1775, the Proprietaries' Land Office, operated by the descendants and heirs of William Penn, was effectively closed and the processing of land claims was put on hold.

To complicate matters, Pennsylvania was in a boundary dispute with Virginia. The large area of land, called the District of West Augusta by Virginia in 1776, included a region called Monongalia County which contained much of what Pennsylvania claimed as Westmoreland County. This dispute continued until 1780 when the present-day border of Pennsylvania was established by extending the Mason-Dixon Line as agreed by both States. Thus, those squatting on land in western Pennsylvania prior to the war continued to do so until the land office opened again years later.[9]

Prior to the Revolution, John Penn (grandson of Pennsylvania's founder William Penn) was Lieutenant Governor of Pennsylvania, and as a principal heir, he was the proprietary owner of much of the state. When the war started, Penn was a Tory supporter (British loyalist) and was arrested for a brief time before being placed on parole. The Divesting Act of 1779 transferred ownership of most of the remaining 22 million acres of the Penns' proprietary lands to the Commonwealth of Pennsylvania. John Penn was paid £130,000 as compensation for the loss of his inherited right to one quarter of the State.

In 1781, the Revolutionary Era State Assembly created a new State Land Office consisting of a secretary, a receiver general, and a surveyor general who were assigned the records and responsibilities of their proprietary predecessors of the same titles. A Board of Property, similar to Commissioners of Property under the Penn government, was also created in 1782 to hear and determine cases of disputes arising from Land Office business.[10]

As previously mentioned briefly, Harbaugh had named 1767 as the year of migration for Lewis-I to Pennsylvania. This proposed year of migration was examined closely because in 1767, all of Western Pennsylvania still belonged to the Six Nations. If Lewis-I and family did indeed migrate in that year, they did so in the face of the proclamations made by the Crown and the Governor of Pennsylvania prohibiting such action. They also subjected themselves to the threat of death, if not by their own government, then at the hands of the Six Nations who could strike with impunity.[11] However, it may also be remembered that if the Davidsons did anxiously move west of the Alleghenies in 1767 they were certainly not alone. One estimate places about one hundred and fifty families, or about 800 persons, in the region now defined as Fayette County in 1768.[12] This estimate is rough and did not include other areas in the surrounding region.

Specifically, Harbaugh mentions a tract of land deeded to Lewis-I dated 29 June 1767, filed at Greensburg (Westmoreland County), which would confirm the year of migration.[13] A request to that office for a copy of the deed yielded a disappointing response. It seems that Greensburg does not have any records that old. Since Westmoreland County wasn't formed until 1773, it was thought that the wrong County government was referenced by Harbaugh. In 1767, the Davidsons' tracts would have been located in Cumberland County. So inquiries were made with the town of Carlisle, the center of government for that County. However, the deed mentioned by Harbaugh was not found there either. Just for closure, the same search was ordered for Bedford County, again without luck. This was unusual since all other verifiable records pertaining to William-III, as cited by Harbaugh, were found to be reliable, leaving us to ponder the mystery of this one anomaly.

Efforts were redoubled and further land records involving the Davidsons were sought. This persistence ultimately paid off. The indenture was found in Westmoreland County, just as Harbaugh had said. This conveyance of land was transacted before any legal authority existed in the frontier and likely amounted to a gentleman's agreement and a handshake at the time it was contracted. In order to locate such indentures, one must know the date the instrument was recorded. In this case, the document drawn up in June 1767 wasn't recorded until March 1781, nearly fourteen years later![14] Since all the previous searches had been conducted for business transacted in 1767, the document was missed. This is a good tip for researchers who should always include the date deeds were recorded when citing land transactions, a vital piece of information not supplied by Harbaugh.

Interestingly, the conveyance of 1767 is also referenced in another indenture in which Lewis-I deeded 420 acres of land to his son William-III. This is a good example of why it is important to carefully read the language in these old documents even though they are often times mundane. The reader will find that this 420 acre parcel of land was part of a larger tract previously "conveyed" to Lewis-I by James Gilmore on 29 June 1767![15] So there is not one, but two documents placing Lewis-I in southwestern Pennsylvania in June 1767, just as Harbaugh had said. This second indenture was also found at Greensburg, again matching Harbaugh's reference. So, the indenture recorded in 1781 firmly establishes the presence of Lewis-I in southwestern Pennsylvania in June 1767.

Although this section is intended for Pennsylvania records, it is timely to briefly consider one of the real estate transactions that took place in Delaware. One of the more important of the Delaware land transactions occurred on 30 November 1771, when "Lewis Davidson of Bedford Co., Pennsylvania, yeoman," sold his last known parcel of Delaware land.[16] This event is important because it helps to support the fact that the Lewis Davidson in Delaware is the same Lewis that had already relocated to Pennsylvania by that time. This time period is complimented by examination of the Pennsylvania tax return of 1773 for Bedford County, actually prepared in 1772, in which we find "Lewis Davison" included in Springhill Township.[17] The existence of several persons residing near Lewis-I who also appear on this tax list is adequate confirmation of both the location and the identity of our Lewis-I.[18,19] The 1771 Delaware land transaction also tells us that Lewis-I was a yeoman. Generally speaking, a yeoman was a British term for a freeholder beneath the gentry or ruling class. In other words, he was a landowner who was not a member of the nobility.

One other interesting observation regarding Lewis-I's purchases in Pennsylvania and the sale in Delaware is found in the long delay between these transactions. Lewis-I waited nearly 3½ years to sell his last Delaware parcel. He knew moving to the frontier was a dangerous and risky venture so he retained ownership of the Delaware land as his insurance policy. If the instability on the frontier proved to be too hazardous, as it was for many, the family would have a place to which they could safely return. It is easy to picture the family occasionally meeting to discuss the conditions on the frontier and the events occurring all around them to decide whether they should remain or retreat.

It is stressed that a comprehensive review was not performed of the land transactions in Pennsylvania. However, from the transactions uncovered, it can be shown that Lewis-I owned quite a lot of property. Unfortunately, the indenture for the 1767 tract, the earliest and possibly the largest purchase he made, does not include the number of acres the parcel contained. This is likely because it occurred before the warrant system was installed, so it was probably never surveyed. But, this tract is described as "…a large purchase of improvements and land." The part retained by Lewis-I was much larger than the 420 acres he sold to William-III.[20] It is also very possible that the boundaries of Lewis-I's initial claim extended some distance beyond Gilmore's settlement, enclosing adjacent land not yet claimed by other settlers.

In addition to the large tract purchased in 1767, Lewis-I purchased a 50 acre tract of land called *Fortune* from John Crawford who had made application on 19 October 1773. This parcel was described as "lying on the East Side of Monungehail [Monongahela] River opposite the mouth of Muddy Creek lying down the river in West Moreland [*sic*] County." Crawford also obtained a warrant for the land having the same date as the application and executed by John Penn. The warrant legally entitled Crawford to a survey which was conducted 30 June 1786, much delayed for the reasons already discussed. The parcel purchased by Lewis-I was estimated to consist of 50 acres and the return of the survey in June 1786 confirms this expectation, but somehow Lewis-I ended up with 170 acres, possibly because Crawford's parcel adjoined the larger tract of Lewis-I.[21,22]

The survey states, "Lewis Davidson in right of John Crawford." This means that Lewis-I purchased the land from Crawford after the warrant was issued, but before the land was surveyed, clearly making Crawford the first legal claimant. Although John Crawford had the first legitimate claim of the *Fortune* tract, he never obtained a patent and therefore never technically owned the land. The parcel was patented to Lewis-I on 11 April 1787.[23] This was the parcel of land to which Crawford's Ferry was attached. When Lewis-I assumed the operation it became known as Davidson's Ferry and later Davidson's Upper Ferry. The latter reference was used to distinguish between Lewis-I's ferry and another ferry later established by David Davidson, a son or later descendent of William-III (see the later chapter *Families*).

In October 1775, Lewis-I sold a tract called *Hickory Level* to his son, Thomas. The acreage was not specified, but the price was ten shillings.[24] In March 1781, he sold a 300-acre tract of land to his stepson, William Conwell, for the sum of seven pounds and ten shillings.[25] Later that same month, Lewis-I sold the 420 acre tract to William-III for a mere two pounds and ten shillings.[26] The amounts of these sales were all token sums and the parcels adjoined one another. Even after the sale of these parcels to his family, Lewis-I still owned 170 acres defined in his *Fortune* tract.

Based on these records, Lewis-I may be viewed as a patriarch figure who forged his way to southwestern Pennsylvania, when it was still Indian Territory, to lay early claims on large parcels of open land. Lewis-I rewarded his family by carving off parcels of his large real estate holdings which he effectively gave to his sons and stepson, all the while keeping the family physically close together. The language in the indenture to son Thomas is particularly touching and betrays the fatherly affection he expressed for his children, "for the natural love he has for his son..."[27] Lewis-I purchased and sold several parcels of land over the decades, both in Delaware as well as Pennsylvania.

Jehu Conwell has not so far been included in this discussion, but he should not be omitted. It was found that he purchased a tract of land from another pioneer named James Bredin in January 1772 for £60. This transaction identifies Jehu as a shoemaker.[28] This purchase is the only case found in which one of Lewis-I's sons or stepsons initially purchased land from someone other than Lewis-I. It is here thought that Jehu's purchase was financed by Lewis-I as it would seem unlikely he would help everyone except Jehu. However, it is also possible that other deeds remain yet undiscovered in Pennsylvania.

We turn now to William-III's land transactions. It will be remembered that his father sold William-III a 420-acre parcel on the east side of the Monongahela River for £2 and 10 shillings. This transaction was dated 27 March 1781.[29] However, on 15 May 1778, we find that William-III sold part of this tract to Thomas Stockley for £54. Although this indenture specifies 120 acres, William-III retained a 303½ acre claim. This order of events is evidence that William-III was promised this tract by Lewis-I almost three years before the parcel actually changed hands by deed. It also shows that land in this area was being purchased and sold in transactions occurring on a private level, with the principals accepting the tomahawk claims of their neighbors as legitimate.

According to William-III's land application, improvements were first made on the parcel he claimed by March 1779.[30] The application, written on plain paper, was witnessed by John Allen and James Finley, two Justices of the Peace. However, Allen and Finley didn't sign the application until 23 December 1784. They certified William-III's parcel with the "...beſt Information we have had..." that the land "...was improven [sic] in the year one thousand Seven hundred and Seventynine."[31] Therefore, it appears that William-III squatted on his land for almost five years before taking appropriate steps to purchase the parcel he would later call *Dispute Ended*. This was not necessarily his intention since by 1779 the Land Office was closed due to the war, the boundary dispute between Pennsylvania and Virginia was ongoing, and no official determination as to the control of the Penns' land was yet made.

A warrant was issued for William-III's claim in August 1785. The estimate provided for 250 acres "...including an Improvement on Monongahela River adjoining lands of William Conwell on the upper side & Thomas Stokely on the lower side of said river and Aaron Hackney and Mr. Gilpin..." As a point of clarification, the "upper side" was based upon the flow of the Monongahela, but William Conwell's tract was actually south of William-III's parcel. The Warrant specified that William-III was to pay "...Ten Pounds per Hundred Acres..." with interest commencing from the "...first day of March 1779." The warrant here confirms that William-III had indeed squatted on his land since the collection of interest was back dated to 1779. The warrant was executed by John Dickinson, Esq, President of the Supreme Executive Council and was addressed to John Lukens, Eſq, Surveyor General.[32]

William-III's parcel was surveyed 25 October 1786 by Alexander McClean, but a note written on this survey says that "John Stokely is diſsatisfyed with this Survey & defered me to Return the same disputed and defers that Patent may not be Granted until he has an hearing before the board of property."[33]

The first hearing found in the available records was granted before the Board of Property on 3 March 1788, entitled *William Davidson* v. *John Stokely*.[34] The entire record is reproduced here:

> The parties being heard chose James Hamon & Henry Swindler who are together with the Dep'y Surveyor to go to the land & make the Surveys of Davidson & Stokely in such a manner as to leave Stokely as much towards filling his Warrant by extending Davidson's Survey towards Thomas

Stokely's and Hamon's Surveys will admit of, of which the said Gentlemen are desired to report to this board by the first monday in September next, to which time this Caveat is continued.[35]

Apparently, John Stokely thought he was entitled to a certain number of acres and he felt that William-III's and Thomas Stokely's property lines overlapped his claim thereby unfairly reducing the acreage contained in his parcel. The only other record found relating to this event was for the following hearing held 19 May 1789:

> The report of James Hamon, Henry Swindler, Archibald Scott and Alexander McClean together with a Draught made by said McClean pursuant to order of Board of 3 March, 1788 being considered it is judged proper to postpone the determination of this Case to the first Monday in October next as Mr. McClean declares that the said Draught is not perfect there being an unaccountable error which he cannot rectify without going on the ground again, which he says he will do as soon as possible.[36]

The survey was redrawn and noted as corrected, but the new survey bears the same date as the first and attributes 303½ acres to William-III. The surveyor states the earlier survey "…was found to be erronous, the errors are now corrected and the survey altered Agreeably to the opinion of the Auditor appointed by the Honorable Board of Property altho it is found to Contain more [acreage] than they expected." A note written by the surveyor says, "…the dotted lines in the draught represent the claim of Thomas Dobbin."[37] The "dotted lines" mentioned by the surveyor would have dramatically reduced the acreage claimed by William-III. Unfortunately, further records of the hearings were not found.

William "Ranger" Davidson

In subsequent land records it is evident that William-III's parcel remained unchanged so he apparently was allowed to maintain his claim as it was depicted on the corrected survey. He was issued a Patent dated 17 December 1790, nearly six years to the day after his application was prepared and nearly eleven years after he officially assumed possession in 1779. No doubt it was owing to this long-lived boundary disagreement that William-III at first called his land *Dispute* as recorded on the reverse side of the corrected survey and later *Dispute Ended* as shown on the patent. So it seems that William-III was not without a sense of humor. The patent specifies that William-III made his final payment in the amount of nine pounds and seven shillings for the land, but in total William-III paid £44 and 7 shillings for *Dispute Ended*.[38-41] More than £34 of William-III's payments were made using Continental Certificates, more than £9 was in the form of State Certificates, common forms of currency during that era.

Examination of the Application for William-III's *Dispute Ended* tract reveals that the year of occupation was originally written as "one thousand seven hundred and seventy." The handwriting is very clear. In what appears to be a different handwriting, the number "nine" was added and crowded into the small space between the year and the following words in the document. This turned, what was originally, 1770 into 1779.

Remember that the "official" period of March 1779 is known to be incorrect, since we have already shown by the Cumberland County Tax records that William-III was in residence no later than 1768. He was married in 1769, ten years prior to his reported date of occupation. He also sold 120 acres of this parcel in May 1778 to Thomas Stockley as mentioned previously! These details seem to point to a much earlier date of occupation than the one recorded on the application. Allen and Finley, who certified William-III's Application did so years after the settlement was established. Their source as to when William-III's improvements were begun is not known, but William-III himself may have provided that information.

Other Pennsylvania Records

One obvious reason exists to want the date changed to a later year. Interest would accrue from the reported date of improvement or occupation. By reporting the later year, William-III would avoid the payment of several years of accrued interest on the purchase of his claim. The interest on land purchases during this era was 3% and given the amount paid by William-III, he saved £8.2, almost one fifth the overall cost of the tract, a significant sum.[42] While there could be other explanations or possible reasons for the date to be changed, this just discussed seems probable.

As previously mentioned, much of the land located in Westmoreland County was also claimed by Virginia until 1780 when it was ceded to Pennsylvania. Virginia called this area the District of West Augusta, which also included a portion of West Virginia. The region in which William-III and Lewis-I's tracts were located was called Monongalia County by Virginia. Some sources indicate that frequently a duplicate set of land records is archived by both Pennsylvania and Virginia. Since William-III applied for his land in 1779, inquiry was made with the Library of Virginia which houses such records, but they indicated that their holdings really only include records of tracts that were ultimately determined to be in Virginia and West Virginia.

As noted previously, Lewis-I sold parcels of land to his sons and also to at least one of his stepsons, William Conwell. These sales were documented in the form of indentures because these were private sales. However, patents were also purchased for some of these same parcels which at first may seem confusing. In these cases, Lewis-I was entitled to first claim on the large tracts of land which, when combined, probably contained close to, if not more than 1,000 acres.[43] However, since this tomahawk claim was carved from Indian Territory, as a squatter, his claim was not legally recognized. Lewis-I apparently granted his sons permission to settle on his land and several years later, subdivided his claim and sold parcels to his children for token sums. Although this resolved the matter on a personal or private level, the claims were still unsettled with the government. Consequently, after paying Lewis-I, the purchasers subsequently had to make a second payment for their parcels to the government, for which they received patents.

1768 TAX ASSESSMENT. One of the most significant tax assessments of interest was taken in Cumberland County from the region called the Cumberland Valley (which later became the southwest portion of Bedford County). This was the earliest of any document found showing the presence of William-III in southwestern Pennsylvania.[44,45] William Conwell is also listed. This document and its significance has been discussed in some detail in earlier chapters. One additional interesting fact disclosed in this document is discussed in a later section in this chapter.

1769 TAX ASSESSMENT. This record, when used in conjunction with the next one, yields some subtle evidence. In 1769, William-III is listed with the freemen of the county. This meant that he was single, at least 21 years of age or older, and owned land. In the 1770 record, he is listed with the married men, which serves to narrow the possible dates of his first marriage to Rosanna Hutchinson and affirms the marriage year given by Harbaugh as 1769.[46,47]

1770 - 1773 TAX ASSESSMENTS. Although William-III was listed in the Cumberland Tax records in 1768, 1769, and 1770, Lewis-I was not included in 1770.[48] While Lewis-I appears in Springhill Township in the 1773 Bedford County tax record (prepared in 1772), William-III does not.[49,50] There are many possible reasons for these anomalies. Considering all the information, it is here supposed that Lewis-I or William-III were omitted in error when the respective tax lists were first drawn up.

Another obvious possibility is that the person of interest was simply not present when the tax list was prepared. It has been recorded that Jehu Conwell returned to Delaware for a period of time due to the hostile activities occurring on the frontier in 1772.[51] It was also common for frontiersmen to journey back east for supplies which could take months. It is possible that Lewis-I and William-III, during the separate dates noted, had temporarily withdrawn from the frontier, or were otherwise absent when the tax lists were prepared. All these possibilities of course are speculation. It was disappointing that these disparities could not be resolved with any degree of certainty.

It was also noted that William-III appears in the 1771 Cumberland County tax record in which he is recorded as owning one horse and one cow.[52] Lewis-I is missing from this record, but it is known that he sold his remaining tract of land in Delaware in that year and may have been absent for that reason.

OTHER TAX RECORDS. At first glance it may seem that there are potentially many tax lists that may contain information about the Davidsons while they resided in Pennsylvania. However, many of these records amount to little more than a list of names and the amount of the assessment. Care must also be taken to respect the changing boundaries of the counties when researching these elusive documents.

The Bedford County tax list of 1773 has already been discussed. Although tax lists survive for Bedford County in 1774, 1775, 1776, and other years, the Davidsons are not included there because the boundaries changed and the region in which the family resided became a part of Westmoreland County in February 1773.

For Westmoreland County, the next available document is the Census of 1783 in which we find William-III where expected in Menallen (or Manallen) Township.[53,54] Although other neighbors of William-III are found in Menallen Township, which confirms his identity, it is not known why William-III's father, Lewis-I, is absent. Another later Westmoreland tax list survives from 1786, but by then the boundaries had changed again and we must look to records held by Fayette County.

Both William-III and Lewis-I (spelled "Levis" in the Pennsylvania Archives transcript) are found in the 1785 Tax list of Luzerne Township in Fayette County. Lewis-I paid 10 shillings, 3 pence while William-III paid 12 shillings, 9 pence in taxes. The following year both men are found again in the same location, Lewis-I paying 9 shillings, 3 pence and William-III paying 11 shillings, 4 pence.[55,56]

While some tax lists in different townships recorded the number of horses, cattle, sheep, and persons attributable to each head of household, unfortunately this information was not captured in those lists in which Lewis-I and William-III appear, apart from those mentioned herein.

There are several tax lists available for Fayette County from 1785 through 1798, but most of these do nothing more than show that William-III was still in residence there and that he was primarily a crop farmer.

1798 U. S. DIRECT TAX. This was also called the "window tax" or "glass tax" because it was based on the number of window panes in each house being assessed. This was perhaps the single most interesting tax document located since it describes William-III's house! It was constructed of logs and contained about 880 square feet of living space (22 feet by 20 feet by 2 floors). It had two floors, one door and two windows, each containing six lights or panes of glass. This cabin was only about the size of an apartment by today's standards, but William-III, his wife and several children shared the space. It must be remembered however, that there were no inside bathrooms in those days and the cooking area was part of the main living area.[57-60]

Today fireplaces are mostly ornamental, but the fireplaces in the 18th century were much more functional, often serving in place of a modern day stove. For safety reasons, many pioneers erected a separate structure they called a kitchen where their cooking was done. If the kitchen caught fire, the detached structure posed less of a hazard to the home. The tax records do not indicate that William-III ever constructed a separate kitchen.

SLAVERY IN PENNSYLVANIA. It was surprising to learn that the 1768 tax record lists Lewis-I in the possession of "one negro."[61] However, the 1769 tax record, only one year later, shows that this was no longer the case.[62] Given this short duration, it seems as though Lewis-I may have required assistance in making the journey from Delaware to Pennsylvania and possibly to help the family through initial settlement. The purpose could have been to help clear the land and build a home. It is easy to speculate about this one record and we are only left to guess at the details. Although considerable effort was expended, it was disappointing that attempts to learn anything about this person, including even the name, age, and gender, were not successful. In all other related documents examined, no further record of any such ownership was found in the Davidson lineage.

Boucher describes three predominant types of servitude condoned by legal authorities in Pennsylvania for decades.[63] The indentured servant could generally take two different forms. The first form resulted in one who was indebted to another for a specified term of years as a means of barter. This was often voluntarily done. For example, a father could indenture his son for a debt or one might indenture himself for a conveyance of land. This was considered a relatively harmless type of servitude that was a practiced form of business. The largely agrarian society provided few opportunities, for those attempting to start a livelihood, to earn the capital needed to purchase land. With few opportunities to earn money, the indenture became an accepted form of financing one's debt. In the early years, banks didn't operate on the frontier and therefore business loans were unavailable. The repayment took the form of labor for some specified period of time.

The second type of indentured servant offered persons, often found living in poverty, passage from England or European nations to America. These persons signed a contract called an indenture with the master or owner of the vessel bound for America.[64] The initial vision for this system of indentured servitude offered the participants a means for a new start in exchange for laborers which were greatly needed in the colonies. Once their terms of service expired, the freed laborers earned the right to a certain number of acres of land. However, the system went unregulated for years and all forms of deceit and abuse resulted. The uneducated failed to understand the full nature of the agreements they signed. Many persons were convinced of the misrepresentations told to them by recruiters. Often, their captors relied on trickery to lure their victims aboard ship only to be ushered below deck and forcibly held. Others were kidnapped and sold into bondage, including children.[65]

Alternatively, a redemptioner was a person brought to America without an indenture, but it was agreed prior to embarking that the redemptioner would find relatives or friends at their destination who would pay their travel fare upon arrival and "redeem" them from their bond. Failing this, redemptioners then fell subject to the terms of their master and became indentured servants.[66]

Indentured servants were predominantly white men, women, and children put on the auction block and sold to the highest bidder after arriving in America so their master could recoup their travel expenses plus a lucrative profit. When sold in America, the indenture was transferred to the new owner and the servants were required to work without pay for a term of years. Children generally remained indentured until age 21. In many cases, indentured servants were said to receive only slightly better treatment than African slaves.[67]

The third type of servitude Boucher terms "African Slavery." Native Africans at the source of the lucrative slave trade kidnapped and otherwise forcibly captured other Africans from neighboring tribes or with whom they were at war and sold them into bondage.[68-70] Their European trading partners purchased the captives and transported them to America aboard sailing vessels. The journeys generally took between 60 and 90 days or longer in conditions so abhorrent that an average of 20% of the captives did not survive the transatlantic crawl.[71]

Locally, some African slaves were sold alongside indentured servants for profit at Greensburg (Westmoreland County) on an auctioning block in the town square.[72] The last indentured servant "knocked down," or sold to the highest bidder, reportedly took place there on March 5, 1819.[73]

Slavery was gradually abolished in Pennsylvania beginning with an act dated 1 March 1780, long after Lewis-I's reported ownership had ended. The act required that the children of slaves born in Pennsylvania were to be free upon reaching the age of 28 years.[74] Likewise, slaves brought into the state were to be freed when the age of 28 years was reached. The passage of this act in 1780 caused many settlers, finding themselves on the Pennsylvania side of the Mason-

Other Pennsylvania Records

Dixon Line, to abandon their holdings and move into Maryland, Kentucky, and Virginia.[75] The subsequent passage of additional acts served to strengthen the antislavery movement. The last African slave in Westmoreland County was reported in 1840.[76]

1790 FEDERAL CENSUS. William-III can be found where expected in the Federal 1790 Census in Luzerne Township of Fayette County.[77] His identity is easily validated by comparing several of the names of the other residents to those shown on the Warrantee Township Map.[78] Among them on the same page, the following are included: Nathaniel Breading, Jehu Conwell, William Conwell, George Death, James Death, John Crawford, and Josiah Crawford, all neighbors of William-III.

The "Free white males ages 16 and up" column would include William-III's sons John and Lewis-III and William-III himself for a total of three which ties to the census count. The "Free white males under age 16" column would include only son David Hutchinson Davidson. However, the census shows a count of two. One possibility is that son Abraham was born in 1790 rather than 1791, which is possible. The next column "Free white females" would include Barbara, Comfort, Mary E., Margaret, Elizabeth, and Sarah, for a total of six. However, the census has a count of only five. It is possible that Barbara was accidentally excluded in this count which would reconcile the census. But it is impossible to tell why these variances occurred which could be explained in any number of ways. For the benefit of those unfamiliar with census records, they are often surprisingly informative, but also frequently very wrong.

SEPTENNIAL CENSUS. The State of Pennsylvania performed a census every seven years, beginning in 1779, but it amounts to only a list of names. William-III and Lewis-I are included in the 1786 list in Fayette County.[79,80] The next instance of this census available from this county was conducted in 1800, which is too late, since by this time William-III had left the state of Pennsylvania and Lewis-I was deceased. Source documents for the remaining years were not pursued since they appear to be of little value.

William "Ranger" Davidson

JURY DUTY. One rather obscure record was found in George Albert's "History of the County of Westmoreland, Pennsylvania." In footnote one on page 57 may be found the following, which is interesting. Although it actually adds little to our knowledge of William-III, perhaps an additional dimension of the times will be gained by the reader. From the court sessions of October 1773:

The King v. Luke Picket – Felony

And now a jury being called came to wit, James Kincade, William Lyon, John Armstrong, Henry Martin, William Linn, Robert Meeks, James Carnanghan, Joseph McDowell, Lewis Davison, William Davison, John Wright & Alexander Duglass who being duly impannelled, returned elected tried chosen sworn and upon their respective Oaths do say that Luke Picket is Guilty of the Felony whereof he stands Indited.

Judgment that the said Luke Picket be taken to Morrow Morning (being the 8th Instant) between the hours of eight and ten to the Public Whipping Post and there to receive 21 Lashes on his Bare Back well laid on, that he pay a fine of £32..1..0 to his Honour the Governor that he make restitution of the Goods stolen to the Owner, pay the costs of Prosecution and stand committed until complied with.[81]

The case cited above was the second recorded in which the whipping post was used for punishment in Westmoreland County. Given the early period in which this event occurred there is little doubt that the two "Davison's" are our William-III and his father.

According to Boucher's History of Westmoreland County, the Whipping post was described as a "section of small tree about one foot in diameter, hewn flat on one side and firmly implanted in the ground.

Other Pennsylvania Records

Five feet from the ground was a cross piece about six feet long, thoroughly fastened to it. The whippings were always public performances. When the wrong-doer was about to be whipped, his arms were stretched out and his hands or wrists were tied firmly to the ends of the cross piece." The sheriff or his deputy administered the punishment.[82,83]

1. Edgar W. Hassler, *Old Westmoreland: A History of Western Pennsylvania During the Revolution* (Cleveland, Ohio : The Arthur H. Clark Company, 1900), pp. 188-190, digital version, *Google Books* (http//books.google.com : accessed July 2011).

2. Hanna Benner Roach, FGSP, FASG, *The Pennsylvania Militia in 1777*, reprinted from "The Pennsylvania Genealogical Magazine," Volume XXIII, Number 3, 1964, p. 229, print. The reprint retains the page numbers as the article originally appeared, pp. 161-230.

3. Hassler, Chapter XXVIII, beginning on p. 189, covers the events at the end of the Revolution.

4. James Veech, *The Monongahela of Old* (Pittsburg, PA.: 1858-1892), pp. 96-97, digital version, *Google Books* (http://books.google.com : accessed April 2011).

5. Veech, pp. 97-100, discusses the state of land ownership on the frontier before 1768.

6. Although there were other types of indentures used for a variety of purposes, the discussion in this section is limited to those used to document the transfer of title to land.

7. Veech, pp. 95-97.

8. Fayette County, Pennsylvania, Records of the Land Office, Record Group 17, Survey Book, Volume Y, Page 147, survey of a 303½ acre parcel, called *Dispute Ended*, dated 25 October 1786 (and the corrected version bearing the same date), for William Davidson, photocopies of penned documents, Pennsylvania State Archives, Harrisburg.

9. Veech, Chapter VIII, dedicated to Mason and Dixon's Line, which settled the boundary dispute between Pennsylvania and Virginia.

10. *Records of the Land Office*, RG-17, *Pennsylvania Historical & Museum Commission* (http://www.phmc.state.pa.us/bah/dam/rg/rg17.htm : accessed February 2014), Pennsylvania State Archives, Harrisburg. This web page describes transition of land ownership from the Penns to the state of Pennsylvania.

11. Veech, pp. 89-90, the early settlers were threatened with the death penalty in February 1768.

12. George Dallas Albert, *History of the County of Westmoreland Pennsylvania* (Philadelphia: L. H. Everts & Co., 1882), p. 41, digital version, *Google Books* (http://books.google.com : accessed August 2011).

13. Elizabeth Davidson Harbaugh, *The Davidson Genealogy* (Ironton, Ohio : self-published, 1948; Ann Arbor, Michigan : Lithoprinted, Edwards Brothers, Inc., 1949), p. 128, print, OCLC: 23167553.

14. Westmoreland County, Pennsylvania, Recorder of Deeds, Deed Book A: 239, "Indenture, James Gilmore to Lewis Davidson," 29 June 1767, recorded 22 May 1781, photocopy of penned document, Greensburg, Pennsylvania. Technically, both James Gilmore and Lewis-I were squatters and neither had legal ownership of the land other than Tomahawk Claim. However, they did have the conveyance documented and executed it in 1767, as evidenced by their signatures, reproduced in the recorded copy.

15. Westmoreland County, Pennsylvania, Recorder of Deeds, Deed Book A: 237, "Lewis Davidson to Wm Davidson," 27 March 1781, recorded 22 May 1781, for 420 acres for £2 s. 10, photocopy of penned document, obtained January 2012, Greensburg, Pennsylvania.

16. Sussex County, Delaware, Deed Book L: 235-236, "Isaac Draper from Lewis Davison," dated 30 November 1771, recorded 6 May 1772, Record Group 4555, digital copies of penned indenture for seven acres, obtained November 2015, Delaware Public Archives, Dover.

17. *Bedford County, 1773-1775, 16th, 17th, 18th of the 18 Penny Tax, Springhill Township, Continued, 1773*, p. 33, 48th entry for Lewis Davison, unnumbered, digital copy of penned document, Tax and Exoneration Lists, 1762-1794, Series 4.61;

Other Pennsylvania Records

Records of the Office of the Comptroller General, Record Group 4, Pennsylvania State Archives, Harrisburg. Lewis-I was assessed £0..3..6.

18. John H. Campbell, Chief Draftsman, *Warrantee Township Map: Fayette County, Luzerne Township* (Harrisburg, Pennsylvania: Records of the Land Office, 1920), Record Group 17, Series 17.522, Pennsylvania State Archives, digital version, *Commonwealth of Pennsylvania's Enterprise Portal* (http://www.portal .state.pa.us : March 2011).

19. Comparing the names of residents on the *Warrantee Township Map* to those on the Bedford County tax list of 1773 provides confirmation as to the identity of Lewis Davidson. In addition to Lewis-I are William Conwell, William Crawford, Henry Enoch, Aaron Hackney, Thomas Scott, and others.

20. The language found in the indenture recorded in 1781 says that the land purchased by William-III from Lewis-I was "part of a large purchase of improvements and land joining thereto which may more largely and particularly appear by a conveyance from James Gilmore…" This indicates that Lewis-I had amassed a lot of property in southwestern Pennsylvania. This is further evidenced by the several sales made by Lewis-I to his sons and stepson.

21. Fayette County, Pennsylvania, Records of the Land Office, Record Group 17; Survey Book, Volume C, Number 34, Page 3, Survey of a 50 acre parcel, called *Fortune*, 30 June 1786, for "Lewis Davidson in Right of John Crawford," photocopies of penned documents, Pennsylvania State Archives, Harrisburg.

22. Fayette County [formerly Westmoreland], Pennsylvania, Records of the Land Office, Record Group 17; Patent Book, Volume P, Number 8, page 410, patent application for John Crawford, 19 October 1773 [same as the Warrant date]; warrant number 30 to John Crawford, 19 October 1773; patent to Lewis Davidson, for a 50 acre tract of land called *Fortune*, 6 April 1787, photocopies of penned documents, Pennsylvania State Archives, Harrisburg.

23. Ibid.

24. Westmoreland County, Pennsylvania, Recorder of Deeds, Deed Book A: 326, "Lewis Davidson to Thomas Davidson," 30 October 1775, recorded 13 April 1783, photocopy of penned document, Greensburg, Pennsylvania.

25. Westmoreland County, Pennsylvania, Recorder of Deeds, Deed Book A: 239, "Lewis Davidson to Wm Conwell," 7 March 1781, recorded 22 May 1781, photocopy of penned document, Greensburg, Pennsylvania.

26. Westmoreland County, Pennsylvania, Recorder of Deeds, Deed Book A: 237, "Lewis Davidson to Wm Davidson," 27 March 1781, recorded 22 May 1781, photocopy of penned document, obtained January 2012, 420 acres for £2 s. 10, Greensburg, Pennsylvania.

27. Westmoreland County, Pennsylvania, Recorder of Deeds, Deed Book A: 326, "Lewis Davidson to Thomas Davidson," 30 October 1775, recorded 13 April 1783, for a parcel called *Hickory Level*, photocopy of penned document, Greensburg, Pennsylvania.

28. Westmoreland County, Pennsylvania, Recorder of Deeds, Deed Book A: 239, "Ja[s] Bredin to Jehu Conwell," 27 January 1773, recorded 22 May 1781, photocopy of penned document, Greensburg, Pennsylvania. The acreage was not stated.

29. Westmoreland County, Pennsylvania, Recorder of Deeds, Deed Book A: 209, "William Davidson to Thomas Stockley," 15 May 1778, recorded 23 January 1781, 120 acres from the west side of *Dispute Ended*, photocopy of penned document, obtained August 2012, Greensburg, Pennsylvania.

30. Fayette County, Pennsylvania, Records of the Land Office, Record Group 17; Patent Book, Volume P, Number 15, page 421, patent application, dated 23 December 1784; warrant number 13, dated 8 August 1785; and patent, dated 18 December 1790, for William Davidson, for a 303½ acre tract called *Dispute Ended*, photocopies of penned documents, Pennsylvania State Archives, Harrisburg.

31. Ibid.

32. Ibid.

33. Ibid.

34. Pennsylvania Archives, Series 3, Volume I, p. 582, digital version, *Fold3* (http://www.fold3 .com : accessed October 2012).

35. James Hamon was probably James Hammond, a neighbor residing near William-III, as was Henry Swindler, as shown on Campbell's *Warrantee Township Map: Fayette County, Luzerne Township.*

36. Pennsylvania Archives, Series 3, Volume I, p. 652, digital version, *Fold3* (http://www.fold3 .com : accessed October 2012).

37. The nature of Thomas Dobbin's claim was not established; he does not appear on the *Warrantee Township Map.*

38. Fayette County, Pennsylvania, Records of the Land Office, Record Group 17, Ledgers, 1701-1710, 1712-1955, series 17.369, Ledger K, 1785-1786, p. 300, page untitled, entry for William Davidson on 8 August 1785, recording payments for a 303½ acre tract of land, photocopy of penned document, Pennsylvania State Archives, Harrisburg.

39. Fayette County, Pennsylvania, Records of the Land Office, Record Group 17, Ledgers, 1701-1710, 1712-1955, series 17.369, Ledger M, 1790-1792, p. 149, page untitled, entry for William Davidson for payments made on a 420½ acre tract of land, several transactions from 17 December 1790 thru 26 July 1792, photocopy of penned document, Pennsylvania State Archives, Harrisburg.

40. Fayette County, Pennsylvania, Records of the Land Office, Record Group 17, Journals, 1701-1710, 1712-1955, series 17.368, Journal K, 1785-1786, "Philadelphia 8th August 1785," p. 252, three entries for William Davidson recording payments for a 303½ acre tract of land, photocopy of penned document, Pennsylvania State Archives, Harrisburg.

41. Fayette County, Pennsylvania, Records of the Land Office, Record Group 17, Journals, 1701-1710, 1712-1955, series 17.368, Journal M, 1790-1792, "Philadelphia 17th December 1790," p. 190, two entries for William Davidson in payment of a 303½ acre tract of land, photocopy of penned document, Pennsylvania State Archives, Harrisburg.

42. The amount William-III saved in interest may be calculated as (303.5 acres ÷ 100) × £10 per hundred acres × 3% interest × 9 years (1770 to 1779) = 8.1945 pounds.

43. Sales by Lewis-I included: 50 acres to son Thomas [conservatively guessed since the acreage was not stated in the indenture] + 300 acres to William Conwell + 420 acres to William-III + 170 acres held by Lewis-I after he purchased *Fortune*

= 940 acres. These may not represent all the land transactions by Lewis-I; a comprehensive search was not conducted in Greensburg and the staff there (Joe in particular) repeatedly resisted requests for even the smallest amount of assistance.

44. *Tax Rates Book, 1768-1770*, Book 004, "Cumberland Rates 1768," Cumberland County, Cumberland Township, p. 31, 2nd entry for Lewis Davison, assessed eight pounds, eight shillings, four pence province tax and four pounds county tax, digital copy of penned document online, Commissioners Record Series, *Cumberland County Archives* (http://www.ccpa.net/ : accessed January 2016), Carlisle, Pennsylvania.

45. *Tax Rates Book, 1768-1770*, Book 004, "Cumberland Rates 1768," Cumberland County, Cumberland Township, p. 33, 4th entry under "Cumberland freemen" for William Davison, assessed 15 shillings province tax and 9 shillings county tax, digital copy of penned document online, Commissioners Record Series, *Cumberland County Archives* (http://www.ccpa.net/ : accessed January 2016), Carlisle, Pennsylvania.

46. *Tax Rates Book, 1768-1770*, Book 004, "Cumberland Townp 1769," Cumberland County, Cumberland Township, p. 240, 2nd "Freemen," entry for Wm Davison, digital copy of penned document online, Commissioners Record Series, *Cumberland County Archives* (http://www.ccpa.net/ : accessed January 2016), Carlisle, Pennsylvania.

47. Harbaugh, p. 129.

48. *Tax Rates Book, 1768-1770*, Book 004, "Cumberland 1770," Cumberland County, Cumberland Township, p. 426, 19th entry for William Davison, assessed 15 shillings, four pence province tax and 2 pounds county tax, digital copy of penned document online, Commissioners Record Series, *Cumberland County Archives* (http://www.ccpa.net/ : accessed January 2016), Carlisle, Pennsylvania.

49. *Bedford County, 1773-1775, 16th, 17th, 18th of the 18 Penny Tax, Springhill Township, Continued, 1773*, p. 33, 48th entry for Lewis Davison, unnumbered, digital copy of penned document, Tax and Exoneration Lists, 1762-1794, Series 4.61; Records of the Office of the Comptroller General, Record Group 4, Pennsylvania State Archives, Harrisburg. Lewis-I was assessed £0..3..6.

Other Pennsylvania Records

50. Transcript of Taxables in the County of Bedford for the Year 1773. On the transcript, a man named William Dawson was listed. The source document for this record was ordered on the suspicion that this was actually our William-III and that his surname was misspelled in the transcript. In this case, it was found that the transcript was accurately recorded.

51. John W. Jordan and James Hadden, *Genealogical and Personal History of Fayette County, Pennsylvania*, Volume II (New York: Lewis Historical Publishing Company, 1912), p. 604, *Internet Archive* (http://www.archive.org : accessed October 2013).

52. *Tax Rates Book, 1736-1930*, Book 005, "Cumberland rates 1771," Cumberland County, Cumberland Township, p. 47, last entry on page for William Davison, assessed for one horse and one cow, digital copy of penned document online, Commissioners Record Series, *Cumberland County Archives* (http://www.ccpa.net/ : accessed January 2016), Carlisle, Pennsylvania.

53. *Pennsylvania, Tax and Exoneration, 1768-1801*, Westmoreland County, Menallen Township, penned document, untitled, p. 5, fourth "D" entry for Willm Davidson, assessed 17 shillings, ten pence, state tax and seven shillings, county tax in 1783, digital image 4 of 30, *Ancestry* (http://www.ancestry.com : accessed 2011), citing *Tax & Exoneration Lists, 1762–1794*, Series No. 4.61; Records of the Office of the Comptroller General, Record Group 4; Pennsylvania State Archives, Harrisburg.

54. *Pennsylvania, Tax and Exoneration, 1768-1801*, Westmoreland County, Menallen Township, penned document, untitled, p. 4, fourth "D" entry for Wm Davidson, assessed one pound, ten shillings, three pence, state tax and seven shillings, 11 pence, county tax in 1783, digital image 14 of 30, *Ancestry* (http://www.ancestry.com : accessed 2011), citing *Tax & Exoneration Lists, 1762–1794*, Series No. 4.61; Records of the Office of the Comptroller General, Record Group 4; Pennsylvania State Archives, Harrisburg.

55. *Pennsylvania, Tax and Exoneration, 1768-1801*, Fayette County, Luzerne Township, penned document, untitled, p. 47, 13th "D" entry for William Davidson, assessed 12 shillings, nine pence in 1785, digital image 1 of 17, *Ancestry* (http://www.ancestry.com : accessed 2011), citing *Tax & Exoneration Lists, 1762–1794*, Series No. 4.61; Records of the Office of the Comptroller General, Record Group 4; Pennsylvania State Archives, Harrisburg.

56. *Pennsylvania, Tax and Exoneration, 1768-1801*, Fayette County, Luzerne Township, penned document, untitled, p. 47, eighth "D" entry for Lewis

Davidson, assessed ten shillings, three pence in 1785, digital image 1 of 17, *Ancestry* (http://www.ancestry.com : accessed 2011), citing *Tax & Exoneration Lists, 1762–1794*, Series No. 4.61; Records of the Office of the Comptroller General, Record Group 4; Pennsylvania State Archives, Harrisburg.

57. *Pennsylvania, U.S. Direct Tax Lists, 1798*, Schedule *A*, penned document, page unnumbered, untitled, line 21, entry for Wm Davidson, Fayette County, Luzerne Township, digital image 29 of 426, *Ancestry* (http://www.ancestry.com : accessed 2011), citing microfilm M372, Tax Lists for the State of Pennsylvania, Records of the Internal Revenue Service, 1791-2006, Record Group 58; National Archives and Records Administration, Washington, D.C.

58. *Pennsylvania, U.S. Direct Tax Lists, 1798*, Schedule B, penned document, page unnumbered, untitled, line 51, entry for Wm Davidson, Fayette County, Luzerne Township, digital image 144 of 426, *Ancestry* (http://www.ancestry.com : accessed 2011), citing microfilm M372, Tax Lists for the State of Pennsylvania, Records of the Internal Revenue Service, 1791-2006, Record Group 58; National Archives and Records Administration, Washington, D.C.

59. *Pennsylvania, U.S. Direct Tax Lists, 1798*, Schedule D, penned document, page unnumbered, untitled, line 21, entry for Wm Davidson, Fayette County, Luzerne Township, digital image 281 of 426, *Ancestry* (http://www.ancestry.com : accessed 2011), citing microfilm M372, Tax Lists for the State of Pennsylvania, Records of the Internal Revenue Service, 1791-2006, Record Group 58; National Archives and Records Administration, Washington, D.C.

60. *Pennsylvania, U.S. Direct Tax Lists, 1798*, Schedule E, penned document, page unnumbered, untitled, line 51, entry for Wm Davidson, Fayette County, Luzerne Township, digital image 346 of 426, *Ancestry* (http://www.ancestry.com : accessed 2011), citing microfilm M372, Tax Lists for the State of Pennsylvania, Records of the Internal Revenue Service, 1791-2006, Record Group 58; National Archives and Records Administration, Washington, D.C.

61. *Tax Rates Book, 1768-1770*, Book 004, "Cumberland Rates 1768," Cumberland County, Cumberland Township, p. 31, 2nd entry for Lewis Davison, assessed eight pounds, eight shillings, four pence province tax and four pounds county tax, digital copy of penned document online, Commissioners Record Series,

Other Pennsylvania Records

Cumberland County Archives (http://www.ccpa.net/ : accessed January 2016); Carlisle, Pennsylvania.

62. *Tax Rates Book, 1768-1770*, Book 004, "Cumberland Townᴾ 1769," Cumberland County, Cumberland Township, p. 238, entry for Lewis Davison, assessed 19 shillings, four pence, province tax and one pound county tax, digital copy of penned document online, Commissioners Record Series, *Cumberland County Archives* (http://www.ccpa.net/ : accessed January 2016), Carlisle, Pennsylvania.

63. John N. Boucher, *History of Westmoreland County Pennsylvania*, Volume I (New York: The Lewis Publishing Company, 1906), pp. 53-59, digital version, *Google Books* (http://books.google.com : accessed June 2011).

64. Karl Frederick Geiser, *Redemptioners and Indentured Servants in the Colony and the Commonwealth of Pennsylvania* (New Haven, Conn.: The Tuttle, Morehouse & Taylor, Co., 1901), p. 6, digital version, *Google Books* (http://books.google.com : accessed November 2015).

65. Geiser, pp. 20-21.

66. Geiser, p. 6.

67. Boucher, pp. 53-59.

68. Charles Johnson and Patricia Smith, and the WGBH Series Research Team, *Africans in America: America's Journey through Slavery*, video, (New York: Harcourt Brace, 1998).

69. Jennifer Steinberg, "Last Voyage of the Slave Ship Henrietta Marie," *National Geographic Magazine*, August 2002, print.

70. Hugh Thomas, *The Slave Trade* (Simon and Schuster, 1997), print.

71. Steinberg.

72. Boucher, p. 59.

73. Ibid.

74. Boucher, p. 58.

75. S. B. Nelson, *Nelson's Biographical Dictionary and Historical Reference Book of Fayette County Pennsylvania* (Uniontown, PA: S. B. Nelson Publisher, 1900), p. 155, digital version, *Google Books* (http://google.books.com : accessed May 2011).

76. Boucher, p. 59.

77. *1790 United States Federal Census*, population schedule, penned, Luzerne Township, Fayette County, Pennsylvania, p. 39, column 2, 18th entry for William Davidson, digital image 4 of 4, *FamilySearch* (https://familysearch.org : accessed December 2011), citing NARA microfilm publication M637, (Washington D.C.: National Archives and Records Administration, n.d.).

78. John H. Campbell, Chief Draftsman, *Warrantee Township Map: Fayette County, Luzerne Township* (Harrisburg, Pennsylvania: Records of the Land Office, 1920), Record Group 17, Series 17.522, Pennsylvania State Archives, digital version, *Commonwealth of Pennsylvania's Enterprise Portal* (http://www.portal.state.pa.us : March 2011).

79. *Pennsylvania, Septennial Census, 1779-1863*, Fayette County, Luzerne Township, penned document, untitled, unpaged, 12th "D" entry for William Davidson in 1786, digital image 16 of 30, *Ancestry* (http://www.ancestry.com : accessed 2011), citing *Septennial Census Returns, 1779–1863*, Box 1026, Records of the House of Representatives, Records of the General Assembly, Record Group 7; Pennsylvania State Archives, Harrisburg.

80. *Pennsylvania, Septennial Census, 1779-1863*, Fayette County, Luzerne Township, penned document, untitled, unpaged, eighth "D" entry for Lewis Davidson in 1786, digital image 16 of 30, *Ancestry* (http://www.ancestry.com : accessed 2011), citing *Septennial Census Returns, 1779–1863*, Box 1026, Records of the House of Representatives, Records of the General Assembly, Record Group 7; Pennsylvania State Archives, Harrisburg.

81. Albert, p. 57.

82. Ibid.

83. Boucher, p. 52, discusses the whipping post.

9

Families

The families of the ancestors we have discussed so far must not be left out. When this chapter was initially conceived, it was intended to cover the family of William-III by his two wives. However, it was later decided to expand the content to include the families of William-II and Hannah, and Lewis-I and his two wives, in addition to William-III.

Unfortunately, there were really very few vital records located that pertain to these early families. Instead, we must look to the works of Hardesty (1882), Lewis H. Davidson (1890), Evans (1903), and

Harbaugh (1949) whose combined works hold more information about these families than any others found.[1-4] Much of the information in this chapter is based upon the works of these authors. The information in the above-mentioned sources largely came from descendant testimonials whose identities have long since been lost.

Other essential sources may include census records, land records, and wills when readily available, but the reader must be informed that limited research was conducted on the persons of interest in this chapter. The names and vital dates of children of these descendants were only included if they were found in a census, a will, if a photograph of the grave was found online, or other similar credible sources.

Traditional naming conventions that use the parent's names for children are not uncommon in various parts of the world. This practice was introduced by immigrants to America and was often continued by their descendants. This is particularly exemplified in the Scandinavian countries where patronymics and matronymics were used for centuries. The rules used were regional and not always strictly followed.

For example, the first son was frequently named after the father's father. The second son was named after the mother's father. The third son was named after the father. For girls, the same naming order was followed for the wife's side of the family. Additional children were sometimes given their aunt's and uncle's names. Middle names that sound like surnames were also used respecting the maiden names of the father's mother, the wife's mother, the mother, and so on.

Subtle evidence helping to confirm some of the family relationships may be found by considering the choice of names for William-III's children. William-III's second child was named after his father, Lewis-I. His third and eleventh children were named after William-III's mother, Comfort Warrington. His fourth and eleventh children were named after his first wife, Rosanna Hutchinson. William-III himself was likely named after his grandfather. These occurrences are too numerous to be coincidence.

Families

1. William Davidson (William-II) and Hannah. William-II was thought to have been born in Somerset County, Maryland. He married Hannah, whose unmarried surname has so far been undiscovered. From the survey and land records associated with William-II and Hannah, we can determine that this family was intent on moving from Maryland to Delaware by 1731.[5,6]

Lewis-I, born in 1712, is believed to be the first child of William-II and Hannah, which could put their marriage year around 1711. If William-II and Hannah were, say 28 years of age when they married, then they would have been born about 1683 and in 1731 they would have been about 48 years old when they moved to Delaware, but all these assumptions are only very rough estimations.

Hannah is described as a widow in the survey conducted by Shankland on November 16, 1731, so we know that William-II was deceased prior to this date. In partnership with Joshua Stockley, William-II had purchased a 179-acre tract of land in Delaware from Thomas Warrington. His death occurred in Somerset County, Maryland and given that he had recently formed a business partnership, his death was apparently unexpected and possibly sudden.

Hannah went on to have their parcel of land in Delaware surveyed and the indenture was made out in her name. The indenture describes Hannah as the "widow & relict of…Willm Davidson of Sumorset County in the Province of Maryland" indicating the location of her husband's demise.

Harbaugh presents an "acc't of her administration…" reporting that Hannah died in 1747.[7] This latter record used her same surname, indicating that Hannah never remarried. This single record cited by Harbaugh was not found in the Delaware records and was not separately examined.

Beginning no later than February 1732, Hannah and her son Lewis-I and her two daughters lived on the family farm located on the north side of Bracey Branch (a small creek) in Indian River Hundred, on Angola Neck, Sussex County, Delaware. The farm was sold in 1753 by Lewis-I, Mary, and Sarah, children and heirs of Hannah.[8]

William "Ranger" Davidson

Lewis-I, Mary, and Sarah were consistently named in the order just given in at least two Delaware land records, which we shall here presume to be the order of their births.

1.1 **Lewis Davidson (Lewis-I)**. We have already covered many details about Lewis-I, however, a summary is provided a little later in this chapter.

1.2 **Mary Davidson**. We know almost nothing of Mary except that she was reportedly born in Somerset County, Maryland and probably died in Sussex County, Delaware.[9] There was no further record of her found. If we assume that she was the second child of William-II and Hannah, then we could guess that she may have been born about 1714 or about two years after Lewis-I.

1.3 **Sarah Davidson**. If we make similar assumptions about Sarah as we did for her sister, being the third child of William-II and Hannah, then we might guess that she was born about 1716. Sarah was married to John Arderly by August 1753, when Hannah's heirs sold her farm.[10,11] Sarah was deceased by 6 May 1784 as evidenced by another Delaware land record.[12]

2. Lewis Davidson (Lewis-I) and Comfort Warrington. Lewis was born in 1712. Harbaugh says he was born in Somerset County, Maryland and the Delaware land records point to this area as the location where his parents, William-II and Hannah, formerly resided.[13,14] Lewis-I grew up in Maryland, leaving there at about 19 years of age, when his mother, Hannah, and his two sisters relocated to Sussex County, Delaware. His father, William-II, died just prior to their migration, placing an extra burden on the family.

The first evidence that Lewis-I struck out on his own is found in 1750 when he purchased a tract of land.[15] But, according to Harbaugh, Lewis-I was married about 1746 to his first wife, Comfort

162

Warrington.[16] There is sufficient evidence that Lewis-I was a farmer as were his parents.

Several Delaware land transactions between the Warrington and Davidson families show the close proximity of these two clans.[17] The last will of William M. Warrington, father of Comfort, provides evidence that Comfort was the mother of both William Davidson (William-III) and Lewis Davidson (Lewis-II).[18] William M. Warrington died in 1755 and left an inheritance to the two children of his daughter Comfort, named as "William and Lewis Davidson." Since Comfort herself was not named in the will we may reasonably conclude that she was deceased prior to 1755, but Harbaugh says she died about 1749, without providing any citation.[19]

2.1 **William Davidson (William-III).** William-III was born on November 20, 1747 on a tract of land adjoining or near Rehoboth Bay, in Indian River Hundred, on Angola Neck, in Sussex County, Delaware. His mother died when he was only about two years of age. He was likely cared for by his two aunts, Mary and Sarah, in his earliest years. He spent the first eight or nine years of his boyhood in Indian River Hundred, probably skipping stones on Rehoboth Bay, receiving an education, and working on the family farm. The next nine or ten years of his life were spent in Broadkill Hundred near the banks of Broadkill Creek. William-III next migrated to southwestern Pennsylvania in June 1767 with his family.

When his father, Lewis-I died in 1793, William-III was to receive £18 in "creature cattle or produce," from his father's estate, the value of which was to be determined by William-III's half-brother Jeremiah.[20] Lewis-I goes on to say in the will that if the fair value could not be agreed upon, they should then find another person to render an estimate of the fair value. Was Lewis-I anticipating an argument between two siblings?

William-III is the man central to this entire book, so we shall leave his further history for later.

2.2   **Lewis Davidson (Lewis-II)**. Lewis-II was born about 1749, the same year that his mother, Comfort, died. The locations of his birth and childhood are the same as his older brother, William-III.

Lewis-II likely moved west to southwestern Pennsylvania with his family in June 1767, but returned east and settled near Fort Cumberland, Maryland where he purchased at least six parcels of land totaling 282 acres which he cleared and farmed.[21] He also cultivated honey as evidenced by his possession of two beehives.[22] He appears in both the 1800 and 1810 federal census records in Cumberland Township, Allegany County, Maryland.[23,24]

Lewis-II married Nancy Todd about 1769 and they had 14 children. Harbaugh recorded that Nancy was an orphan born in England and that she was raised by a wealthy English woman who brought her to America.[25]

In 1793, Lewis-II was bequeathed a similar inheritance from his father as was his brother, William-III, £18 in "creature cattle or produce," the value of which was to be determined by his half-brother, Jeremiah.[26]

The family remained in the Fort Cumberland area for the remainder of their days. Nancy preceded Lewis-II, but her date of death is unknown. Several years before his death, Lewis-II lost his eyesight. In 1814, he and three of his daughters and two of his grandsons contracted typhoid fever which caused their deaths. All six passed away within a few days of one another. They were buried in the family cemetery on their farm. Harbaugh reported in 1948 that no grave markers then remained.[27]

Lewis-II includes the following persons in his will, which was reproduced by Harbaugh: daughters Elizabeth, Comfort Ann, Margaret, Mary, Hannah, Rosanna; sons William, Samuel,

Lewis, John, Thomas; daughters Ann, Rebecca, and Sarah. Sons Lewis and John were named executors.

Additionally, daughters May and Ann are included in the will, but were not separately addressed by Harbaugh. Harbaugh further adds daughter Nancy who was born about 1785 and died young. Nancy's absence from the will is evidence of her early decease.

3. Lewis Davidson (Lewis-I) and Elizabeth Claypoole-Conwell.

Lewis-I secondly married Elizabeth Claypoole about five years after the death of his first wife, Comfort Warrington. This marriage took place in Sussex County, Delaware about 1754 based upon the approximate birthdate of their first child.

Evidence of the marriage between Lewis-I and Elizabeth is found in a chancery case that took place in Lewes, Delaware in 1759.[28] For all those fortunate descendants of this union, there is evidence that the Claypoole lineage may possibly be traced to Emperor Charlemagne: a genealogical home run![29]

Elizabeth was born in Sussex County, Delaware. Prior to her marriage to Lewis-I, she was married to Thomas Conwell about 1745. Their two sons were William Conwell, born in 1746, and Jehu Conwell, born in 1749.[30,31]

Lewis-I was recorded in several real estate transactions in Sussex County. Perhaps the most significant was a move in March 1755 to Broadkill Hundred in, or very near, the town of Conwell's Landing, today called Milton. In this neighborhood, in March 1757, Lewis-I purchased a seven acre parcel of land containing an orchard and a house in which he and Elizabeth and probably their younger children resided for the next ten years. The family moved there to take advantage of a 235-acre tract of land left to William and Jehu Conwell by their father, Thomas, deceased.[32]

As has already been discussed in some detail in a previous chapter, the family next migrated west to southwestern Pennsylvania and settled in what is Luzerne Township of Fayette County today. This migration occurred by June 1767, when the region was still in the territory owned by the Six Nations, at least 50 miles west of any land that could be legally claimed and settled at the time.

His trek to Pennsylvania was Lewis-I's last migration. He operated a farm and also Davidson's Ferry that ran across the Monongahela River. This land was located several miles south of Redstone (now Brownsville) and he and Elizabeth resided there until they died. Lewis-I died 16 November 1793; Elizabeth died there, only about five months later, on 24 April 1794.[33] They were buried next to each other in the nearby Dunlap's Creek Presbyterian Church cemetery where they were recorded as church members.[34,35] Lewis-I left a last will in which his wife and all of his surviving children were remembered.[36]

3.1   **Thomas Davidson**. Thomas was born about 1755 in Sussex County Delaware. He came to current-day Luzerne Township, Fayette County, Pennsylvania with his mother and father in June 1767.

It may be remembered from a previous chapter that Lewis-I was technically entitled to first claim of all the land on which his sons and stepson settled in Pennsylvania. Thomas purchased a parcel called *Hickory Level* from Lewis-I for a token sum in 1775.[37] Since *Hickory Level* represented a personal transfer of ownership, Thomas still needed to make the purchase official by purchasing his tract from the government by patent, signifying that Thomas was the first owner of record.

Thomas received an additional parcel from his father as his inheritance in 1793. According to the will of Lewis-I, Thomas was to receive "the land on which he [Thomas] now lives..."[38]

He owned at least 201 acres of land called *Winchester* on the east side of the Monongahela River in Luzerne Township, Fayette County, adjoining his father's parcel.[39]

Thomas married Mary Stokely in 1776. Mary was born in 1760 in Sussex County, Delaware. She was the daughter of John and Mary Baynes Stokely.[40]

Families

Some members of the Stokely family also owned land in Delaware and migrated to southwestern Pennsylvania as did the Davidsons. Thomas Stokely warranted a claim for a 170-acre tract west of William-III. John Stokely warranted a 259-acre land claim adjacent to that of Thomas Davidson in 1784.[41] However, it was not discovered whether this John Stokely was the father of Mary, wife of Thomas Davidson.

Ellis recorded that a man who had travelled from Hagerstown, Maryland to Luzerne Township accidentally suffered a broken leg. Being alone, poor, and in need of help, eight men gathered and built a "hammock" on which they carried the man about 140 miles back to Hagerstown, delivered him to a surgeon, and paid for the physician's services. Only the names of five of these men were known when Ellis recorded this story: Thomas Davidson, John Conwell, Michael Cox, Eli Virgin, and William Roberts.[42]

According to tax records in 1798, the settlement built by Thomas included three separate structures, a two story log cabin that was 18 by 16 feet in size, a separate kitchen 16 by 14 feet in size, and a barn 40 by 18 feet in size.[43,44] The kitchens in those days were often erected as separate structures to reduce the possibility of accidentally setting the main house ablaze.

Harbaugh says that Thomas died between 1845 and 1850.[45] The upper number in the range given would make Thomas 95 years old when he died. However, Thomas can only be found in the federal census records from 1790 through 1820.[46-49] Mary Davidson next appears in the federal census record of 1830.[50] This information suggests that Thomas likely died in his 70's between 1821 and 1829 and that his wife, Mary, assumed ownership of their farm following the loss of her husband.

Harbaugh further says of Mary that she died 26 April 1828.[51] However, as mentioned, Mary appears in the federal census record of 1830. The fact that Harbaugh provided an exact date easily leads to the speculation that the date of Mary's death should have read 26 April 1838 and that the year given by Harbaugh was incorrectly recorded. However, this was not verified.

Thomas and Mary were members of the Dunlap's Creek Presbyterian Church and their graves have since been lost.[52] They had 11 children.[53]

3.2 **Hannah Davidson**. Hannah was born about 1757 on the family farm in Delaware. She was about ten years of age when she was brought to southwestern Pennsylvania with her family in 1767.

In 1780, Hannah married James McMechen. James and Hannah migrated to Ohio County, Virginia where they settled and established a farm that adjoined the Ohio River and included more than 260 acres of land.[54,55] Today, their farm would be found in Franklin District, Marshall County, West Virginia, across the Ohio River from the modern-day town of Clarington, Ohio.[56]

Harbaugh recorded a family tradition that Hannah saved three of her young daughters from attack by the Six Nations by poling a canoe several miles up a river. In the meantime, their cattle were driven away from the river by servants in the hope that their attackers would pursue the livestock. It was said that the family home had been burned three times.[57] When and where these events occurred were not recorded, but given their general location, and the ages of her children, we could suppose these events occurred on the Ohio River, probably about 1787, following the birth of their third daughter.[58]

Hannah's father died in 1793. Lewis-I specified in his will that Hannah was to receive one "ewe and lamb."[59] Lewis-I's farm was located more than 60 miles east and across the Monongahela River from the neighborhood of the McMechen's farm. It is not known whether Hannah returned to her old home to retrieve her inheritance.

Families

Fortunately, James McMechen left a will in which he names Hannah as his wife and thus provides assurance as to his identity.[60] He died between 26 July 1823 and April 1824, after his will was signed and before it was proved in court. He bequeathed a total of 260 acres of land to three of his children and his wife, Hannah. Daughters Rachel Wells, Sally Williamson, and Elizabeth Burris were to receive the unspecified "ballance" of land not already bequeathed, indicating that their farm was larger than the 260 acres specified.[61]

In addition to 100 acres of land, Hannah was left in the possession of their house, orchard, and barn, as well as their livestock which included six sheep, two cows, and four hogs. Two cows were also left to his daughter Ruth.[62]

Hannah and James had eight children together. In his last will, James named: Hannah, his wife, daughters Orphy, Ruth, Sally Williamson, Polly Williamson, Jane, Rachel Wells, and Elizabeth Burris. Charles Wells, executor.[63]

In 1830, James Davidson, husband of Hannah's daughter Orpha, acquired a patent for 154 acres of land in Vermillion County, Indiana.[64] Hannah also removed to Vermillion County.[65] She resided south of the town of Eugene, in Eugene Township until she died in 1840. She left a will from which it was learned that she owned a tract of land in the county of her death and she had $300 in cash when she died. She left her family instructions to use her assets for the education of her grandchildren. It appears from her will that she had also retained ownership of the land in Virginia from which she continued to receive income. This was bequeathed to Charles Wells, the husband of her daughter Rachel.[66,67]

In her last will, Hannah named the following persons: grandchildren William Davidson, Fleming Davidson, Hannah Jane Davidson, Finely Davidson, and James Davidson; daughter Orpha, beloved son George Archer; Charles Wells of

Marshal (Marshall County), Virginia. Orpha Davidson, executrix and grandson David Davidson, executor.[68]

3.3   **Elizabeth Davidson**. Elizabeth was born about 1763 in Sussex County, Delaware. She married George James. Elizabeth was to receive "one saddle, one feather bed together with the necessary covering and one cow and calf" according to Lewis-I's last will.[69] Further information about this family was not found.[70]

3.4   **Rachel Davidson**. Rachel was born in 1765 in Sussex County, Delaware, as were all her siblings. Rachel was about two years old when the family migrated to southwestern Pennsylvania.

According to Harbaugh, Rachel married Samuel McKee who was likely born about 1753. They were residing in Franklin County, Ohio when Samuel applied for a pension in 1818 for his service in the Revolutionary War.[71-74]

As with her sister Hannah, Rachel was to receive "one ewe and lamb" according to her father's will.[75] It will be recalled that Lewis-I died in 1793. The distance from Franklin County, Ohio to her father's farm in Luzerne Township, Fayette County, Pennsylvania was nearly 200 miles. It is unknown whether Rachel travelled to her former home to retrieve her inheritance.

Samuel McKee's pension file says that he enlisted in November or December 1775 in the 6th Regiment, of the Pennsylvania Line of the Continental Army under the command of Colonel Irwin. Samuel served as a private in Captain James Wilson's company for 13 months. He was honorably discharged 16 February 1777 at Ticonderoga, New York. He was sworn and testified before a judge at a Court of Common Pleas on 25 May 1818, in Franklinton, that he fought at the *Battle of three Rivers* in the Province of Canada.[76-78]

There is documented evidence that Samuel McKee saw some action during his service. Captain James Armstrong

Families

Wilson, under whom Samuel served, commanded Company "E." Captain Wilson was captured at Isle Aux Noix, Canada on 24 June 1776. The company's first lieutenant was also taken prisoner and the only other officer, ensign Joseph Culbertson was also killed the same day.[79]

Samuel testified a second time before the Court of Common Pleas on 17 June 1820, certifying an inventory of his few belongings to justify his plea for financial assistance. His only possessions at that time were listed as one horse and colt, two cows, six chairs and plates, six knives and forks, one iron pot, a kettle, a tea kettle, and a set of cups, all valued at $57.44.[80] Samuel stated that he was a weaver by occupation and that he was constantly disabled from a "soreness in the leg." The judge attested in a letter on 25 March 1819 that Samuel McKee was a "lame, infirm man" and that he was "living in want."[81]

In his deposition of 1820, Samuel stated that he had no other family except his wife.[82] This sworn testimony, before a judge in a Court of Common Pleas, suggests that he and Rachel were childless, or that their children predeceased them.

Samuel further stated in his deposition of 1818 that he was 58 years of age; in 1820 he deposed that he was 67 years of age and that his wife was 55 years of age, but unfortunately her name was not given in the record.[83]

Samuel qualified for an "invalid" pension for which he received the equivalent of $8 per month (in six month installments) from 25 May 1818 until he died. His last payment was recorded in September 1823. Samuel died 20 July 1823, thought to be about 69 years of age, at Franklin County, Ohio where all of his pension payments were remitted. Administrators of his estate were appointed in Franklin County, Ohio on 30 August 1823, indicating that his estate was probated there, but no will was found.[84] No further record of

Rachel was found, but we know from Samuel's testimony that she was alive on 17 June 1820.

3.5   **Jeremiah Davidson**. According to the headstone of Jeremiah, he was born 10 June 1768.[85,86] Harbaugh recorded that Jeremiah was born in Allegheny County, Maryland. However, the birthdate suggests that he was possibly born in Pennsylvania, given that the family had settled in today's Fayette County by June 1767. It is here supposed that some members of the family traveled back east with Elizabeth to safer surroundings until Jeremiah was born.

On 7 September 1790, Jeremiah married Anne Alexander. Anne was born in 1772.[87] She was the daughter of Huto or Hoto Alexander and second wife Esther Wyllis.[88] Huto was born in 1726 in County Antrim, Ireland and came to America in 1741. He died 26 August 1796. Esther was born in 1747 and died 26 August 1800.[89]

In 1793, Lewis-I died and bequeathed to his son Jeremiah, "the plantation I now live on together with the ferry and everything there unto pertaining…"[90] Jeremiah's parcel thus adjoined the banks of the Monongahela River.[91]

Jeremiah was also given the responsibility by his father to care for his mother, Elizabeth, who died only about five months following the death of Lewis-I.

Ellis says, in addition to being a farmer, Jeremiah was a boat builder who constructed barges for himself and for sale to others. According to Ellis, Jeremiah made journeys on the river trading farm produce with other settlers and he reportedly continued to operate his father's ferry across the Monongahela River.[92]

Harbaugh says that Jeremiah served in the War of 1812, however, no record of this service was located. He was a member of the Dunlap's Creek Presbyterian Church, where he and his wife and his parents were laid to rest.[93] Jeremiah reportedly died 30 June 1851.[94] His wife, Anne, died 22 may 1848.[95]

At the time of his death, Jeremiah was considered to be the wealthiest man in Fayette County. He had amassed a large amount of real estate in Fayette County and neighboring Green County. He bequeathed a total of 901 acres to his children not including a lot in Merrittstown. He was also a 50% owner with a man named William Armstrong in a grist mill and saw mill businesses located at the mouth of Muddy Creek.[96]

Named in Jeremiah's last will are his wife Anne, sons Alexander L. Davidson, Clark Davidson, James Barnes Davidson, daughters Rhoda who married James Barnes, Elizabeth who married George Brown, Anne Delina who married Westly Frost, Helen Mar who married Alfred Armstrong, and Orpha who married John McDougle. Also named was grandson Jeremiah Davidson, son of Alexander L. Son James Barnes Davidson, was named sole executor.[97]

4. William Davidson (William-III) and Rosanna Hutchinson.

Lewis-IV's work appears to be the earliest record regarding Rosanna. However, even Harbaugh, who likely drew much information from Hardesty and Evans, has few details as to William-III's first wife. Both Evans and Harbaugh spelled her name "Rosanna Hutchinson," setting aside perceived typographical errors. The only source document offered is the baptism of Rosanna by Rev. John Cuthbertson, spelled Cuthberton by Harbaugh, who only gives us a clue as to her source being "…records published by Helen S. Fields." This same event was found published in another earlier work by Glasgow.[98-100]

Cuthbertson achieved some notoriety as a traveling reverend who wandered the frontier of Pennsylvania preaching wherever he was welcomed and had only been in America a few weeks when he recorded the baptism of Rosanna. In his journal, below the heading, "September 1, 1751," the entire entry of interest reads, "…at this time he baptized…Rose Ann, daughter of Joseph Hutchison." The event took place at Rock Creek, Adams County, Pennsylvania, about one mile northeast of present day Gettysburg. Unfortunately there is no further information that would solidly link this "Rose Ann" to our subject at hand. Harbaugh recorded that "Roseanna" was the daughter of John Hutchinson, while the baptismal record cited names him as Joseph Hutchison.[101]

The Cumberland County tax records from 1768 and 1769 (discussed previously) support the marriage year of William-III and Rosanna in 1769. The birthdate of their first child, John, in December 1770 is consistent with their marriage year. Since John was reportedly born in Westmoreland County, it is further supposed that this was also the location of their marriage. William-III and Rosanna were about 22 and 18 years of age respectively when they were married. They had five children together. According to Harbaugh, Rosanna died about 1782 in Fayette County, Pennsylvania where she and William-III were then residing. Technically, however, this should be listed as Westmoreland County since Fayette did not exist before 1783. The timing of Rosanna's death coincides with the possibility of a sixth pregnancy, two years following the birth of their previous child. Associated complications could supply the cause of her death, but no records were found that would confirm this suspicion.

Presuming the children were born on or near the family farm, all of their children were born in today's Luzerne Township, Fayette County, Pennsylvania. The farm was located about eight miles south of Brownsville (also formerly known as Redstone Old Fort and Fort Burd). They had five children together.

4.1   **John Davidson.** John was born 12 December 1770 and grew up on his father's farm on the east side of the Monongahela River. On 26 November 1793, he married Margaret Armstrong at Redstone. Margaret was born 8 August 1776.

In 1801, this family migrated to Ohio by keelboat as did William-III in 1799. The year is confirmed by his presence on a tax record created in September 1801.[102-104]

Families

John settled where the town of Burlington stands today in Fayette Township of Lawrence County, Ohio. It appears he purchased a tract of land together with William Montgomery, and William Lynn, that consisted of all of fractional section two in township one of range 17 (S2-T1N-R17W, Ohio River Survey).[105] John was a farmer and a merchant.[106]

John died 25 May 1828 at the age of 58 years and Margaret died 5 July 1828 at the age of 52 years. Given that they were relatively young and died little more than a month apart suggests the cause was an illness. Both are buried in Burlington Cemetery. They had seven children.[107]

4.2   **Lewis Davidson (Lewis-III).** Lewis was born 23 March 1773. In July 1798 at Redstone, he was married to Mary Davidson, his first cousin (daughter of William-III's brother, Lewis-II), by Rev. James Roberts. Mary was born 25 September 1778 near Fort Cumberland, Maryland.[108]

They migrated down the Ohio River to South Point, Ohio in 1800.[109-114] Their water craft was described as, "large canoes fastened together."[115] They next reportedly moved to Scioto County in 1804. In March 1809, they decided to return to Pennsylvania. After loading two horses with their belongings, they set off on their journey which took the family through Zanesville where they forded the Muskingham River. On the way, one of their horses died which halted their journey and caused them to settle nearby.[116,117] Lewis-III purchased about 160 acres (quarter section) by patent in Tuscarawas County, which later became Freeport Township in today's Harrison County, Ohio. Their tract was located a few miles west of the town of Freeport, where they built a log cabin, cleared their land, and established a working farm.[118,119]

According to his son, Lewis H. Davidson (Lewis-IV), Lewis-III was willing, but unable, to serve in the War of 1812. Lewis-IV, described a condition he termed rheumatism which manifested in such severity that his father was unable to work and even unable to walk for a period of time.[120]

After settling in Harrison County, Lewis-III and Mary were reportedly visited on occasion by a man named Joseph Pyles. Joseph related the fate of William-I, who had been taken captive or was murdered by the Indians before the Revolutionary War and was never seen or heard from again. Joseph was a grandson, or possibly a great-grandson, descended from the second wife of William-I and her second husband. It was through these persons that the account of William-I has survived.

Lewis-III died and was buried on his farm between 1 September 1832 and 8 April 1833 (after his will was created and before it was proved).[121] He was about 60 years of age. Mary died 27 September 1840 and was buried in Hartford, Blackford County, Indiana, where she had gone to visit her children. They had twelve children.[122]

Lewis-III named the following persons in his last will: Wife Mary, daughter Mary M. Davidson, son Jesse Davidson, son Thomas L. Davidson, son Joseph C. Davidson, son Jonathan S. Davidson; he also stated that he had ten children in all. John L. Grubb and Lewis H. Davidson, were named executors.

4.3 **Comfort Davidson.** Comfort was born about 1775. About 1793, she married Alexander McCourtney at Redstone, today's Brownsville, Fayette County, Pennsylvania. This couple apparently moved to present-day South Point, Ohio about the same time as William-III and Barbara. They later moved to Missouri where Harbaugh says land patents in Alexander's name were found on file in Jefferson City. The tracts were located in St. Louis and Charles Counties in the years 1798 and 1799.[123]

4.4   **David Hutchinson Davidson**. David was born in 1777 in today's Fayette County, Pennsylvania. He grew up on his father's farm on the east side of the Monongahela River.

In 1800, he married Mary Williams. Mary was born in 1785. She was the daughter of James Williams (b. 1750; d. 11 July 1839) and Elizabeth (b. 1755; d. 5 July 1838).[124]

David was a farmer and a ferryman. He reportedly went with his father to Ohio in 1799 and stayed for a short time in Kentucky before returning to Pennsylvania.[125] It was David who kept a part of his father's *Dispute Ended* tract in the family by purchasing the northern 120 acres of the parcel from his father and mother for $600 in October 1807.[126]

A David Davidson, on *Dispute Ended*, later established a steam powered ferry across the Monongahela River, however, it is uncertain whether this David was the son of William-III or a later descendent. David's ferry became known as *Davidson's Lower Ferry* to distinguish it from *Davidson's Upper Ferry* which was purchased from Crawford and operated by Lewis-I then subsequently passed on to his son Jeremiah Davidson after Lewis-I died. At some point, the novelty of David's steam ferry wore down and it was discontinued.[127]

David and Mary remained in Luzerne Township, Fayette County, and continued working their farm for decades. This is easily confirmed by examining the 1800, 1810, and 1820 census records in Luzerne Township, Fayette County, Pennsylvania. David died 29 February 1828 at the age of 51 years and was buried in the Williams' family cemetery in Fayette County.[128,129]

Mary reportedly married Shepherd Conwell after David died and removed to Marion County, near Morgantown, West Virginia where she died on 27 May 1855.

David and Mary had nine children.[130] Two of their children were under the age of 14 years when David died and they were named in an Orphan's Court hearing in Fayette County as: Orpa David and Eliza Jane.[131] In another later record, three children were named: Orpa Davidson Conwell, Eliza Jane Davidson, and Mary Davidson now Clayburgh.[132]

4.5   **Mary E. Davidson**. Mary was born 23 May 1780 in today's Fayette County, Pennsylvania. She married Mordicai Williams in 1795 at Redstone.

Mordicai was born in 1777. His father, James, was born in 1750 and died in 1838. His mother was Elizabeth. Both of Mordicai's parents were buried in the Williams' Cemetery in Fayette County, Pennsylvania.

Mary and Moridcai remained in Fayette County until 1799 when they migrated to South Point, Ohio. Some years later they moved to today's Kilgore, Carter County, Kentucky where Mordicai died in 1834 at the age of 57 years.[133]

Harbaugh located the last will of Mordicai Williams in which he named his wife Elizabeth, son James, grandson James D. Williams, granddaughter Mary Armstrong, son Mordicai, daughter Susanna Dearth, daughter Mary Conwell (previously the wife of David Davidson, deceased), great-granddaughter Ann Craft, and William Craft (possibly Ann's father).[134]

Mary is found as the head of household in the 1840 census.[135] She is listed again in the 1850 census at age 70, along with Samuel Williams, age 33, presumably her son. There were also four laborers residing on their farm with them.[136] She does not appear on the 1860 census in the same area.

Mary and Mordicai had eight children together.[137]

5. William Davidson (William-III) and Barbara McDowell.

According to Harbaugh, about two years after Rosanna died, William-III married second wife Barbara McDowell. Barbara and William-III were married about 1784, probably in Fayette County, Pennsylvania.[138]

Harbaugh offers several spelling variations of Barbara's surname, including McDowell, McDewell, McDole. Hanna puts forth McDale, but this is thought to be a typographical error.[139] In the course of reviewing the many hundreds of records associated with the preparation of this work, many families and individuals found going by the name "McDowell" were conspicuous. Only perhaps one or two "McDole" families were observed. Due to this overwhelming frequency of McDowell's in southwestern Pennsylvania, it is supposed that this is most likely the correct spelling of Barbara's surname. Evans uses the spelling "McDole" and says that she was born in Wales, information not seen elsewhere, nor supported by any citation.[140]

Presuming their children were born on or near the family farm, the birthplace of their first six children would be modern-day Luzerne Township, Fayette County, Pennsylvania. The last four children were born on or near *Fractional Section 5* (S5-T1N-R17W) where their farm was located in Fayette Township, Lawrence County, Ohio.

Harbaugh was the first author found to supply Barbara's birth date of 8 January 1768. Harbaugh further states, "…the place of her birth and the names of her parents not established…," but she then fails to record how Barbara's birth date was obtained.[141] The author further gives the approximate marriage year of 1884, for which it must be assumed that 1784 was intended. The estimated marriage year was probably based on the reported birth date of William-III and Barbara's first child, Margaret, recorded as 29 November 1785.[142] This means that Barbara was only about 16 years old when she married William-III, who was then 37 years of age.

Apart from testimonials regarding the date of Barbara's death and her place of burial, which will be discussed in the later chapter *Final Years*, Barbara only appears in a handful of other known records. She is named in two indentures in Pennsylvania as the wife of William-III. The first, dated March 1799, occurred when William-III and Barbara sold a portion of their *Dispute Ended* tract to Jonathan Ridge. Again in May 1807, William-III and Barbara sold the remaining 123 acres of *Dispute Ended* to their son David Davidson, where Barbara is explicitly named as the wife of William-III and the mother of David.

Fortunately for us, William-III left a last will. This is a third document in which Barbara is recorded. In this important record, all the surviving children of William-III from both marriages are remembered. The names of the children are given here, but a more detailed discussion as to the content of the will is deferred to the later chapter *Final Years*. The brief information provided is mostly as it was found recorded by Harbaugh.[143] Their ten children were:

5.1 **Margaret Davidson**. Margaret was born 29 November 1785 in Fayette County, Pennsylvania and was about fourteen years of age when the family relocated to the Northwest Territory. In about 1805, Margaret married John Riley Francis. John was born 5 September 1782 in Ohio.

The area in which they permanently settled became Fayette Township in Lawrence County, Ohio where they operated a farm.[144,145]

John died 6 June 1850 and was buried in the "old cemetery" at South Point, Ohio. Margaret died 31 July 1854. They had ten children.[146] Margaret is called "Peggy Francis" in William-III's last will.

5.2 **Elizabeth Davidson**. Elizabeth was born about 1787. Elizabeth married William Lynd about 1806, probably in Lawrence County, Ohio.[147] William Lynd is found in the 1830 and 1840 Federal census records in Fayette Township, Lawrence County.[148-150] They had five children.[151] Elizabeth is called "Betty Lynd" in her father's will.

5.3 **Sarah (Sallie) Davidson**. Sarah was born about 1789 on or near the family farm on the east side of the Monongahela River, in today's Luzerne Township, Fayette County, Pennsylvania.[152-156]

Sarah married William McKee in 1807 in Kanawha County, Virginia.[157] William was reportedly born in 1785 in County Down, Ireland and came to the United States at 14 years of age with his father, William.[158]

Families

William served in the War of 1812, although no record of this service has been found.[159-161] He and Sarah remained in Fayette Township, Lawrence County, Ohio where they purchased and sold several parcels of land, including one tract by patent for 44 acres, located northeast of South Point.[162,163]

William died 24 April 1858 in Lawrence County. Sarah died on 19 September 1873 in Fayette Township, Lawrence County, and was likely buried next to her husband in the *First Davidson Cemetery* (see the later chapter *Final Years*) on *Fractional Section 5* in South Point. William left a will in which he mentions his wife and his children, but no names are given.[164] Sarah is called "Sarah McKee" in her father's will (William-III). William and Sarah had fifteen children.

5.4   **Abraham A. M. Davidson**. Abraham was born in 1791 in Fayette County, Pennsylvania. He was about eight years of age when he was brought to the Northwest Territory with his parents.

Abraham married Leticia (Ankrim) Lynn about 1813. Leticia was born about 1787 in Pennsylvania. Leticia was the daughter of Samuel Ankrim, Senior (1742-1827) and Jennie Anne Ankrim (1748-1836).[165]

Abraham and Leticia were engaged in farming in Fayette Township, where they permanently resided. It is thought that Abraham died in February 1850 in Fayette Township.[166] Leticia continued operation of their farm with the assistance of her children. She died after 1860.[167,168]

In the Will of William-III, Abraham is named "Abraham A. M. Davidson." No reference was found for the meaning of "A. M." Other sources use the middle initial "D" which Harbaugh says stood for Duncan.

Abraham and Leticia had five children: William Duncan (b. 1814); Jane Ann (1815-1840); Samuel (b.1823); Sarah (b. 1825); and Joseph L. (b. 1828).[169,170]

5.5   **Thomas Davidson**. Thomas was born about 1794 in Fayette County, Pennsylvania. He was brought to present-day South Point, Ohio with his parents in 1799.

On 9 January 1819, Thomas married Mary Croley. Mary died in 1819 at South Point. Thomas and Mary had one son, Jesse (1819-1864).[171]

In 1821, Thomas married Jane (Dye) McKee. Jane was a widow with daughter Phoebe, when she married Thomas. Jane was born about 1800 in Pennsylvania.[172] Thomas and Jane relocated after 1830 to St. Marys, Auglaize County, Ohio where Thomas died in 1834 and was buried at the Old St. Marys Cemetery.[173,174]

Harbaugh says that following the death of Thomas, Jane subsequently married George Bruce; and still later, Archie Richenson. Jane died in 1854 in St. Marys.[175]

Thomas and Jane had three children together: Isaac (abt 1822-1861); Andrew (b. abt 1829); and Mathias (b. abt 1832).[176]

5.6   **Rev. William Warrington Davidson (William-IV)**. William-IV was born 6 November 1798. He was the last child of William-III and Barbara to be born in Luzerne Township, Fayette County, Pennsylvania. He was brought to the Northwest Territory by his father and mother at about six months of age in the spring of 1799.[177]

On 31 May 1821, William-IV married first wife Sarah Short in South Point, Ohio. Sarah was born 26 March 1803 in West Virginia or Kentucky. Sarah died 23 October 1834. They had five children: Ira (1822-young); William Fuson (1825-1887); Peyton Short (1827-1901); Matilda (1829-1862); and Sarah (1832-1918).[178]

On 30 November 1837 at Ironton, Ohio, William-IV married Nancy (Lawson) Davison (widow of John Davison). Nancy was born 3 December 1803 at Portsmouth, Ohio. She died 5 December 1853 and was buried in South Point Cemetery. They had four children: Nancy (1839-1912); Thomas Lawson (1840-1913); Joseph (1842-1855); and Jeremiah Jay (1845-1932).[179]

On 5 October 1854 at Hanging Rock, Ohio, William-IV married Lavina Yingling. Lavina was born 7 July 1815 at Hanging Rock, Ohio. She died 18 December 1893 at South Point and was buried in White Cottage Cemetery.[180] They had three children: Lavina (1855-1879); Robert Yingling (1857-1900); and Marry Kelly (1858-1947).[181]

William-IV was a Baptist Minister and a farmer. For many years he was the pastor of the Baptist Church at South Point, which was built on land where he grew up and was previously owned by his father in *Fractional Section 5*. He died 5 October 1883 at South Point, Ohio.[182] He was buried in White Cottage Cemetery, South Point, Fayette Township, Lawrence County.[183]

5.7 **Rose Davidson**. Rose was born in 1801 at South Point, Ohio. She died young. Rose is buried in South Point Cemetery.[184]

5.8 **Jesse Davidson**. Jesse was born in 1803 at South Point, Ohio. He died 14 February 1814 at about 11 years of age. Jesse was buried in the *First Davidson Cemetery* (see the later chapter *Final Years*) on his father's farm.[185]

5.9 **Joseph William Davidson**. Joseph was born 26 December 1806 at South Point, Ohio. Joseph owned and operated boats on the Big Sandy River and was a farmer.[186]

On 3 November 1826, he married Jane Bryson in Lawrence County, Ohio. Jane was born 9 September 1809 in Washington County, Pennsylvania.[187]

Joseph died 16 August 1872 at South Point. Jane died 30 August 1889. Both were buried in the Davidson Cemetery, South Point, Fayette Township, Lawrence County, Ohio.[188-190]

Joseph and Jane had thirteen children together: 1) Sarah Short (1828-1865); 2) Jonathan Croley (1829-1888); 3) James Bryson (1831-1832); 4) Emmanuel Grubb (1832-1912); 5) Elizabeth L. (1834-1918); 6) Emeline (1836-1836); 7) Isaac William (1837-1911); 8) Josephus (b. 1839); 9) Delilah M. (1841-1912); 10) Benjamin Johnston (1843-1927); 11) Umphrey Montgomery (1844-1927); 12) Alonzo (1846-1848); 13) Archibald Paul (b. 1848).[191]

5.10   **Cynthia Davidson.** Cynthia was born 29 August 1809 at South Point, Ohio. On 16 June 1831, Cynthia married Jonathan Croley at South Point, Ohio. Cynthia died 10 September 1840. Jonathan died 9 July 1869.[192]

Cynthia and Jonathan had five children together: Sarah Jane (d. young); John Silverthorn (1834-1881); James Bryson (b. 1836); Isaac Harvey (1837-1898), Mary Ellen (1838-1913).[193]

---

1.   Elizabeth Davidson Harbaugh, *The Davidson Genealogy* (Ironton, Ohio: self-published, 1948; Ann Arbor, Michigan : Lithoprinted, Edwards Brothers, Inc., 1949), 482 pages, print, OCLC: 23167553.

2.   Nelson W. Evans, *History of Scioto County, Ohio* (Portsmouth, Ohio: Self-published, 1903), reprint (Markham, Virginia: The Apple Manor Press).

3.   *Commemorative Biographical Record of the Counties of Harrison and Carroll, Ohio* (Chicago: J. H. Beers & Co., 1891), article: "Lewis H. Davidson," pp. 446-453, digital version, *Google Books* (http://books.google.com : accessed April 2013).

4.   *Atlas of Lawrence County, Ohio, Hardesty 1882 and Lake 1887 (Combined)*, 1st edition reprint (Ironton, Ohio: Lawrence County Historical Society, 1985).

5.   Sussex County, Delaware, Shankland Survey Book 2: pages 71-72, Survey for "Hanah Davidson" (untitled), 16 November 1731, Record Group 4555, digital

copy of penned document, obtained December 2015, Delaware Public Archives, Dover.

6. Sussex County, Delaware, Deed Book I: 29-30, "Deed of Sale Thom[s] Worington to Hannh Davison," 7 February 1732, recorded 6-9 February 1732, Record Group 4555, digital copy of penned document, obtained November 2015, Delaware Public Archives, Dover.

7. Harbaugh, p. 125.

8. Sussex County, Delaware, Deed Book I: page 68, "Jacob Warrington from Lewis Davidson and sisters Deed," dated 6 August 1753, recorded 7 February 1754, Record Group 4555, digital copy of penned document, obtained November 2015, Delaware Public Archives, Dover.

9. Harbaugh, p. 126.

10. Sussex County, Delaware, Deed Book I: page 68, "Jacob Warrington from Lewis Davidson and sisters Deed," dated 6 August 1753, recorded 7 February 1754, Record Group 4555, digital copy of penned document, obtained November 2015, Delaware Public Archives, Dover.

11. Harbaugh, p. 126.

12. Elaine Hastings Mason and F. Edward Wright, *Land Records of Sussex County, Delaware 1782-1789, Deed Book N No. 13* (Westminster, Maryland: Willow Bend Books, 2002), p. 4, print.

13. Harbaugh, p. 128.

14. Sussex County, Delaware, Shankland Survey Book 2: pages 71-72, Survey for "Hanah Davidson" (untitled), 16 November 1731, Record Group 4555, digital copy of penned document, obtained December 2015, Delaware Public Archives, Dover.

15. Sussex County, Delaware, Deed Book I: 30-31, "Thomas Warrington and Jacob Warrington's Bond to Lewis Davison," dated 17 December 1750, recorded 11 May 1751, Record Group 4555, digital copy of penned document, obtained November 2015, Delaware Public Archives, Dover.

16. Harbaugh, p. 128.

William "Ranger" Davidson

17. See the *Delaware* chapter for details.

18. William M. Warrington, Will of William Warrington and Probate Records, untitled, Sussex County Probate, Record Group 4545.009: 1755 – 1796, 11 pages, dated 20 January 1755, proved 27 June 1755, digital copies of typewritten and penned documents obtained November 2015, Delaware Public Archives, Dover.

19. Harbaugh, p. 128.

20. Lewis Davidson, Will of Lewis Davidson (Lewis-I), untitled, Register of Wills, Will Book 1, p. 86, photocopy of penned document, dated 6 July 1787, recorded 28 November 1793, proved 4 February 1794, Uniontown, Fayette County, Pennsylvania.

21. "Maryland Register of Wills Records, 1629-1999," Allegany County, Cumberland Courthouse, *Vol. A 1790-1850*, pp. 123-125, will of Lewis Davidson (Lewis-II), untitled, dated 31 July 1809, proved 14 June 1814, penned document, digital image 79 of 379, *FamilySearch* (https://familysearch.org/ : accessed 20 May 2014), citing Prerogative Court, Hall of Records, Annapolis. Lewis-II named his parcels which are given here with the number of acres in parentheses: Hazle Hollow (20), Walnut Valley (62), Davidson's Choice (70), Davidson's Wish (65), Precious Spring (49), and Penn's Spring (16).

22. "Maryland Probate Estate and Guardianship Files, 1796-1940," Allegany County, county courts, *Davidson, Lewis 1814-1816, Adm. Lewis Davidson & John Davidson*, penned, unpaged, digital images 1 through 26, *FamilySearch* (https://family search.org/ : accessed 20 May 2014), citing county courts, Maryland.

23. 1800 United States Census, population schedule, penned, Cumberland Township, Allegany County, Maryland, p. 11, entry 19 for Lewis Davidson, unnumbered, digital image 1 of 6, *FamilySearch* (https://familysearch.org : accessed 10 June 2015), citing NARA microfilm publication M32, (Washington D.C.: National Archives and Records Administration, n.d.).

24. 1810 United States Census, population schedule, penned, Cumberland Township, Allegany County, Maryland, p. 14, entry 3 for Lewis Davidson unnumbered, digital image 9 of 10, *FamilySearch* (https://familysearch.org :

accessed 1 December 2015), citing NARA microfilm publication M252, (Washington D.C.: National Archives and Records Administration, n.d.).

25. Harbaugh, p. 336.

26. Will of Lewis Davidson (Lewis-I).

27. Harbaugh, p. 336.

28. Sussex County, Delaware, Court of Chancery, Case File C, number 25, documents dated between 12 December 1758 and 10 February 1759, Record Group 1225.026, photocopies of penned documents, obtained September 2016, Delaware Public Archives, Dover. Evidence of the marriage between Lewis Davidson (Lewis-I) and Elizabeth Claypoole before 1759.

29. J. Orton Buck & Timothy Field Beard, *Pedigrees of some of the Emperor Charlemagne's Descendants*, Volume III (Baltimore: Genealogical Publishing Co., Inc., 1996), print, 360 pages. Also, Harbaugh, p. 95.

30. Harbaugh, pp. 360, 367.

31. T. C. Conwell, *The Conwell's of Dyer's Delight*, not published, dated 1984, p. 30 of 91 typewritten pages, digital version, *Ancestry* (http://www.ancestry.com : accessed October 2013).

32. Mason & Wright, p. 98.

33. Franklin Ellis, *History of Fayette County Pennsylvania with Biographical Sketches of many of its Pioneers and Prominent Men* (Philadelphia: L. H. Everts & Co., 1882), pp. 735-736, digital version, *Internet Archive* (http://www.archive.org : accessed April 2011).

34. Ibid.

35. Harbaugh, p. 360, Lewis-I and Elizabeth Claypoole.

36. Will of Lewis Davidson (Lewis-I).

37. Westmoreland County, Pennsylvania, Recorder of Deeds, Deed Book A: 326, "Lewis Davidson to Thomas Davidson," 30 October 1775, recorded 13 April 1783, for a parcel called *Hickory Level*, photocopy of penned document,

William "Ranger" Davidson

Greensburg, Pennsylvania. A parcel of land called *Hickory Level* was purchased by Thomas for 20 shillings; the size of the parcel was not recorded.

38. Will of Lewis Davidson (Lewis-I).

39. John H. Campbell, Chief Draftsman, *Warrantee Township Map: Fayette County, Luzerne Township* (Harrisburg, Pennsylvania: Records of the Land Office, 1920), Record Group 17, Series 17.522, Pennsylvania State Archives, digital version, *Commonwealth of Pennsylvania's Enterprise Portal* (http://www.portal .state.pa.us : accessed March 2011).

40. Harbaugh, p. 368.

41. Campbell, *Warrantee Township Map: Fayette County, Luzerne Township*.

42. Ellis, pp. 640-641.

43. *Pennsylvania, U.S. Direct Tax Lists, 1798*, Schedule B, penned document, page unnumbered, untitled, line 55, entry for Thos Davidson, Fayette County, Luzerne Township, digital image 144 of 426, *Ancestry* (http://www.ancestry.com : accessed 2011), citing microfilm M372, Tax Lists for the State of Pennsylvania, Records of the Internal Revenue Service, 1791-2006, Record Group 58; National Archives and Records Administration, Washington, D.C.

44. *Pennsylvania, U.S. Direct Tax Lists, 1798*, Schedule E, penned document, page unnumbered, untitled, line 55, entry for Thomas Davidson, Fayette County, Luzerne Township, digital image 346 of 426, *Ancestry* (http://www.ancestry.com : accessed 2011); citing microfilm M372, Tax Lists for the State of Pennsylvania, Records of the Internal Revenue Service, 1791-2006, Record Group 58; National Archives and Records Administration, Washington, D.C.

45. Harbaugh, p. 368.

46. 1790 United States Census, population schedule, penned, Springhill Township, Fayette County, Pennsylvania, p. 26, entry one in column two, unnumbered, for Thomas Davison, digital image 2 of 5, *FamilySearch* (https://familysearch.org : accessed 14 May 2015), citing NARA microfilm publication M637, (Washington D.C.: National Archives and Records Administration, n.d.).

Families

47. 1800 United States Census, population schedule, penned, Luzerne Township, Fayette County, Pennsylvania, page unnumbered, entry 40, unnumbered for Thomas Davidson, digital image 2 of 5 of penned document, *FamilySearch* (https://familysearch.org : accessed 10 June 2015), citing NARA microfilm publication M32, (Washington D.C.: National Archives and Records Administration, n.d.).

48. 1810 United States Census, population schedule, penned, Luzerne Township, Fayette County, Pennsylvania, p. 965, entry 28, unnumbered for Thomas Davison, digital image 3 of 6, *FamilySearch* (https://familysearch.org : accessed 1 December 2015), citing NARA microfilm publication M252, (Washington D.C.: National Archives and Records Administration, n.d.).

49. 1820 United States Census, population schedule, penned, Luzerne Township, Fayette County, Pennsylvania, page unnumbered, entry 19, unnumbered, for Thomas Davidson, digital image 5 of 6, *FamilySearch* (https://familysearch.org : accessed July 2015), citing NARA microfilm publication M33 (Washington D.C.: National Archives and Records Administration, n.d.).

50. 1830 United States Census, population schedule, penned, Luzerne Township, Fayette County, Pennsylvania, p. 233, entry 20, unnumbered, entry for Mary Davidson, digital image 13 of 18, *FamilySearch* (https://familysearch.org : accessed August 2016), citing NARA microfilm publication M19 (Washington D.C.: National Archives and Records Administration, n.d.).

51. Harbaugh, p. 368.

52. Ellis, p. 735-736

53. Ibid.

54. Harbaugh, pp. 371-374.

55. "West Virginia Will Books, 1756-1971," *Will Book No. 1, 1810-1823, County Clerk, Circuit Court, Ohio County*, pp. 24-25, will of James McMahon (McMechen), untitled, dated 26 July 1823, proved April 1824, digital image 33 of 41, *FamilySearch* (https://familysearch.org : accessed June 2016). The first line of this typewritten copy of the will has the deceased's name spelled "McMahon," however the signature and certification use the correct spelling "McMechen."

56. Harbaugh, p. 391.

57. Harbaugh, p. 374.

58. Harbaugh, pp. 374-375, 389.

59. Will of Lewis Davidson (Lewis-I).

60. It appears that several McMechens who settled in Ohio County, Virginia were related to an early pioneer named William McMechen. William reportedly came to Ohio County, Virginia in 1773 and settled where the town of McMechen stands today. William established a large estate a few miles south of Wheeling in the pan handle of today's West Virginia.

It may be possible that our James McMechen was the son of William, the pioneer. William moved his family east to the Redstone area (Brownsville), Pennsylvania, about 1777 due to the ongoing violent activities in Ohio County. This would provide an opportunity for our Hannah Davidson to have met William's son, James. It will be recalled that Hannah's father Lewis-I, was then residing on the east side of the Monongahela River below Redstone.

William and his family returned west to reclaim their land following the Revolutionary War and his son James was said to have removed some 28 miles south of Wheeling, which is in the neighborhood where our James McMechen and his family reportedly settled, in today's Franklin District, Marshall County, West Virginia.

While these details fit neatly together, it is easily shown that more than one person going by the name "James McMechen" was in the same general area as the one here discussed. Also, the surname "McMechen" is unfortunately prone to a wide variety of spelling variations, including McMachan, McMahon, McMichin, McMeekin, among others and which are valid family names of possibly other unrelated lineages. These issues combine to render positive identification of a particular "James McMechen," named in any given record, difficult. This has given rise to the many details regarding this family that conflict from one source to another.

Some of the descendants of our James McMechen have tried to link him to William, the pioneer, however, no documentation was found during this admittedly limited research effort that would conclusively show such a connection actually exists.

61. Will of James McMahon (McMechen).

62. Ibid.

63.   Ibid.

64.   Bureau of Land Management, General Land Office Records, Crawfordsville Land Office, Vol. 110, p. 180, state volume land patent for James Davidson for 154.4 acres in Eugene Township, Vermillion County, Indiana, consisting of the NW¼ of S19-T17N-R9W of the 2nd principal meridian, issued 2 December 1830, certificate 11457, digital image of penned document, *General Land Office Records* (http://www.glorecords.blm.gov/ : accessed December 2015). The mapping service on the web page confirms the location of the parcel.

65.   Harbaugh, p. 374.

66.   Harbaugh, p. 371.

67.   Indiana, Circuit Court, Vermillion County, "Vermillion County, Indiana, Will Records, 1829-1929," pp. 82-83 and 100, "Hannah McMichen Will," dated 28 July 1840, proved 12 January 1841, digital images 72-73 and 81 of typewritten document, *Ancestry* (http://www.ancestry.com : accessed December 2015), citing Indiana County, District and Probate Courts.

68.   Ibid.

69.   Will of Lewis Davidson (Lewis-I).

70.   Harbaugh, p. 397.

71.   Ibid.

72.   "United States Revolutionary War Pension Payment Ledgers, 1818-1872," Ledgers of payments, 1818-1872, to U.S. pensioners, under Acts of 1818 through 1858, from records of the office of the Third Auditor of the Treasury, State of Ohio, Franklin County, penned, p. 495, entry 14, unnumbered, Samuel McKee, 15 May 1818, digital image, *FamilySearch* (https://familysearch.org/ : accessed 22 December 2016), citing Ohio, United States, NARA microfilm publication T718 (Washington D.C.: National Archives and Records Administration, 1962), Series T718, roll 1. Samuel received $48 per year from 15 May 1818 to March 1823.

73.   United States Senate, *The Pension Roll of 1835, 4 vols, 1968 Reprint, with index*, (Baltimore: Genealogical Publishing Company, 1992), Volume 4, p. 184, sixth

line, unnumbered, entry for Samuel M'Kee, digital image 58, *Ancestry.com* (http://www.ancestry.com : accessed October 2015). Samuel was placed on the pension roll 26 April 1819, his pension commenced 25 May 1818. This record gives Samuel's date of death as 20 July 1823, age 69 years.

74. Harbaugh does not provide a source for her information, but it undoubtedly came from family members contributing to her work. Harbaugh's information was used to locate the matching pension record.

75. Will of Lewis Davidson (Lewis-I).

76. "U.S., Revolutionary War Pension and Bounty-Land Warrant Application Files, 1800-1900," Pennsylvania pension file for Samuel McKee number S. 41.853, pension certificate 9805, digital images of 24 pages of penned documents, unpaged, *Ancestry* (http://www.ancestry.com : accessed October 2015), citing Revolutionary War Pension and Bounty-Land Warrant Application Files (NARA microfilm publication M804, 2,670 rolls); Records of the Department of Veterans Affairs, Record Group 15; National Archives, Washington, D.C.

77. Although the Pension File cited aligns with the information supplied by Harbaugh, there is not enough information in the file itself to confirm that the record pertains to the correct Samuel McKee. However, a letter from an archivist at NARA is included in this file affirming that this was the only person named Samuel McKee in their records, presumably residing in Franklin County, Ohio, to receive a Revolutionary War pension and who died before 1832.

78. Franklinton is a neighborhood of Columbus, Franklin County, Ohio.

79. John B. B. Trussell, Jr., *The Pennsylvania Line Regimental Organization and Operations, 1776-1773* (Harrisburg: Pennsylvania Historical and Museum Commission, 1977), pp. 93-95, print.

80. Pension file for Samuel McKee number S. 41.853.

81. Ibid.

82. Ibid.

83. Ibid.

Families

84. Franklin County, Probate Court, Columbus, Ohio, "The Estate of Samuel McKee, Dec'd," Administration Docket I, page 187, administrators appointed to the estate of Samuel McKee on 30 August 1823, digital copies of penned documents, *Ohio History Connection*, formerly *Ohio Historical Society* (http://catalog.ohiohistory.org/ : accessed December 2015), citing Estate accounts [microform], 1803-1879, 1977; (Case files) [State Archives Series 3819], arranged numerically by case. The administrators were George Anthony, George B. Harvey, and Orrin Parrish.

85. *Find A Grave* (http://www.findagrave.com : accessed November 2015), memorial 7409004 for Jeremiah Davidson (1768-1851), citing Dunlap Creek Presbyterian Church Cemetery, Redstone Township, Fayette County, Pennsylvania, digital photograph added 23 June 2011. The transcript provided by the contributor was necessary due to the poor condition of the headstone which rendered the years shown on the photograph illegible. This information is being provided here on the assumption that it is accurate, inscription: Father, J. Davidson, Born June 10, 17[68], Died June 30, 18[51].

86. Harbaugh, p. 397. Harbaugh appears to have several of the details for Jeremiah confused, recording that he was born 10 June 1869 in Alleghany County, Maryland and in the fall of that year his parents migrated to Pennsylvania. However, the year is a typographical error. If 1769 is substituted, it would seem in line, but we know that Lewis-I had already purchased land in Pennsylvania by June 1767. The *Find A Grave* memorial for Jeremiah indicates he was born in June 1768. It is thought that some members of the family returned east to safer country with Elizabeth until Jeremiah was born.

87. *Find A Grave* (http://www.findagrave.com : accessed November 2015), memorial page 7409008 for Ann Alexander (1772-1748), citing Dunlap Creek Presbyterian Church Cemetery, Redstone Township, Fayette County, Pennsylvania, digital photograph added 23 June 2011. Inscription: Ann, Wife of Jeremiah Davidson, Died May [22, 18]48, in the 76 year of her Age. Her age on the headstone yields her birth year of 1772. Harbaugh spells her name with an "e" which is omitted on the headstone.

88. Harbaugh, p. 397. Harbaugh uses two different spellings for the name of Ann's father within the same paragraph: Hoto; Huto.

89. Harbaugh, p. 397.

90. Will of Lewis Davidson (Lewis-I).

91. Campbell, *Warrantee Township Map: Fayette County, Luzerne Township*.

92. Ellis, p. 636.

93. Ellis, pp. 735-736.

94. *Find A Grave* (http://www.findagrave.com : accessed November 2015), memorial 7409004 for Jeremiah Davidson (1768-1851), citing Dunlap Creek Presbyterian Church Cemetery, Redstone Township, Fayette County, Pennsylvania, digital photograph added April 2015. Inscription: Father, J. Davidson, Born June 10, 17[68], Died June 30, 18[5]1.

95. *Find A Grave* (http://www.findagrave.com : accessed November 2015), memorial page 7409008 for Ann Alexander (1772-1748), citing Dunlap Creek Presbyterian Church Cemetery, Redstone Township, Fayette County, Pennsylvania, digital photograph added June 2011. Inscription: Ann, Wife of Jeremiah Davidson, Died May [22, 18]48, in the 76 year of her age.

96. Greene County, Pennsylvania, "Will Books, 1796-1918 ; Index to Wills and Estates, 1796-1967," Register of Wills, Volume 7-8, 1892-1900, Volume 8, case number 4496, pp. 8-11, "Exemplification of Record from Fayette County, Penna. Will of Jeremiah Davidson, Filed and Recorded June 18, 1897," will dated 4 December 1847, proved 9 July 1851, probated in Greene County, Pennsylvania, digital images 369 and 370 of penned document, *Ancestry* (http://www.ancestry.com : accessed December 2015), citing Pennsylvania County, District and Probate Courts.

97. Ibid.

98. Harbaugh, p. 129.

99. Helen S. Fields, *Register of Marriages and Baptisms Performed by John Cuthbertson*, 1934, Reprint, (Baltimore, Maryland: Clearfield Company by Genealogical Publishing Company, 2009), particularly pp. 70-71. Includes a transcript of the baptism of Rosanna Hutchinson, first wife of William-III.

100. William Melancthon Glasgow, *History of the Reformed Presbyterian Church in America* (Baltimore: Hill & Harvey, Publishers, 1888), digital version, *Google Books* (http://books.google.com : accessed November 2011). This work includes a

transcript of the baptismal record for Rosanna Hutchinson, first wife of William-III.

101. Ibid.

102. Harbaugh, p. 134.

103. Evans, p. 1225.

104. *Tax Duplicate 1801*, "Ohio Tax Records, 1800-1850," page untitled and unnumbered, penned document, entry for John Davison, assessed in September 1801, digital image 20 of 59, *FamilySearch* (https://familysearch.org/ark:/61903/1:1:JS5Z-NMS : accessed November 2012), citing Auditor, Gallipolis Township, Washington County, Ohio, Historical Society Library, Columbus; FHL microfilm 945,761.

105. Bureau of Land Management, General Land Office Records, Chillicothe Land Office, credit volume patent, Vol. 7, p. 204, for James Davidson, William Montgomery, and William Lynn in Gallia Township, Washington County, Ohio consisting of fractional S2-T1N-R17W, Ohio River Survey, certificate unnumbered, issued 20 February 1809, digital image of penned document, *Bureau of Land Management, General Land Office Records* (http://www.glorecords .blm.gov/ : accessed December 2015). The mapping service on the web page confirms the location of the parcel. John Davidson may have purchased other tracts of land around the area of fractional section 2.

106. Harbaugh, p. 134.

107. Ibid.

108. Harbaugh, p. 157.

109. Ibid.

110. Charles Augustus Hanna, *Historical Collections of Harrison County in the State of Ohio* (New York: privately printed, 1900), p. 484, digital version, *Internet Archive* (http://www.archive.org : accessed April 2011).

111. *Commemorative Biographical Record of the Counties of Harrison and Carroll, Ohio*, pp. 446-453.

William "Ranger" Davidson

112. 1800 Census of the Northwest Territory.

113. *Tax Duplicate 1801*, "Ohio Tax Records, 1800-1850," page untitled and unnumbered, penned document, entry for Lewis Davison, assessed in September 1801, digital image 20 of 59, *FamilySearch* (https://familysearch.org/ark:/61903/1:1:JS5Z-NMS : accessed November 2012), citing Auditor, Gallipolis Township, Washington County, Ohio, Historical Society Library, Columbus; FHL microfilm 945,761.

114. All accounts from local history sources agree that Lewis-III migrated to Ohio in 1801, however he appears on the 1800 Census of the Northwest Territory with William-III, as well as the 1801 tax record.

115. *Commemorative Biographical Record...*, p. 446.

116. Ibid.

117. Harbaugh, p. 157.

118. Bureau of Land Management, General Land Office Records, Steubenville Land Office, credit volume patent, Vol. 27, p. 10, for Lewis Davidson, in Tuscarawas County in today's Freeport Township, Harrison County, Ohio, consisting of the southeast quarter of S29-T11N-R7W, Ohio River Survey, certificate unnumbered, issued 6 November 1815, digital image of penned document, *Bureau of Land Management, General Land Office Records* (http://www.glorecords.blm.gov/ : accessed December 2015). The mapping service on the web page confirms the location of the parcel.

119. *Commemorative Biographical Record...*, p. 451.

120. Ibid.

121. Ohio, Probate Court, Harrison County, *Ohio, Wills and Probate Records, 1786-1998*, Will Record, Vol A-C, 1813-1878, Vol. A, pp. 305-306, The last will and testament of Lewis Davidson [Lewis-III], untitled, dated 1 September 1832, proved 8 April 1833 at Cadiz, digital images 171-172 of penned document, *Ancestry* (http://www.ancestry.com : accessed December 2015), citing Ohio County, District and Probate Courts.

122. Harbaugh, p. 157.

196

Families

123. Harbaugh, p. 227.

124. Harbaugh, p. 228, citing the headstones of the Williams' which have since been lost.

125. Ibid.

126. Fayette County, Recorder of Deeds, Deed Book F: 197, William Davidson (William-III) to David Davidson, untitled, dated 4 May 1807, recorded 26 October 1807, photocopy of penned document, Uniontown, Pennsylvania.

127. Ellis, p. 636.

128. Harbaugh, p. 228.

129. *Find A Grave* (http://www.findagrave.com : accessed November 2015), memorial 85119785 for David Davidson (1777-1828), added 17 February 2012, citing Williams Cemetery, Luzerne Township, Fayette County, Pennsylvania, digital photograph added 16 April 2015. Inscription: In Memory of, David Davidson, who departed this life, Feb. 24 [1828], Aged [51] Years. This information is provided on the assumption that the contributor supplied data in square brackets that could be read on site, but not in the photograph.

130. Harbaugh, p. 228.

131. "Pennsylvania Probate Records, 1683-1994," Orphans' Court records v. 1-3 1783-1844, Fayette County, Volume 2, p. 341, entry for "Davidson, David Dec'd on the petition of Mary Davidson widow...," untitled, penned, 23 October 1828, undated, digital image 352 of 695, *FamilySearch* (http://www.familysearch.org : accessed November 2015), citing county courthouses, Pennsylvania. Jeremiah Davidson and John Coorvert [Covert] were named as joint guardians of Orpa David & Eliza Jane under the age of 14 years.

132. "Pennsylvania Probate Records, 1683-1994," Orphans' Court records v. 1-3 1783-1844, Fayette County, Volume 3, p. 279, entry for "Davidson, David Dec'd, Samuel Roberts acting Ex^r of the last will & testament of David Davidson late of Fayette County..." untitled, penned, 3 September 1840, undated, digital image 608 of 695, *FamilySearch* (http://www.familysearch.org : accessed November 2015), citing county courthouses, Pennsylvania. In this

record, are named Orpa Davidson Conwell, Eliza Jane Davidson, and Mary Davidson, now Clayburgh.

133. Harbaugh, p. 232.

134. Harbaugh, p. 232, citing Will Book 2, p. 146.

135. 1840 United States Census, population schedule, penned, Carter County, Kentucky, unpaged, entry for Mary Williams, digital image 7 of 33, *FamilySearch* (https://familysearch.org/ : accessed November 2015), citing NARA microfilm publication M704, (Washington D.C.: National Archives and Records Administration, n.d.).

136. 1850 United States Census, population schedule, penned, District 2, Carter County, Kentucky, unpaged, entry for Mary Williams, digital image 24 of 144, *FamilySearch* (https://familysearch.org/ : accessed November 2015), citing family 143, NARA microfilm publication M432 (Washington, D.C.: National Archives and Records Administration, n.d.).

137. Harbaugh, p. 232.

138. Harbaugh, p. 249.

139. Hanna pp. 483-484, the spelling of Barbara's surname as McDale.

140. Evans, p. 1224, recorded in 1903 that Barbara McDowell was born in Wales. Hanna, pp. 483-484, recorded in 1900 that William-III's first wife Rosanna Hutchinson, was born in Wales which was also reported by Lewis-IV in 1890.

141. Harbaugh, p. 249.

142. Ibid.

143. Ibid.

144. 1820 United States Census, population schedule, penned, Fayette Township, Lawrence County, Ohio, unpaged, entry 4 for John Francis, unnumbered, digital image 3 of 3, *FamilySearch* (https://familysearch.org/ : accessed October 2015), citing NARA microfilm publication M33, (Washington D.C.: National Archives and Records Administration, n.d.).

145. 1830 United States Census, population schedule, penned, Fayette Township, Lawrence County, Ohio, p. 316, entry 15 for William Lynd, digital image 5 of 8, *FamilySearch* (https://familysearch.org/ : accessed November 2015), citing NARA microfilm publication M19, (Washington D.C.: National Archives and Records Administration, n.d.), roll 134; FHL microfilm 337,945.

146. Harbaugh, p. 249.

147. This marriage year for Elizabeth Davidson and William Lynd was approximated based upon the birth date of their first child, Jane in 1807, as given by Harbaugh, p. 257. Their marriage location is here inferred based upon their residence in the 1830 and 1840 census records.

148. 1830 United States Census, population schedule, penned, Fayette Township, Lawrence County, Ohio, p. 316, entry 16 for William Lynd, digital image 5 of 8, *FamilySearch* (https://familysearch.org/ : accessed November 2015), citing NARA microfilm publication M19, (Washington D.C.: National Archives and Records Administration, n.d.), roll 134; FHL microfilm 337,945.

149. 1840 United States Census, population schedule, penned, Fayette Township, Lawrence County, Ohio, unpaged, entry 28, unnumbered, Wm Lynde, digital image 9 of 18, *FamilySearch* (https://familysearch.org/ : accessed August 2015), citing NARA microfilm publication M704, (Washington D.C.: National Archives and Records Administration, n.d.).

150. It is apparent by looking at the two census records cited that Elizabeth was alive when the 1840 census was taken. Although not explicitly named in either record, a female is in the same age bracket as William Lynd in both records which is assumed to be Elizabeth.

151. Harbaugh, p. 257.

152. Harbaugh, p. 258.

153. 1850 United States Census, population schedule, penned, Fayette Township, Lawrence County, Ohio, p. 881, line 29, entry for Sarah McKee, digital image 11 of 28, *FamilySearch* (https://familysearch.org/ : accessed January 2017), citing family 80, NARA microfilm publication M432, Roll 701 (Washington, D.C.: National Archives and Records Administration, n.d.). Sarah was 58 years of age.

154. 1860 United States Census, population schedule, penned, Fayette Township, Lawrence County, Ohio, p.71, line 24, entry for Sarah McKee, digital image 39 of 40, *FamilySearch* (https://familysearch.org/ : accessed April 2016), from "1860 U.S. Federal Census - Population," database, *Fold3* (http://www.fold3.com : n.d.), citing NARA microfilm publication M653, Roll 997 (Washington, D.C.: National Archives and Records Administration, n.d.). Sarah McKee, age 68 years, born in Pennsylvania.

155. 1870 United States Census, population schedule, penned, Fayette Township, Lawrence County, Ohio, p. 26, line 31, entry for Sarah McKee, digital image 26 of 54, *FamilySearch* (https://familysearch.org/ : accessed May 2014), citing NARA microfilm publication M593, Roll 1231 (Washington, D.C.: National Archives and Records Administration, n.d.). Sarah was 78 years of age.

156. The three census records cited consistently put Sarah's birthdate in 1792, in which case she would have been 15 years of age when she married William McKee.

157. "War of 1812 Pension and Bounty Land Warrant Application Files, 1812-ca. 1900," file number 2196, widow's pension application file for Sarah McKee claiming soldier William McKee, for service in "Capt. Gardner, Miller, and Titus' Co's Ohio Mil," applied 21 April 1871, digital copies of penned documents, *Fold3* (http://www.fold3.com : accessed January 2017); citing NARA, Department of the Interior, Bureau of Pensions, 1849-1930, Record Group 15: Records of the Department of Veterans Affairs, 1773 - 2007, War of 1812 Pension Roll: RG15-1812PB-Bx2283. This application was rejected 17 December 1872 due to inability to provide proof of marriage, despite the sworn testimony of witnesses. However, it is now thought that Sarah's application was actually denied for other reasons not stated in the file. See note 161 below.

158. Harbaugh, p. 258, gives the marriage year of William McKee and Sarah Davidson as 1803.

159. "War of 1812 Pension and Bounty Land Warrant Application Files, 1812-ca. 1900," file number 2196, widow's pension application file for Sarah McKee.

160. "War of 1812 Pension and Bounty Land Warrant Application Files, 1812-ca. 1900," file number 182 bounty land warrant 8569-80-50 issued 16 June 1837 and 1577 for bounty land warrant 32408-80-55, soldier's pension application file for William R. McKee, for service as a private in "Capt Timothy Titus' Co Ohio Mil," digital copies of penned documents, *Fold3* (http://www.fold3.com :

accessed January 2017); citing NARA, Department of the Interior, Bureau of Pensions, 1849-1930, Record Group 15: Records of the Department of Veterans Affairs, 1773 - 2007, War of 1812 Pension Roll: RG15-1812PB-Bx2283. Discharged 15 March 1814.

161. It appears that when Sarah applied for a widow's pension, her claim was identified with the wrong soldier, William R. McKee. This can be easily shown when comparing the two above-referenced files (see notes 157 and 160 above). It is known that our William resided in Fayette Township, Lawrence County, Ohio from 1807 until he died in 1858. However, examination of the bounty land certificate reveals that the land was in Kansas and was sold there by William R. McKee who resided in Brown County, Kansas for many years. William R. McKee testified in 1856 that he was then 64 years of age. This yields a seven year age discrepancy between him and our William McKee who would have been about age 71 at that time. By the time Sarah applied for a widow's pension, William R. McKee had already received his benefits. Given that Sarah applied for a widow's pension is evidence that our William McKee had some involvement in the War of 1812 even though no record for him was found.

162. Bureau of Land Management, General Land Office Records, Chillicothe Land Office, state volume patent, Volume 126, p. 394, cash entry for William McKee for 40.1 acres in Fayette Township, Lawrence County, Ohio, consisting of the NW¼ of the NE¼ of S33-T2N-R17W, Ohio River Survey, certificate 9430 issued 25 June 1841, digital image of penned document, *Bureau of Land Management, General Land Office Records* (http://www.glorecords.blm.gov/ : accessed June 2012). The mapping service on the web page confirms the physical location of the parcel.

163. Land entry file, NARA: February 2017.

164. "Ohio Probate Records, 1789-1996," Lawrence County, Record of Wills, Volume 1, pp. 308-310, last will and testament of William McKee, untitled, penned, dated 18 August 1855, proved 28 July 1858, digital image 191 of 574, *FamilySearch* (https://familysearch.org/ : July 2014); citing county courthouses, Ohio.

165. Harbaugh, p. 268.

166. "United States Census (Mortality Schedule), 1850," unpaged, line 34, entry for Abram Davidson, age 62, died February 1850 of quinsy, Lawrence County, Ohio, penned document, digital image 3 of 5, *FamilySearch*

(https://familysearch.org : accessed June 2016), citing Federal non-population census schedules, Ohio, 1850-1880, in the custody of the State Library of Ohio, citing NARA microfilm publication T655 (Washington, D.C.: National Archives and Records Administration, n.d.).

167. 1850 United States Census, population schedule, penned, Fayette Township, Lawrence County, Ohio, unpaged, line 37, entry for Luticia Davidson, digital image 16 of 28, *FamilySearch* (https://familysearch.org : accessed June 2016), citing NARA microfilm publication series M432, Roll 701 (Washington, D.C.: National Archives and Records Administration, n.d.).

168. 1860 United States Census, population schedule, penned, Fayette Township, Lawrence County, Ohio, p. 35, line 14, entry for Letitia Davidson (age 77), digital image 3 of 40, *FamilySearch* (http://familysearch.org : accessed June 2016), citing *Fold3* (http://www.fold3.com : n.d.), citing NARA microfilm publication M653, Roll 997 (Washington, D.C.: National Archives and Records Administration, n.d.).

169. Harbaugh, p. 268.

170. 1850 United States Census, population schedule, penned, Fayette Township, Lawrence County, Ohio, unpaged, line 37, entry for Luticia Davidson, digital image 16 of 28, *FamilySearch* (http://familysearch.org : accessed June 2016), citing NARA microfilm publication M432, Roll 701 (Washington, D.C.: National Archives and Records Administration, n.d.). Daughter Jane Anne does not appear in this record.

171. Harbaugh, p. 270.

172. 1850 United States Census, population schedule, penned, St. Marys, Auglaize County, Ohio, p. 264, dwelling 432, entry for Jane Davidson, digital image 6 of 16, *FamilySearch* (http://familysearch.org : accessed June 2016), citing NARA microfilm publication M432, Roll 660 (Washington, D.C.: National Archives and Records Administration, n.d.). Jane was 50 years of age in 1850.

173. Harbaugh, p. 270.

174. 1830 United States Census, population schedule, penned, Fayette Township, Lawrence County, Ohio, p. 316, entry 25, unnumbered, for Thomas Davidson, digital image 5 of 8, *FamilySearch* (http://familysearch.org : accessed June 2015),

citing NARA microfilm publication M19, Roll 134-135 (Washington D.C.: National Archives and Records Administration, n.d.).

175. Harbaugh, p. 272, recorded that Jane was 90 years of age when she died in 1854, however the 1850 Census, already cited, indicates Jane was born about 1800.

176. Harbaugh, p. 272.

177. Harbaugh, p. 273.

178. Harbaugh, pp. 273-276.

179. Harbaugh, pp. 276-280.

180. *Find A Grave* (http://www.findagrave.com : January 2015), memorial 55664424 for Lavina (Yingling) Davidson, created 31 July 2010, digital photograph, citing White Cottage Cemetery, South Point, Fayette Township, Lawrence County, Ohio. Inscription: Lavina Davidson, 1815 – 1898.

181. Harbaugh, p. 282.

182. Ibid.

183. *Find A Grave* (http://www.findagrave.com : January 15), memorial 40072966 for Rev. William W. Davidson, created 30 July 2009, digital photograph, citing White Cottage Cemetery, South Point, Fayette Township, Lawrence County, Ohio. Inscription: Rev. William W. Davidson, Born Nov. 6, 1798, Died Oct. 5, 1883, Aged 84 ys, 10 m, & 29 ds.

184. Harbaugh, p. 284.

185. Harbaugh, p. 284.

186. Harbaugh, p. 285.

187. Ibid.

188. Ibid.

189. *Find A Grave* (http://www.findagrave.com : June 2016) memorial 43987316 for Joseph W. Davidson, created 6 November 2009, digital photograph, citing Davidson Cemetery, South Point, Fayette Township, Lawrence County, Ohio. Inscription: Jos. W. Davidson, born Dec. 26, 1806, died Aug. 16, 1872, aged 65 y, 7 m, 20 d.

190. *Find A Grave* (http://www.findagrave.com : June 2016) memorial 43987439 for Jane (Bryson) Davidson, created 6 November 2009, digital photograph, citing Davidson Cemetery, South Point, Fayette Township, Lawrence County, Ohio. Inscription: Jane, His Wife, 1809 – 1889.

191. Harbaugh, pp. 285-333.

192. Harbaugh, p. 334.

193. Ibid.

Ohio

A t the close of the Revolutionary War, the British agreed to cede the Northwest Territory to the United States. The U.S. had further passed the Land Ordinance of 1785 and the Northwest Ordinance of 1787. These acts gave the United States government jurisdiction over all unsettled lands and established public domain. These developments led to a renewed expansion of settlers heading west of the Ohio River.

For the most part, the Six Nations had retreated, officially by treaty, into the Northwest Territory, a large portion of which later became the state of Ohio. This Territory included all lands east of the Mississippi River, but north and west of the Ohio River, which formed a natural boundary between the Six Nations and the settlers. Many of the Six Nations, who had not been invited to the peace talks with Great Britain and never agreed to the transfer of sovereignty over the Northwest Territory, formed a confederacy resisting further encroachment on Indian lands.

As settlers began rapidly crossing the Ohio River the natural result was the clashes that occurred between greedy settlers and mistreated Indians. About five years before William-III migrated to the Northwest Territory, General "Mad" Anthony Wayne was called out of retirement by General George Washington to quell the uprising of the Western Indian Confederacy. In August 1794, peace was achieved through Wayne's victory at the Battle of Fallen Timbers.

The Treaty of Greenville, honored by the Six Nations, was signed in 1795 and in 1797 a line was drawn confining the Six Nations to the northwest quadrant of the Northwest Territory and beyond.[1] These events along with the execution of several additional major treaties with the various tribes opened the way for western settlement. Ohio was the first state created from the Northwest Territory exercising the rules established by the Enabling Act of 1802. Ohio officially became a state in March 1803.

Once again, the Indian lands were reduced and the displaced tribes were pushed further west over the land of broken promises. Weary of battle, and unable to stop the aggression, they retreated. Just as the Six Nations killed many members of the Alligewi tribe and violently forced them from the region a century or more before, the Six Nations were forcibly pushed further west. The flintlock replaced the stone tipped arrow and open range was eventually fenced.

Evans published in 1903 that William-III and family migrated to the Northwest Territory by floating down the Monongahela and Ohio Rivers on a keelboat.[2] Evans was possibly one source Harbaugh drew from when she published her work in 1948. Evans failed to provide a source for this information, but it likely came from testimonials given by descendants of William-III's son, William Warrington Davidson (William-IV), whose brief biography appears in the earlier work of Hardesty (1882).[3] William-IV was contemporary with the author that compiled Hardesty's work, which makes Hardesty's book a valuable resource for researchers. The details given in Hardesty were quite possibly dictated by William-IV himself. William-IV died at South Point, Ohio on 5 October 1883.

Certain details about the keelboat journey are also given in the obituary of James Davidson, another source rich in genealogical information. James was a son of John Davidson and wife Margaret Armstrong.[4] John was the first child of William-III and first wife, Rosanna Hutchinson. John also came to the Northwest Territory from Pennsylvania with his family aboard a keelboat in 1801 and settled in the area that later became known as the town of Burlington, a short distance up the Ohio river from his father's settlement.

The date of William-III's journey has been vaguely given in different sources as 1798 and 1799.[5-8] The discrepancy is surely due to the failing memories of old pioneers and the careless memories of youngsters only casually interested in the old stories of their grandparents and great-grandparents.

Frequently people tend to better remember when certain events occurred by associating them with other significant events in their lives. For example, Hardesty says of William-IV, that he was born in Fayette County, Pennsylvania on November 6, 1798 and that he "came to Ohio with his father in 1799 when he was only six months old."[9] This information was probably recalled by William-IV himself, based on what his parents had told him. Remembering that he was six months of age when he was brought to Ohio is easier than remembering the specific departure and arrival dates. The year 1799 also agrees with the testimonial given by another direct descendent in the obituary of James Davidson.[10]

We also know that William-III was in Pennsylvania as late as March 1799 when he signed an indenture in which about two thirds of his *Dispute Ended* tract was sold to Jonathan Ridge (see the later chapter *Final Years*).[11] Although he may have explored parts of southern Ohio in 1798, this transaction is evidence that he was still in Pennsylvania in March 1799.

William "Ranger" Davidson

Counting six months from the birth of William-IV in November 1798, we calculate the migration period as May 1799. Although speculative, this all fits neatly together. In the fall of 1798, William-III probably scouted some land in the Northwest Territory. After returning, he raised some cash by selling a portion of *Dispute Ended*. He probably needed to purchase supplies for the journey, possibly even a keelboat. He would also need money to purchase land for a new farm.

Two months later everything was packed and the family pushed off from the banks of the Monongahela. In the absence of any documentation or event pointing to 1798 as the year of departure and considering all the relevant records, it seems most likely that William-III and his family set off for the Northwest Territory in the spring, probably around May of 1799.

There are many possible ways a settler could handle the logistics for such a move. It simply depended upon the individual situation of the family. A few possibilities are discussed here, but we don't actually know how the Davidson family worked it out.

Just as families do today, when they decided to relocate, one or more members of pioneer families typically went out in advance to scout a desirable location. We may safely suppose that William-III along with one or more of his sons rode out to the Northwest Territory to locate a suitable place to settle. It could be that they simply searched for a good general location with plenty of unoccupied land and a source of fresh water. They then returned home as quickly as possible to retrieve their families and belongings. On the other hand, one or more members of the family may have formed a camp and stayed behind to guard the claim and began clearing the parcel while the others returned home to inform the family back east. When they stepped aboard their boat, Barbara was caring for William-IV, then an infant, and they would need rest and shelter after their long journey westward.

Given this scenario, Barbara would have been carrying a child at the time their new land claim was being scouted. This doesn't mean that Barbara was left alone while William-III rode west. Four of

Ohio

Barbara's step-children were married by that time and two of her own children were ten years of age and older. These family members likely assisted Barbara during William-III's absence.

In May 1799, William-III was 51 years old and Barbara was 31 years of age. At that time, they had eleven children ranging in age from 28 years to six months. But, not all of the children migrated to Ohio with their mother and father for permanent settlement. The younger children certainly did travel with their parents and this would include (approximate ages): Margaret, 13; Elizabeth, 12; Sarah, 10; Abraham, 8; Thomas, 5; and William-IV, 6 months.

Several of the older children may have accompanied William-III in the traveling party. Our knowledge of this comes from descendent testimonials as reported through Harbaugh. Included in the migration was William-III's oldest daughter, Comfort (age 24) who was then married to Alexander McCourtney.[12] Also, William-III's daughter, Mary (age 20) who had married Mordicai Williams in 1795 and had one son, age 3 at that time.[13]

Harbaugh says that David (age 22) came to Ohio with William-III, and later returned to Pennsylvania.[14] However, David was married to Mary Williams in 1800 and her family was residing in Pennsylvania, presumably the location of their marriage. Given this short duration of time, it appears that David may have been temporarily enlisted by his father for logistical help on the journey. He was said to have stayed in Kentucky for a short time, then promptly returned to Fayette County, Pennsylvania. He then resumed farming the remaining portion of *Dispute Ended*, still in the ownership of William-III. A short time later David was betrothed to Mary Williams.

Harbaugh also says that Lewis-III, second son of William-III, age 26, migrated to Ohio in 1801.[15] But, Lewis-III appears on the census of the Northwest Territory with William-III in June 1800.[16] This could indicate that Lewis-III actually took part in the migration with his parents and intended to settle in the Northwest Territory by May 1799. Lewis-III had also married Mary Davidson in July 1798 in Fayette County, Pennsylvania. However, their first son, William, was reportedly born near Fort Cumberland, Maryland in November 1799.[17] This is difficult to reconcile, but perhaps Lewis-III took Mary to stay with her parents (brother and sister-in-law of William-III) at Fort Cumberland for the duration of her pregnancy. Lewis-III then assisted William-III in his move to Ohio after which he later reunited with his wife. This is very speculative, but the information available supports this conclusion, if all the dates and locations were reported correctly.

William-III's first son, John, reportedly came to the Northwest Territory in 1801 and the records support this date. John was not listed on the Territorial Census taken in 1800, but he does appear on tax records beginning in 1801.[18]

So the migration party certainly included William-III and Barbara and their six youngest children. But also, possibly Comfort and her husband Alexander McCourtney, Mary and her husband Mordicai Williams and their son William (age 3), David, and possibly Lewis-III. With as many as fifteen persons in the traveling party, it is also very possible that more than one boat was used in the journey.

William-III was credited by Hardesty as the first settler in what later became Fayette Township in Lawrence County, Ohio where he also built a cabin.[19] Ferguson has pointed out, that since his land straddled the boundary line, William-III was also the first landowner in Perry Township, however this appears to be incorrect as will be shown later in this chapter.[20] Hardesty gives credit to Philip Salliday as the first settler of Perry Township since he was the first to build a dwelling on that side of the township line. However, Hardesty does not address whether Salliday owned the land on which he settled. Solida Creek in Fayette Township was named for Salliday, whose name was misspelled and undoubtedly mispronounced.

It should be pointed out that even though William-III, having arrived in the spring of 1799, is considered a pioneering settler he was far from being the first person to traverse the area. As early as 1794, two keelboats were reportedly making regular trips between Pittsburgh and Cincinnati taking a month each way.[21] One estimate says that in a year from November 1787 to the end of November of 1788, some 967 boats had floated down the Ohio River.[22] By 1802, it was estimated that there was about 45,000 inhabitants in the Northwest Territory.[23]

From the existing accounts we can easily reconstruct the Davidson's path westward. William-III's *Dispute Ended* tract in Pennsylvania adjoined the Monongahela River which flows northward to Pittsburgh where it joins the Allegheny. Together these rivers form the Ohio River which initially flows north, then bends southward and eventually passes by the tract of land settled by William-III in southern Ohio.

The river journey was about 380 miles (measured using modern maps). By comparison, one example was recorded in which a 200 mile river journey took 31 days.[24] This is roughly two weeks per hundred miles! In another description made by George Washington, he estimated that even going up stream with poles, a four man crew could likely make 20 miles a day or five days per hundred miles.[25] The great difference in these estimates is probably due to the condition of the river, the season traveled, and many other factors. This makes estimating the length of time the Davidsons spent on the river difficult, however we may safely say it took a minimum of 20 days, but likely longer.

There were relatively narrow windows of time in which settlers could effectively use the river. In winter, the Ohio frequently froze over and in summer it often ran too low to accommodate river craft.[26] There were also many water hazards slowing the boatman's journey. In 1866, it was estimated that there were 285 dangerous obstructions in the Ohio including snags, logs, and wrecked boats, and this didn't consider the many reefs and bars on which boats could run aground and sometimes become stubbornly lodged.[27] This was much later than the Davidson's journey, but it is unlikely that the conditions of the river were any better in 1799.

One type of water obstacle pioneers called a "planter" was an immoveable log embedded in the river bottom or along the bank and protruding from the surface of the water vertically or at an angle to the water surface. Another type was called a "sawyer" which was a tree trunk, large limb, driftwood, or other debris lodged tight at the upper end while the lower end was kept in motion by the current of the river causing the object to sway or "saw" back and forth.[28]

Common use of the flatboat likely started after the Revolutionary War ended in 1783.[29] Although there were many styles and designs, Hulbert recorded that the average flatboat was about 50 feet long and generally between nine and 12 feet in width.[30] In contrast to Hulbert, Lawyer describes a larger craft "from sixty to one hundred feet long and about fifteen feet wide…which drifted with the current."[31] These hulks reportedly could hold several wagon-loads of freight.[32] It is well documented that the pioneers took wagons and their horses, cattle, sheep, hogs, and other livestock aboard.[33] It is difficult to improve upon the description provided by Hulbert:

> The first craft of the pioneer era, however, was the flatboat or barge; the "broadhorn" was a common name for it; if called a "Kentucky broadhorn," its destination was along the Ohio River; if called a "New Orleans broadhorn" the destination was known to be on the Mississippi River, and the craft was (supposedly) a little heavier and more strongly put together. As a house may be anything from a tottering shack to a millionaire's mansion, so the flatboat or barge may have been anything from a creaking raft with a drygoods box on it to a strong, roomy house with a little barn in the rear. The names barge and flatboat were used almost synonymously, but technically speaking a flatboat was a raft with a house on it while a barge was a square, tub-like boat with a cabin in the centre…[34]

Lawyer says the keelboat was more commonly constructed by experienced boat-builders and sold at a profit. These were generally better constructed, more elaborate, more comfortable, and swifter than the flatboat. The keelboat was also known to carry cannons for defense. Only wealthier emigrants could afford the price of a keelboat. Keelboats are often depicted having a vee-shaped hull and prow which served to improve speed and maneuvering. Some authors make the further distinction that generally the "flatboat" was most often homebuilt. Ellet describes one example of the homebuilt variety as being constructed of green oak planks fastened to a frame of timber by wooden pins, and caulked with tow (rope fibers) or other available materials.[35]

Although careful distinctions are here made between the flatboat and the keelboat, unless one has conducted such research it is likely that these terms are frequently inappropriately used interchangeably for any of the early types of watercraft. Both Harbaugh and Evans use the term "keelboat" in their narratives and this same term is used in the obituary of James Davidson, however, in truth it is now impossible to say with any certainty what type of boat was actually used by Davidson.

Some readers might reason that William-III, being a pioneer who had long since learned to become self-sufficient on the frontier, would most likely have built himself a flatboat. In fact, one of William-III's half-brothers, Jeremiah, was recorded as being a boat-builder who also resided on the Monongahela River. William-III may have acquired the assistance of Jeremiah in building himself a boat.

On the other hand, another might argue that being a successful farmer for many years and having reached middle age, William-III would have had the money and would not have risked the lives of his family in a homebuilt craft, but would more likely have purchased a more reliable keelboat. In fact, boats could be purchased at the busy nearby boatyards of Brownsville (formerly Redstone Old Fort).[36] As previously mentioned briefly, William-III had also raised some money by selling a portion of *Dispute Ended* (see the later chapter *Final Years*), so he had the cash available to make such a purchase. In this case, whether William-III built or bought, the reader must choose.

In either case, these boats were propelled and steered using long "setting-poles" or "pike-poles." Many boats had "running boards" on each side along which the "crew" walked while pushing their poles against the bottom of the river or on a nearby log or rock.[37] Often flatboats used long oars for propulsion situated near the bow called "gougers" and a long steering oar at the stern used as a rudder.[38]

It is easy to picture the children uneasily stepping aboard their boat, tremendously excited and perhaps a little scared. They likely waved goodbye to family and friends who remained behind and gathered at the shore to see them off. One may imagine them hurrying to the rail to memorize the last glimpses of their beloved Pennsylvania cabin before it shrank in the distance and finally disappeared from view as their vessel snaked around the bends in the Monongahela.

There are many documented cases in which pioneer families floating down the Ohio River were attacked and killed and their possessions stolen. Sometimes a decoy would lie in wait by the shore and hail the flatboats going by, imploring them to heave to and make rescue. Once the unsuspecting pioneers neared the shore, the attack commenced. Sometimes hostages were made to act as decoys at threat of death to accomplish this goal. In some cases, the attack was started when a boat simply came near enough to shore to give effective musket fire from nearby woods and then the enemy would give chase in pursuit of the weakened and terrorized pioneers.[39]

One source says that the last hostile Six Nations activity reported in southern Ohio occurred in 1794.[40] However, another says that hostile activity was ongoing in the Scioto River Valley until 1802, but this probably occurred some forty miles north and west of the Davidson settlement.[41]

It is said that William-III first landed on the south side of the river where Catlettsburg, Kentucky stands today. Evans adds that he "soon crossed the Ohio River and took up land" on the Ohio side.[42] This is also confirmed in the obituary of James Davidson, discussed earlier.[43] Ferguson states, "As Davidson built his cabin, he retreated at night to the point between the two rivers for a better defense against any renegade Indians roaming the area."[44] The point referenced is located between the Big Sandy River and Catlett's Creek on the south shore of the Ohio River. While this is supposition on the part of Ferguson, there is a very good chance he was correct for several possible reasons.

The idea has been put forth that northern Kentucky and the region of West Virginia bordering the Ohio River were hunting grounds for the Six Nations and they did not generally reside in their hunting grounds.[45] Further, the Ohio River had become the natural boundary between the Six Nations and the settlers beginning with the treaty at Fort Stanwix in 1768. Since then, the country north and west of the Ohio River had been considered Six Nations land, so Six Nations activities may have occurred more recently to the north.[46] By camping across the river, William-III might have reduced exposure to "renegade Indian" activity originating inland on the Ohio side of the river. But, as stated previously, today it is uncertain whether such a threat actually existed by the time the Davidsons arrived. This isn't to say that other forms of danger did not exist, but it would seem that the possibility of attack by the Six Nations might not have been the foremost concern.

Perhaps the real reason the Davidsons temporarily camped on the southern shore, which eluded previous researchers, is that many other pioneers had already settled near the southern shore. A list of more than forty families, who had established themselves near the mouth of the Big Sandy River before 1798, was recorded by Ely![47] This area, which later became known as Catlettsburg, Kentucky, would have afforded better protection simply because there were many other settlers there. The Davidsons could also have bartered or traded with those families for needed supplies until their farm was established. Just for reference, today, the Ohio River at this crossing is roughly one third of a mile from shore to shore.

Why William-III chose his particular stretch of land is not known and we are left to guess that perhaps he preferred the lay of the land, the fertility of the soil, the relative density of the forest, or perhaps erosion on the northern bank seemed less severe. It may also simply have been that more land was still available and unsettled to the north, since Virginians had long since migrated rapidly into the lands south of the southern shore.[48]

William "Ranger" Davidson

We have no information regarding the size or construction of William-III's home in Ohio, but one could safely suppose that it was constructed as much for protection as for comfort, and much in the same way and using the same tools and materials as his former home in Pennsylvania. He would also need to clear the land of the forest which would be replaced by productive farm fields.

One tool or machine we know that William-III owned in Ohio was called a horse gear or horse gears.[49] This device was used by hitching one or more horses or oxen to a long pole which was attached to a central drum. The drum could vary in size, but could be as large as eight feet in diameter. The animals employed walked in circles around the drum which turned a large gear. The central gear was attached to one or more shafts which provided a mechanical means of performing any of a number of possible tasks. Unfortunately, we don't know what William-III used the horse gears for, but it could have been used to drive a mechanism for threshing grain or milling wheat into flour or corn into meal. It could also have been used to draw water from a well or the nearby Ohio River for irrigating his fields. It is also possible that if William-III was operating a mill he may have been doing so as a side business, providing the service for area farmers. Also among his possessions was a steelyard, a type of scale that could be used to weigh commodities, such as sacks of grain or flour.[50] The steelyard could have been used to confirm the weight of a product being sold so its cost could be determined. Conversely, William-III could also have used his steelyard to confirm the weight of purchases he had made from others.

Next, the hunt was on for the location of William-III's Ohio parcel. General inquiry with the Ohio Historical Society resulted in the legal description where the tract was located, a good starting point for researchers. The parcel was in Section 5, Township 1 North, Range 17 West (or S5-T1N-R17W for short), Ohio River Survey.

A land entry file should exist for William-III's land claim in Ohio. Inquiry began with the Ohio Historical Society who suggested that the Bureau of Land Management (BLM) and the National Archives and Records Administration (NARA) should be contacted for more information. After NARA replied that the land entry file was not located, the BLM subsequently opened a title resolution case with NARA to obtain an official reason the Ohio land entry file could not be found. NARA replied to the BLM that William-III's Ohio land entry file was "either damaged or destroyed" before it could be preserved by their archivists.[51] This is most unfortunate because the application in that file would show the date that William-III actually took possession and began improvements of his tract.

The land entry file may also have included a survey depicting the size, shape, and location of William-III's Ohio parcel. Although the survey could not be found, the patent certificate is available. Patent certificates include the legal description of the purchase which resolves this dilemma. As it turns out, William-III's purchase was not just a part of section 5, but the entire section![52]

As is typical in genealogy research, every answer raises more questions. At the time William-III explored and settled in the Northwest Territory, it was mostly a wilderness. Prior to research, it was supposed that William-III had paced off his parcel and marked his boundaries as he had done in Pennsylvania. But, how did William-III know where the boundaries were located so that his parcel would exactly coincide with all of section 5? Read on.

The section, township, and range boundaries were originally surveyed by commissioned surveyors hired by the government. The township where William-III settled was first surveyed by a man named Levi Whipple. A copy of this survey is available and may be obtained from NARA. Whipple's survey was conducted in November 1798, only about six months before William-III migrated to Ohio![53] When such surveys were conducted, the surveyors marked the boundaries using piles of rocks, by carving markers into the trunks of live trees, or by using stakes.[54] This explains how William-III was able to enter this wilderness area and defend a claim that exactly coincided with the boundaries of section 5: the markers were already there!

Whipple's survey does not show land ownership, but it does reveal the shape of the parcel, the acreage contained in the section, and also provides a basic description of the land. Based upon this survey, it was learned that all of section 5 contained 242.98 acres.[55] The surveyor's notes describe Section 5 as, "Creek bottom and excellent wheat hills, tim[ber] oak, hickory, etc." Other types of trees in the area were poplar, spruce, and dogwood.

The boundary lines of the section, township, and range of William-III's land, as depicted in 1798 by Whipple, remain unchanged today. The Ohio River forms the southern boundary of the tract causing it to be irregular in shape, roughly triangular, and smaller than the 640 acres normally found in a full-sized rectangular section. Thus, section 5 is known as a fractional section. William-III called this parcel his *Fractional Section 5* in his last will.[56]

Some readers may wish to obtain a copy of a Lawrence County map which depicts the precise location of *Fractional Section 5*.[57] For those who find this inconvenient, the boundaries of *Fractional Section 5* may be closely located using a modern-day map. First, locate the Village of South Point. Then draw a north/south line to the river bank, beginning at the point where Solida Road meets N. Kenova Road. Next, draw an east/west line from the previous starting point, west to the Ohio River bank. Interestingly, this line should run along the edge of Davidson Street on the west side. If extended across the river, the east/west line should strike the Kentucky side of the river north of the mouth of Catlett's Creek. The area of land on the Ohio side of the river delineated by the two lines is where the triangular-shaped *Fractional Section 5* is situated.

Armed with all of the information so far gathered, the Bureau of Land Management was able to provide a copy of the two pages from the original tract book pertinent to William-III's purchase.[58] This document shows that William-III purchased his land making installments as required by the rules defined by the Land Office at that time.[59] His initial deposit was recorded on 15 May 1804 (considered the purchase date). His final payment was made 15 May 1809 and he was issued final certificate (FC) or patent number 1003, dated 21 September 1810, issued during the presidency of James Madison. This means

William-III obtained legal ownership of his land only just over a year before he died. He paid a total of $621.98 in three installments for his Ohio parcel.

The "true quantity" of acres recorded in the tract book was 242.99. This is remarkably close to Whipple's survey plat, the two differing by only 0.01 acres! This further confirms that William-III actually did own all of *Fractional Section 5*.

Fractional Section 5 was part of the "Congress Lands" which simply meant that William-III's land fell outside any of the other special use regions of land set aside by the government, such as the U.S. Military Lands, the Virginia Military District, and others.

William-III filed his claim through the land office at Chillicothe, which had opened in 1801. On 1 March 1803, Ohio became a state and in April that same year *Fractional Section 5* was made part of Gallia County. One might expect that the news of these widely published and much discussed events would have inspired William-III to formally claim his land, but he made no effort to do so until May 1804. At that time, he saddled his horse, possibly the one he called Fox, and rode about 80 miles to Chillicothe to apply for a patent. This journey would have taken two to four days each way!

What about the claim that William-III also owned land that fell in Perry Township (north and west of *Fractional Section 5*)? This information was reported by Ferguson possibly based upon his interpretation of an entry recorded by Hardesty.[60] Hardesty incorrectly lists "William W. Davidson" as the first settler in Perry Township in 1799. But, William W. would have been less than one year old at that time. It is possible that Ferguson interpreted Hardesty's entry as a typographical error and instead attributed the first settler claim in Perry Township to William-III. No records were found for any land in Perry Township to have ever been in William-III's ownership. Examination of early maps show that all of *Fractional Section 5* was contained in Fayette Township from 1798 (Whipple's Survey) to present day.[61] No other purchases of land were found for William-III in Ohio. While it is possible that another purchase was made by William-III in Perry Township, no surviving documentation was found to prove it.

Before moving forward, a couple additional issues should here be addressed. Harbaugh recorded that William-III made the river journey to Ohio "…where he had previously purchased a large tract of land."[62] Examination of the Tract Book entry does not bear this out. In fact, according to the Tract Book, William-III did not even purchase the land until May 1804.[63] Apparently, William-III took possession of the land as a squatter for several years before making application at the General Land Office, in similar fashion as he did in Pennsylvania.

Another misconception regarding the Ohio parcel is found in Ferguson's work. Ferguson, writing for South Point's Centennial Committee in 1988, says that the Ohio parcel was land William-III "had received for military service."[64] On this point, Ferguson is incorrect. Nearly all land granted in exchange for military service in the state of Ohio was located in one of two defined regions, the U.S. Military District or the Symmes Purchase.[65] No part of either of these regions is within 30 miles of South Point. Further, searches conducted at the National Archives, the Pennsylvania Archives, and the Virginia State Library failed to produce a bounty land warrant file for William-III. Later research revealed that William-III did not even qualify for a pension or bounty land, and consequently, he never would have applied for such benefits.[66]

A search of the patent records at the Bureau of Land Management, General Land Office records, does reveal a patent issued to William Davidson in Ohio on January 14, 1799. However, this patent was for a different man named William Davidson who was from Virginia and had served as a private in that state's Continental Line. Also, the land was located in the Virginia Military District. It is thought that perhaps Ferguson mistakenly identified this patent with our William-III.[67]

In summary, we have determined that William-III owned a roughly triangular-shaped parcel of land consisting of all of fractional section 5-T1N-R17W, located in today's southwestern Fayette Township,

Lawrence County, Ohio. The southern side of this 242.99 acre parcel was defined by a stretch of the Ohio River over a mile in length.

Often when the pioneers reached their destination by river, they dismantled their boat and used the lumber to construct a cabin or other structures such as a barn.[68-70] Since there were no sawmills anywhere near *Fractional Section 5* at the time, it seems likely that William-III would have used the lumber from his boat to his advantage. The family would soon have begun clearing the land, just as they did in Pennsylvania on *Dispute Ended.* This was William-III's final move where he spent the next eleven years developing and building a working farm for himself and his family.

Harbaugh recorded that William-III's cabin was located between the Ohio River and the brick house built by one of William-III's sons, Joseph Davidson (1806-1872). In 1948, Harbaugh further said that Joseph's brick house was then still in "good condition" and was occupied by a great-granddaughter. This landmark has since been razed. In 1988, Ferguson wrote that William-III's house or cabin was located "on the river bank facing the Old River Road near the junction of today's Second Street and Hooper Street." This location would now be 2nd Street East and Hooper Drive.

The "Old River Road" as both Harbaugh and Ferguson refer to it may have been Front Street which can only be seen on early maps of South Point. In any case, both the road and William-III's cabin were eventually lost to the combined effects of erosion and the periodic flooding of the Ohio River.[71]

NORTHWEST TERRITORY CENSUS OF 1800. This document is valuable only in the sense that it places William-III and son Lewis-III in the Northwest Territory on 10 June 1800. Both men are listed as being free male inhabitants, each a head of family, and 21 years of age or older. They are listed in name only in Gallipolis Township of Washington County.[72]

TAX DUPLICATE, 1801. William-III and two of his sons, John and Lewis-III, appear on the tax list in 1801. In this list, both William-III and John are recorded as owning one horse each. William-III owned 9 head of cattle while John and Lewis-III each owned two.[73]

TAX DUPLICATE, 1802. William-III, John, and Lewis-III also appear on the tax list in 1802. By this time, William-III and John each owned two horses. William-III owned 8 head of cattle, John owned two, and Lewis-III owned three.[74]

RIVER SHIPPING. Even by 1820, Ohio was still a wilderness and few towns of any size existed. In the absence of a road system, it was extremely difficult to transport goods from the farm to any market. Many farmers located on or near the Ohio River loaded their produce onto flatboats to transport their goods to other towns located along the river. Some even took their goods all the way to New Orleans by floating down the Ohio and Mississippi river-way.[75] It is not known whether William-III did this, and there is no surviving evidence that he did, but it is possible that he kept his flatboat or keelboat intact for that purpose. He may also have arranged with some of the other family members to handle such river journeys for him.

1. Dr. George W Knepper, *The Official Ohio Lands Book*, first paperback edition (Ohio: Publication of the Auditor of State, 2002), p. 6, digital version, *Auditor of the State of Ohio* (http://ohioauditor.gov : accessed July 2011).

2. Nelson W. Evans, *History of Scioto County, Ohio*, (Portsmouth, Ohio: Self-published, 1903), reprint (Markham, Virginia: The Apple Manor Press), Part 5, p. 1224. The keelboat journey of William-III is mentioned.

3. *Atlas of Lawrence County, Ohio, Hardesty 1882 and Lake 1887 (Combined)*, 1st edition reprint (Ironton, Ohio: Lawrence County Historical Society, 1985), "Rev. William W. Davidson," p. 27.

4. "Obituary. Davidson. James Davidson.", *Ironton Register*, 10 January 1895, Volume 46, No. 26, page 5, printed from microfilm, Hamner Room, Briggs Lawrence County Public Library, Ironton, Ohio.

Ohio

5. Elizabeth Davidson Harbaugh, *The Davidson Genealogy* (Ironton, Ohio : self-published, 1948; Ann Arbor, Michigan : Lithoprinted, Edwards Brothers, Inc., 1949), p. 129, print, OCLC: 23167553. Harbaugh recorded that William-III migrated to Ohio in 1798.

6. Evans, p. 1224, records William-III's migration to Ohio in 1799.

7. *Hardesty 1882 and Lake 1887 (Combined)*, p. 214, says William-III migrated to Ohio in 1798.

8. "Obituary. Davidson. James Davidson.", *Ironton Register*, 10 January 1895, says William-III came to Ohio in 1799.

9. *Hardesty 1882 and Lake 1887 (Combined)*, p. 27.

10. "Obituary. Davidson. James Davidson.", *Ironton Register*, 10 January 1895.

11. Fayette County, Recorder of Deeds, Deed Book C: 1265-1266, "William Davidson to Jonathan Ridge," dated 30 March 1799, recorded 13 May 1799, photocopy of penned document, Uniontown, Pennsylvania. While it is possible that William-III and Barbara later returned to Pennsylvania from Ohio to sign over this deed to Jonathan Ridge, it seems more probable that they would have done whatever was needed so that Barbara would be subjected to the hardships of the journey once rather than twice, especially considering that she was then caring for an infant.

12. Harbaugh, p. 227. It is unknown whether the McCourtney's had any children; they were reportedly married in July 1793. This family reportedly later moved to Missouri. McCourtney was not found in the 1800 Census of the Northwest Territory, but he does appear on the 1800 Federal Census in Fayette County, Pennsylvania.

13. Harbaugh, p. 232. Mordicai Williams reportedly came to Ohio with William-III, but later migrated to Kilgore, Kentucky.

14. Harbaugh, p. 228. According to Harbaugh, David Hutchinson Davidson accompanied William-III to Ohio, settled for a short time in Kentucky then returned to Fayette County, Pennsylvania.

15. Harbaugh, p. 157.

16. 1800 United States Census, population schedule, Gallipolis Township, Washington County, Territory Northwest of the River Ohio, unpaged, penned, 17th entry in column one and 18th entry in column two for William Davesson, digital image 1 of 3, *Ancestry* (https://www.ancestry.com : accessed June 2013), citing "Second Census of the United States, 1800." (NARA microfilm publication roll 1 of M1804, Records of the Bureau of the Census, Record Group 29, National Archives, Washington, D.C.). Certified 10 June 1800. Images reproduced by http://www.FamilySearch.org.

17. Harbaugh, p. 157.

18. *Tax Duplicate 1801*, "Ohio Tax Records, 1800-1850," page untitled and unnumbered, penned document, entry for William Davison, assessed in September 1801, digital image 20 of 59, *FamilySearch* (https://familysearch.org/ : accessed November 2012), citing Auditor, Gallipolis Township, Washington County, Ohio, Historical Society Library, Columbus; FHL microfilm 945,761.

19. *Hardesty 1882 and Lake 1887 (Combined)*, p. 214.

20. Arthur Ferguson, *The History of South Point Village*, not published, (printed by South Point Centennial Committee, Ohio, 1988), spiral bound, Chapter 2, (http://www.villageofsouthpoint.com : accessed 2007). See also, note 60 below.

21. James Patterson Lawyer, *History of Ohio*, Second Edition (Columbus, Ohio : Union Publishing Co, 1905), digital version, p. 97, *Google Books* (http://google.books.com : accessed April 2011).

22. Archer Butler Hulbert, *The Ohio River* (New York and London: G. P. Putnam's Sons, The Knickerbocker Press, 1906), p. 158, digital version, *Google Books* (http://books.google.com: accessed June 2011).

23. Lawyer, p. 95, provides the population in the Northwest Territory.

24. Hulbert, p. 8, travel time on the Ohio River.

25. Hulbert, p. 96, estimate by George Washington of travel time on the Ohio River.

26. Hulbert, p. 8, seasons of travel on the Ohio River.

27. Hulbert, p. 8, obstructions in the Ohio River.

Ohio

28. Hulbert, p. 17, types of obstructions in the Ohio River.

29. Hulbert, p. 139, start of keelboat traffic in 1783.

30. Hulbert, p. 139, size of flatboats.

31. Lawyer, pp. 96-97, size of flatboats.

32. Hulbert, p. 139, capacity of flatboats.

33. Hulbert, p. 158, capacity and cargo of flatboats.

34. Hulbert, pp. 139-140, description of flatboats.

35. Mrs. Ellet, *Pioneer Women of the West*, (New York: Charles Scribner, 1856), pp. 77-78, digital version, *Internet Archive* (http://www.archive.org : accessed November 2013).

36. Hulbert, p. 233, boat construction at Redstone Old Fort.

37. Hulbert, p. 139, steering the flatboat.

38. Hulbert, p. 234, steering the flatboat.

39. Hulbert, p. 140-142, attacks on the Ohio River.

40. Roy E. Vastine, *Scioto – A County History* (Portsmouth, OH.: Knuaff Graphics, 1986), print, 259 pages.

41. William Ely, *The Big Sandy Valley* (Catlettsburg, KY : Central Methodist, 1887), digital version, p. 6, *Internet Archive* (http://www.archive.org : accessed March 2014).

42. Evans, p. 1224, William-III first landed on the Kentucky side of the Ohio River.

43. "Obituary. Davidson. James Davidson.", *Ironton Register*, 10 January 1895.

44. Ferguson, Chapter 2.

45. Hulbert, p. 9, hunting grounds of the Indians.

46. Hulbert, p. 163, Indian land north and west of the Ohio River.

47. Ely, pp. 19-21, pioneer families established in 1798 near where Catlettsburg stands today.

48. Hulbert, p. 162, much land south of the Ohio River was settled before William-III and family arrived there.

49. William Davidson, "William Davidson's Estate," Register of Wills, Will books 1 and 2, Volume A, pp. 232-238, 295, dated 20 June 1810, proved 8 September 1812, Gallipolis, Gallia County, Ohio.

50. Ibid.

51. National Archives and Records Administration, Washington, D.C., Official Title Resolution Case opened by Bureau of Land Management, Kimberly L. Reed, Land Law Examiner, BLM-Eastern States, 7450 Boston Boulevard, Springfield, Virginia 22153, December 2011. This case was opened after it was learned that the purchase documentation for *Fractional Section 5* was not found. The BLM was notified by NARA that the land entry file, which should exist for William-III, was either damaged or destroyed before it could be archived.

52. U. S. Department of the Interior, Bureau of Land Management, General Land Office Records, "Land Patent Search," digital images, *Bureau of Land Management, General Land Office Records* (http://www.glorecords .blm.gov/default.aspx : accessed 2011), entry for William Davidson, accession CV-0009-001, Credit Volume Patent, Volume 9, p. 1.

53. Levi Whipple [surveyor], *Township Survey Plat Map of 1798*, Twp. Plats - OH, Ohio River Survey, R. 17, T. 1 & 2, Record group 49, dated November 1798, digital copy on compact disc, obtained 2012, National Archives and Records Administration, Special Media Archive Services Division (NWCS), Cartographic and Architectural Branch (NNSC), College Park, Maryland. Section 5 was subdivided in 1805 by Joseph Fletcher, surveyor. The actual acreage of *Fractional Section 5* was recorded as 242.98 acres. The surveyor's notes describe the section as, "Creek bottom and excellent wheat hills, tim[ber] oak, hickory, etc." Other types of trees in the area were poplar, spruce, and dogwood.

Ohio

54. C. Albert White, *A History of the Rectangular Survey System* (Washington, D.C.: U.S. Government Printing Office, 1983), pp. 12 & 29, digital version, *Google Books* (http://books.google.com : accessed November 2016).

55. Levi Whipple, *Township Survey Plat Map of 1798.*

56. William Davidson, "William Davidson's Estate."

57. Douglas E. Cade, PE, PS (Lawrence County Engineer), *Highway Map of Lawrence County, Ohio*, 2012.

58. National Archives and Records Administration, Suitland Reference Branch (WNRC), Credit Patent, Chillicothe Land Office, Credit Patents, Tract Book, *Fractional Section 5*, Township 1N, Range 17W, Ohio River Survey, p. 586, entry for William Davidson, photocopy of penned document obtained December 2011 referencing final certificate 1003 (land entry number), NARA, Suitland Reference Branch (WNRC), 4205 Suitland Road, Suitland, Maryland 20746. The Credit Act of May 10th 1800 also known as the Harrison Land Act of 1800, authorized the sale of land for no less than $2 per acre and could be paid in four installments. The buyer would deposit 5% of the purchase price plus survey fees, at the time of sale. Within 40 days he had to pay an additional 20 percent of the purchase money. Additional payments of 25 percent of the purchase price were to be made within two, three, and four years after the date of the sale. For the last three payments the purchaser was charged 6 percent interest per year. The GLO assigned William-III's patent accession number CV-0009-001 and call it a "Credit Volume Patent," a designation of where it is found in their records.

59. Knepper, pp.36-37.

60. *Hardesty 1882 and Lake 1887 (Combined)*, p. 215; also Arthur Ferguson, *The History of South Point Village*. Hardesty incorrectly lists "William W. Davidson" as the first settler in Perry Township in 1799.

61. *Hardesty 1882 and Lake 1887 (Combined)*, plates 39-41.

62. Harbaugh, p. 129, recorded that the Ohio parcel was purchased by William-III prior to his migration.

63. National Archives and Records Administration, Suitland Reference Branch (WNRC), Credit Patent, Chillicothe Land Office, Credit Patents, Tract Book, *Fractional Section 5*, Township 1N, Range 17W, Ohio River Survey, p. 586, entry

for William Davidson, photocopy of penned document obtained December 2011 referencing final certificate 1003 (land entry number), NARA, Suitland Reference Branch (WNRC), 4205 Suitland Road, Suitland, Maryland 20746.

64. Ferguson, Chapter 2.

65. Knepper, pp.40-41, locations of warrants for Revolutionary War military service.

66. U. S. Department of the Interior, Bureau of Land Management, General Land Office Records, "Land Patent Search," digital images, *Bureau of Land Management, General Land Office Records* (http://www.glorecords.blm.gov/default.aspx : accessed 2011), document 346, number 564, entry for William Davidson, et. al.

67. Howard H. Wehmann, "Revolutionary War Pension and Bounty – Land – Warrant Application Files: National Archives Microfilm Publications Pamphlet Describing M804," (National Archives and Records Service, General Services Administration, Washington: 1974), digital version, *National Archives* (http://www.archives.gov/ : accessed 2011), p. 2. This pamphlet documents that only disabled Revolutionary War veterans and widows of deceased veterans were eligible for pensions before 1818.

68. Lawyer, p. 97.

69. Hulbert, p. 233.

70. Ellet, pp. 77-78, describes use of lumber from flatboats and keelboats for cabins.

71. Harbaugh, p. 285.

72. 1800 United States Census, population schedule, penned, Gallipolis Township, Washington County, Territory Northwest of the River Ohio, unpaged, 17th entry in column one and 18th entry in column two for William Davesson, digital image 1 of 3, *Ancestry* (https://www.ancestry.com : accessed June 2013), citing "Second Census of the United States, 1800." (NARA microfilm publication roll 1 of M1804, Records of the Bureau of the Census, Record Group 29, National Archives, Washington, D.C.). Certified 10 June 1800. Images reproduced by http://www.FamilySearch.org.

Ohio

73. *Tax Duplicate 1801,* "Ohio Tax Records, 1800-1850," page untitled and unnumbered, penned document, entry for William Davison, assessed in September 1801, digital image 20 of 59, *FamilySearch* (https://familysearch.org/ : accessed November 2012), citing Auditor, Gallipolis Township, Washington County, Ohio, Historical Society Library, Columbus; FHL microfilm 945,761.

74. *Tax Duplicate 1802,* "Ohio Tax Records, 1800-1850," page untitled and unnumbered, penned document, entry for William Davison, assessed in September 1802, digital image 12 of 40, *FamilySearch* (https://familysearch.org/ : accessed November 2012), citing Gallipolis Township, Washington County, Ohio, Historical Society Library, Columbus; FHL microfilm 945,761.

75. Knepper, p. 37, Ohio was still a wilderness in 1820. Few roads existed causing many farmers to transport their produce by riverboats.

Final Years

I t may be recalled, that William and Barbara Davidson sold a portion of their *Dispute Ended* tract in Pennsylvania to Jonathan Ridge before leaving for Ohio in 1799.[1] Apparently, Mr. Ridge did not understand that it was customary in those days to allow six percent of the acreage for roads and general easements. In 1804, another indenture was created which states, "...the usual allowance of Six Acres p'cent was not comprehended agreeably to the Expectation or desire..." of Jonathan Ridge.[2] Although the boundaries were re-described, the revised document fails to offer new insight into the transaction. But, William-III travelled all the way back to Pennsylvania to sign the corrected indenture!

This would have been quite an inconvenient journey to fix someone else's mistake. But, perhaps William-III paid a visit to son

William "Ranger" Davidson

David, who had stayed behind and continued to farm the remaining portion of *Dispute Ended* that William-III still owned.[3]

One other interesting point of this document is the language in the indenture stating that William-III's "wife not being present by Reason of her removal to an inconvenient distance at present to become a party." William-III made this journey alone or at least without the company of Barbara. She apparently remained at home on *Fractional Section 5* in Ohio.

Another real estate transaction conducted about three years later caused William-III and Barbara to journey together back to Pennsylvania to sell the remaining 120 acre portion of *Dispute Ended* to their son David for the sum of $600. A receipt was produced for the full amount. William-III agreed to this transaction by signature, but Barbara's presence was evidenced by "her mark" (x) which also indicates that she could not write her name. This indenture, recorded on October 26, 1807, was significant since this event marked the end of William-III and Barbara's real estate holdings in Pennsylvania. Another observation is that throughout the body of this document the spelling "Davison" is consistently used, but in the lower section containing the signatures, their name is correctly spelled "Davidson."[4]

William-III received very nearly enough money in this transaction alone to pay the entire cost of *Fractional Section 5*. However, William-III's next payment on the Ohio parcel was not made until the scheduled date. His final cash payment was dated May 13, 1809. William-III's patent was dated 21 September 1810 for *Fractional Section 5*.[5]

Nearly all of the 1810 Federal Census for Ohio was lost in a fire. Although unfortunate, that document would not have provided any new or meaningful information. The 1810 Census only listed the head of household and counts, by number only, of the other family members broken down by age. William-III's presence in Lawrence County is already shown by other documents and the names of the family members are included in his will.

232

Final Years

In October 1811, the first steamboat sailed on the Ohio River and the keelboat began to fade from use.[6] It isn't known whether William-III saw the steamboat, but it would have been interesting to hear his opinion of the newfangled watercraft, with its chugging engine interrupting the quiet and its trail of billowing smoke and steam clouding the sky.

William-III died 16 November 1811, only four days before his 64th birthday.[7-10] He specified in his will that he was to be "intombed in a Decent and orderly manner with Such of my family as are intombed on my Home place." Respecting his last wishes, he was buried in a small cemetery on land he then owned.[11-13] The language from his will also tells us that by the time William-III died, a family cemetery had already been established on his farm.

Evans reported that William-III and Barbara Davidson were buried at the "Old South Point" cemetery. According to Evans, William-III was "buried with his wife, Barbara, at South Point, Ohio, where the inscriptions on their tombstones can yet be easily read."[14] Evans's work was published in 1903.

Ferguson places the cemetery of William-III, his wife, and a "handful of other pioneers," whose names Ferguson did not reveal, "between today's Ferry and Elm Streets with Old 52 on the hillside and the river on the other. High river water and a deepening ditch created 'the hollow' which washed away all but a few graves. As late as the 1930's numerous tombstones still stood." According to Ferguson, periodic flooding of the Ohio River and erosion washed away all traces of the cemetery between 1930 and 1941.[15]

Ferguson goes on to report that "a great-great grandson of Ranger Davidson, Howard T. Ferguson, found the pioneer's" headstone "in the hollow during a search..." This remarkable discovery was coincidentally made just in time for the family reunion during which a monument was dedicated to William-III. Surprisingly and disappointingly, what was engraved on the stone was not divulged by Ferguson. Its general condition was described as being "covered in river silt." This would have occurred in 1941.[16]

William "Ranger" Davidson

If the stone was readable, why didn't Evans, Ferguson, or anyone else, record what it said? If the stone was not readable, then how was it identified with William-III? The recovery of the original headstone would have been rather significant. Harbaugh mentions the lost graveyard, but not the headstone. It seems likely, given the extent of her research, had the stone's recovery been authentic, Harbaugh would have included it in her work, published in 1949. However, this detail was also omitted by Harbaugh.

How unfortunate for us today, and all hereafter, knowing as many as three different persons published information regarding the cemetery and at least two persons saw William-III's tombstone, yet failed to report perhaps the single most important information about it: the inscription! It would seem that persons so devoted to the events of history, and also finding particular interest in William-III, would have taken great pride and care in preserving for future generations what was very nearly lost forever. However, other evidence came to light after further extensive research.

Fortunately for many researchers, members of the Daughters of the American Revolution (DAR) launched a campaign to identify the locations of the graves of Revolutionary War soldiers and to record abstracts of their headstones. This information was recorded in the order it was reported to the DAR (i.e. randomly) by many volunteers working for decades to capture whatever information was available. Readers are here referred to the work of Patricia Law Hatcher, who created an index to these grave abstracts in a four volume set of published books. Hatcher cautions that the information in the abstracts was not proofed, meaning that these records could contain errors and should be supported by other records whenever possible.[17]

The entire entry recorded in the index for William-III reads as follows: *Davidson, William. Bapt. Cem. South Point, O. 43.* This means that an extract of William-III's headstone was created in 1943 by the DAR and that William-III's grave was located at a Baptist Cemetery in South Point, Ohio. From the index, the volume number and chapter of the extract were sent along with a request to the DAR in Washington, D.C.

where the contents of the entry are stored. The DAR response was timely. The results in the record were disappointing.

The extract gives the correct year of death for William-III as 1811. However, his birth year is recorded as 1711, which would make William-III one hundred years old when he died! Using this birth year, he would have served in the Revolutionary War at age 68, which is also improbable. This record references the same two records pertaining to William-III's service in the Revolutionary War that were also cited by Harbaugh from the Pennsylvania Archives, Series 5, Volume IV. There can be little doubt that Harbaugh's work was used when compiling this DAR record.

The DAR abstract indicates that William-III's grave was located at a "Bapt. Cem." Which was thought to be a reference to the nearby First Baptist Church where the memorial to William-III has stood since it was erected in 1941. It was therefore thought that perhaps the headstone was moved to this church in South Point. However, a graveyard does not adjoin the First Baptist Church. It is now thought that the information recorded by the DAR came from William-III's memorial rather than his headstone. This would jibe with the reference to the Baptist Church. The incorrect birth year in the DAR abstract is a typographical error.

As a side note, there is no evidence that William-III was a Baptist, but many of his descendants probably were, which would explain the location of the monument on the old First Baptist Church property. If anything, William-III would most likely have been Presbyterian as was his father. It would seem though, judging from the records, that William-III was perhaps not as attached to faith as was his father, Lewis-I. It will be remembered that Lewis-I, sons Jeremiah and Thomas, as well as stepson, William Conwell, and their wives were members of the Dunlap's Creek Presbyterian Church in Pennsylvania, but William-III is not listed as a member. Lewis-I also includes a respectful reference to God in his last will, but there is no equivalent reference in William-III's final document. In any case, the location of the monument on the First Baptist Church lot is fitting since, as

William "Ranger" Davidson

Ferguson says, it overlooks the land and cemetery where William-III lived and was ultimately laid to rest.

In conjunction with this present work, the services of an amateur genealogist, who resided near South Point, was acquired in 2011 to look for the headstone. Some inquiries were made with a few First Baptist Church members, and a limited physical search was conducted for the headstone without success. Subsequently, contact was made with a member of the Lawrence County chapter of the Ohio Genealogical Society. This contact also reported no knowledge as to the whereabouts of the headstone. A few additional phone messages were left for local residents, possibly having some knowledge of the marker, but these persons failed to respond. All attempts to inspire interest in this topic failed to generate any traction.

Born in part from curiosity and in part from frustration, this author launched a personal effort to locate William-III's headstone. The Village of South Point and the surrounding area were visited and inquiries were made in August 2013.

Before proceeding, the reader must be informed as to the fate of many cemeteries in this region of the country. In the early 19th century, there were few, if any, laws governing burials. Many early resident pioneers were simply buried on their own land, just as were William-III and Barbara Davidson and countless others. Over the following decades, the larger tracts of pioneer farm land were carved up, subdivided, sold, and buildings sprang up around these homegrown burial grounds. In the absence of caretakers, many of the markers became scattered, overtaken by vegetation, and were eventually lost. Today some headstones appear in the yards of ordinary homes where they receive inconsistent degrees of interest and varying levels of care or abandon.

Beginning with Ferguson's description, the "Old Pioneer Cemetery" in South Point could be placed within a village block bounded by 2nd Street West, Ferry Street, 4th Street West, and Elm Street. Ferguson's location was accurate, but not precise enough to enable a single person ground search. More research was successfully

236

conducted at the Hamner Room in the Briggs-Lawrence County Public Library in Ironton where a single document of interest was located. This document by Bruce & Stevens, which amounts to an inventory of headstones, indicated that the cemetery was located behind the South Point Police Department.[18] A quick check of the map revealed that the police station was not within the block specified by Ferguson, but it was thought that perhaps the stone had been relocated there since its apparent recovery in 1941.

In discussing this mission with the library staff, the author was fortunate to acquire the interest of a local volunteer dedicated to making contributions to findagrave.com. This volunteer kindly offered to show the way and to assist in locating the lost cemetery and the missing headstone. Without delay, we set off to the South Point Police Station where we were greeted by fenced lots on which sat a bulk of heavy machinery and equipment, the only open space adjoining the police building. It was soon learned from South Point Police that the location of interest was likely where the old police station formerly stood, but was razed some years prior. The former location was at the corner of Ferry Street and 2nd Street West. This revised location was found to be inside Ferguson's boundary!

If standing at the corner of Ferry Street and 2nd Street West, the remaining grave markers were found almost due north, but slightly west of the vacant lot where the old police station once stood. The location is very nearly dead center in the block circumscribed by Ferguson.

The lost cemetery was found to be located in the backyard of a private residence. Once permission was obtained to enter the area, a search was physically conducted. Almost immediately, three headstones were found atop a grass covered mound from which a small mimosa tree stood along the southwest border of the property. These stones were covered in mud, moss, and other debris and had to be carefully cleaned so their inscriptions could be read. Two of the three remaining headstones found at the site were consistent with those on the inventory of headstones found at the library.[19] This confirmed the location of the old Davidson family cemetery and also validated the inscriptions recorded by the preparers of the document, Bruce & Stevens. Disappointingly, William-III's headstone was not found and must now be presumed lost, yet again.

A low area adjacent to the headstones was observed, which was surrounded by chain-link fence and very densely overgrown with small trees, vines, and other vegetation. This is now thought to be the "hollow" described by Ferguson. Without the appropriate tools, manpower, and permissions, a more thorough search could not be conducted during the short research trip then enjoyed.

Ferguson indicated that erosion and flooding washed away all traces of the cemetery, but since Ferguson's research, some of the headstones have been recovered. Although the stones were there, they had been moved and no longer mark the precise locations of the fallen. The remains of William-III, Barbara, and several others, whose names have been lost with the floods, may yet reside beneath the hollow, but it is also possible they were carried away and lie beneath the muddy bottom of the soupy Ohio River, long since scattered in the violent tossing of high flood waters.

On the brighter side, the inventory of headstones includes the inscription of William-III's marker which is presented here for the first time in print, outside of the inventory created by Bruce & Stevens.[20] William-III's headstone reportedly read:

Wm. Davidson
Died Nov. 1, 1811
Aged 63 Yrs. 11 mos.
26 dys.

Although his actual headstone was not located, the original inscription was finally found. From this information, William-III's birth and death dates are confirmed. Using his age, his birthdate may be calculated to about 5 November 1747. This is reasonably close to the 20 November 1747 birthdate given by descendants.

However, the date of death as recorded on the inventory is different from that given previously of November 16, 1811. Interestingly, if the age is used to calculate William-III's birthdate from the 16th rather than the 1st, then his calculated birthdate equals 20 November 1747 in perfect agreement with the date given by descendants. It is now thought that either the second digit of the date on the headstone was unreadable when Bruce & Stevens saw it or a typographical error was made when typing the inventory. In any case, it should be remembered that calculated dates are only an approximation and the results may vary depending upon the method of calculation used. The corrected version of the headstone would be:

Wm. Davidson
Died Nov. 16, 1811
Aged 63 Yrs. 11 mos.
26 dys.

It is notable that the work of Bruce & Stevens is the only surviving record of the inscription from William-III's headstone by eyewitnesses. All researchers interested in William-III owe a debt of gratitude to these men; especially considering that the headstone has once again been lost. This record is crucial because without it, some of the most basic and important details regarding William-III could not have been verified: his birth and death dates.

Fortunately, William-III left a last will.[21] Harbaugh presented a transcript of this document entitled *William Davidson's Estate*, but did not include the list of possessions belonging to William-III that was also made part of the public record. Interestingly, these items yield several clues regarding the way he and Barbara lived their lives.

As expected, a variety of farming tools and common household items are included, along with some other items, the purpose for which have fallen into obscurity. But, also included in his possessions are found the tools of a true pioneer who was accustomed to self-sufficiency in a frontier setting.

William "Ranger" Davidson

When the inventory was taken, William-III and Barbara owned 15 hogs, four cows and a calf, five heifers, one steer and two sheep. Judging by this small quantity of livestock, we may suppose that William-III was primarily a crop farmer, but the family also had a supply of beef, milk, and bacon that would exceed their needs. Nearly all farmers of that era owned some chickens, although they were omitted from the inventory, it is pretty safe to presume that several routinely scurried around the Davidson farm.

Other livestock included a young 3-year old sorrel stud horse and a 2-year old brown filly. Also included in the list of possessions was a half bushel of horse shoes, so it appears that William-III was also his own blacksmith. Throw in a trammel and this information seems to tell us that William-III was also in the business of breeding horses.[22]

They owned two sheep from which wool would be harvested and spun into yarn on their spinning wheel. They owned a flax hackle, used in making thread from the plant fibers and a loom for weaving cloth and warping bars for making blankets, rugs, and clothing. They owned a shoemaker's toolkit necessary for making and repairing shoes. They had deer skins for making leather moccasins, boots, and other articles of clothing. A flat iron was perhaps used to make his great coat, straight coat, and waist coat presentable for formal occasions. He also owned a pocket book or wallet.

Among the kitchen and cooking items was a churn for making butter and a coffee mill for grinding their morning brew. In the kitchen was found a baking oven, tea kettles, various pots and pans, knives and forks, and ladles. Among the household items were dressers, beds and bedding, tables and chairs, and a chest.

Tools for building and repairing a cabin such as a draw knife, saws, axes, a log chain, and a luting box for mixing and holding the chinking clay were listed. They had several panes of glass for replacing broken windows and the molds for making their own candles, either from sheep tallow or possibly beeswax when available. They also owned the tools to make their own buckets, tubs, and barrels (cooper's adze, compasses, saws, frow, augers). Their farming tools included two ploughs (plows) with double trees, a harrow, a hoe, shovels, and sickles. Also, the horse gears, described in the previous chapter, and hatter chains (probably used with the horse gears). They also had a stone hammer, chisels, and a mill pick; did William-III have a go at mining?

For hunting, self-defense, and travel, they owned a wagon, a handgun with accoutrements, bullet bands, saddle, and locking saddlebags. His horse was a bright bay he affectionately called Fox. Whether the name of his horse is insight into William-III's character or the personality found in his horse we are left to ponder. Bays are dark red to mahogany brown with black legs, mane, tail and muzzle.

Also among their possessions were some fish hooks, which they no doubt cast into the Ohio River while strolling on the mile long shoreline that bordered their southern boundary.

Perhaps one of the more surprising items of interest was William-III's collection of 20 books. This would have been quite a library for a farmer in the first decade of the 1800's. From this we may ascertain that William-III was educated and an avid reader for his day. It would have been extremely interesting to know the titles, but unfortunately they were not recorded.

One of the more curious things perhaps many descendants wonder about is William-III's appearance. Unfortunately, he perished long before the camera came into common usage, and no known oil painting of his likeness exists. Being on the frontier for so many years, it seems likely that he had a beard. However, his list of possessions does include a razor which was stored in a box. This would have been an early straight razor. It is not now possible to say whether it was in regular use, only used for touch-ups, or had long since fallen into disuse.

No one could presume to understand the disparity found in the will regarding the bequests William-III left. The first five children, fathered with Rosanna, were to receive considerably less than the younger ten children. Any number of possible reasons could be cited, but one might hazard to guess it was because these children were considerably older, better established, and had already received assistance from their father during his lifetime.

The first five children received only $1.00 each, except John, the oldest, who was to receive $30. But, for John's bequest, William-III adds "…if not paid in my Life" which sounds as though William-III is repaying an old debt, rather than gifting an inheritance.

His land, *Fractional Section 5*, was to be evenly divided among his five youngest sons "at the death or marriage of their mother." When William-III died, four of the five youngest sons were under the age of 18 years. His youngest daughter, Cynthia was only about two years old when William-III died. Readers are encouraged to review the entire will and list of possessions included in the appendix.

BARBARA DAVIDSON. As with William-III, Evans reported that Barbara's tombstone could be easily read in 1903, but failed to provide the inscription.[23] The now lost headstone is thought to be the unnamed source of her birthdate, presumably preserved by descendants, and given by Harbaugh as 8 January 1768.[24] No further information regarding Barbara's headstone or its inscription was found.

Harbaugh further provided the year in which Barbara and William-III were married, about 1784.[25] This means Barbara was only about 16 years old at the time and she was 21 years younger than her husband. When they were married, Barbara was only two years older than William-III's first son, John! It must also be remembered that in those times it was difficult for pioneers of both genders to find a spouse and marriages having such age differences was not uncommon.

William-III and Barbara's first child, Margaret, was born 29 November 1785. From then, they continued to be blessed with children increasing their number about every two to three years, until William-III died in 1811, with five daughters and five sons. On every occasion William-III refers to Barbara in his last will, he affectionately refers to her as his "beloved wife" (four times).

As a frontier wife and mother, Barbara played an important role in supporting the family. She guarded their home and ran the farm when William-III was away, and provided for the protection and safety of their children while William-III was working in the fields. The life of a frontier wife was frequently dangerous and most women living in the wilderness knew how to load and shoot the firearms of the day.

Most days were consumed with tedious and physically demanding tasks. Every meal had to be prepared from scratch and frequently, it was the wife who dressed and prepared fresh game for meals.

Based upon the items listed in William-III's will, we may surmise that Barbara spun wool into yarn and wove flax into cloth and likely made clothes for the entire family. The men wore leather breeches and hunting shirts from buckskin, linen, or other available fabric. Hunting shirts were generally long, hanging below the waist sometimes reaching to mid-thigh and were usually the pullover type with long sleeves and a collar with a leather thong that could be drawn close at the neck. Shoes were commonly moccasins of buffalo hide or leather. Hats were generally made from fur. The ladies wore long dresses of cloth, sometimes bleached white.[26] The woman's saddle found among the inventory of their possessions when William-III died, indicates that Barbara could ride a horse, another necessity of frontier life for the lady of the house.

It was generally the responsibility of the wife and children to maintain a small garden for personal consumption near the cabin. The vegetables harvested from this important supply of victuals was augmented with roasted or boiled bear meat, venison, goose, turkey, pheasant, fish, and other types of available game. A variety of cornbread called "Johnnycake" or "Journeycake" was made from corn meal which was hand ground using a mortar. This may have been brushed with butter made in their churn. It was also common to collect wild honey and berries.[27]

Unfortunately, few records survive that would tell us more of Barbara's later years. However, we may safely say that Barbara continued to reside on *Fractional Section 5* for nearly 20 years after William-III's death and that she never remarried. These conclusions are based in part upon the timing of a law suit brought to court after Barbara died (see the later chapter *Subsequent Events*), and also in part on the fact that she is found listed in two subsequent census records confirming her place of residence and that her surname remained unchanged.

As stated previously, the 1810 Census for Gallia County was lost in a fire. However, Barbara Davidson is found listed as a head of household in both the 1820 and 1830 Federal Census records in Fayette Township, Lawrence County, Ohio. Unfortunately, both these documents list Barbara in name only.[28,29] However, they do provide a breakdown of the ages of persons found in the household.

It was not possible to reconcile the head counts given in the 1820 census. The numerations do not correspond to the children based upon their ages as they were recorded. It is probable that extended family members were residing with Barbara at the time these records were made.

1820 Census:
1 male between 16 and 18;
1 male between 26 and 45;
1 female under 10;
1 female 45 and older (Barbara);
1 person engaged in agriculture (Barbara).

In contrast, the 1830 census includes Barbara herself (between 60 and 70), and possibly daughter Cynthia (between 20 and 30). Also included is one male under age 5 whose identity remains unknown, but was likely a grandson.

The inventory of possessions listed in William-III's last will became Barbara's for the next twenty years of her life. She would use those things as she needed them and surely sold or gave away certain items, desired by, or needed by, her children. With so many family members and descendants living nearby, she was assuredly well attended by a large support group.

If we presume that William-III did not sell any of his *Fractional Section 5* parcel during his life, then he had 242.99 acres when he died in

Final Years

1811.[30] When Barbara died in 1831, she was in possession of only 52 acres, today located in South Point. During her remaining years, she had apparently sold or gifted nearly 200 acres of land, presumably to augment or finance her retirement needs.

Barbara (sometimes spelled Barbary, the likely pronunciation in the local vernacular of the era) died on 18 October 1831 just a few months prior to her 64th birthday. She was reportedly buried alongside William-III in the "old pioneer cemetery" previously discussed in detail.[31-34] This of course means that her headstone, along with her remains, have been lost to neglect and the inevitable forces of nature.

The name "old pioneer cemetery," and most of the other references used to describe it, are distastefully generic in the viewpoint of this author. The cemetery was on the property of the Davidson family farm, established by William-III, where Davidson, McKee, and other family members were laid to rest. Just as others took the liberty of making up a name, this author would propose this location to be respectfully referred to as the *First Davidson Cemetery*.[35]

1. Fayette County, Recorder of Deeds, Deed Book C: 1265-1266, "William Davidson to Jonathan Ridge," dated 30 March 1799, recorded 13 May 1799, photocopy of penned document, Uniontown, Pennsylvania.

2. Fayette County, Recorder of Deeds, Deed Book F: 5, William Davidson to Jonathan Ridge, untitled, corrected deed, dated 22 February 1804, recorded 11 May 1804, photocopy of penned document, Uniontown, Pennsylvania.

3. David Davidson established a steam powered ferry on *Dispute Ended* that took passengers across the Monongahela River. The location was confirmed, but it is uncertain whether this David was William-III's son or a later descendant.

4. Fayette County, Recorder of Deeds, Deed Book F: 197, William Davidson to David Davidson, untitled, dated 4 May 1807, recorded 26 October 1807, photocopy of penned document, Uniontown, Pennsylvania.

5.   National Archives and Records Administration, Suitland Reference Branch (WNRC), Credit Patent, Chillicothe Land Office, Tract Book, Fractional Section 5, Township 1N, Range 17W, Ohio River Survey, p. 586, entry for William Davidson, photocopy of penned document obtained December 2011 referencing final certificate 1003 (land entry number), NARA, 4205 Suitland Road, Suitland, Maryland 20746.

From this tract book entry it was learned that the tract was estimated to contain 263.69 acres but actually consisted of 242.99 acres for which William-III paid $2 per acre plus fees and interest. The purchase date (first payment) was made 12 May 1804, the final payment was made 13 May 1809. William-III paid a total of $621.98, in three cash payments and received a patent dated 21 September 1810 (NARA entry date). According to NARA, the records that should comprise the land entry file were damaged or destroyed before they could be archived and no longer exist.

The tract was a partial section located in the southwestern portion of Fayette Township, Lawrence County, Ohio. The parcel was bounded on the south by the Ohio River. William-III called this parcel his *Fractional Section 5*.

6.   James Patterson Lawyer, *History of Ohio*, Second Edition (Columbus, Ohio : Union Publishing Co, 1905), digital version, p. 134, *Google Books* (http://google.books.com : accessed April 2011).

7.   Arthur Ferguson, *The History of South Point Village*, not published, (printed by South Point Centennial Committee, Ohio, 1988), spiral bound, Chapter 2, (http://www.villageofsouthpoint.com : accessed 2007).

8.   Elizabeth Davidson Harbaugh, *The Davidson Genealogy* (Ironton, Ohio : self-published, 1948; Ann Arbor, Michigan : Lithoprinted, Edwards Brothers, Inc., 1949), p. 129, print, OCLC: 23167553.

9.   *Atlas of Lawrence County, Ohio, Hardesty 1882 and Lake 1887 (Combined)*, 1st edition reprint (Ironton, Ohio: Lawrence County Historical Society, 1985), "Rev. William W. Davidson," p. 27.

10.   *Commemorative Biographical Record of the Counties of Harrison and Carroll, Ohio* (Chicago: J. H. Beers & Co., 1891), article: "Lewis H. Davidson," pp. 446-453, *Google Books* (http://books.google.com : accessed April 2013).

11.   Harbaugh, p. 129.

12. Ferguson, Chapter 2.

13. *Fayette Township Cemeteries*, not published, hardbound (black cover), Briggs-Lawrence County Public Library, Hamner Room, 321 S 4th St, Ironton, OH 45638; Call number: REF 977.188 Fa; p. FA-4, entry by Bruce and Stevens, undated.

14. Nelson W. Evans, *History of Scioto County, Ohio* (Portsmouth, Ohio: Self-published, 1903), reprint (Markham, Virginia: The Apple Manor Press), Part 5, p. 1224.

15. Ferguson, Chapter 2.

16. Ibid.

17. Patricia Law Hatcher, *Abstract of Graves of Revolutionary Patriots*, Vol. 1 (A-D), (Westminster, Maryland: Pioneer Heritage Press, 2007), print, p. 236.

18. *Fayette Township Cemeteries*, Bruce and Stevens.

19. The two headstones found at the cemetery site, as listed by Bruce & Stevens, were James B. Davidson, d. 19 Aug 1832; and Lewis McKee, d. 17 Jan 1855.

20. *Fayette Township Cemeteries*, Bruce and Stevens.

21. William Davidson, "William Davidson's Estate," Register of Wills, Will books 1 and 2, Volume A, pp. 232-238, 295, dated 20 June 1810, proved 8 September 1812, Gallipolis, Gallia County, Ohio.

22. A trammel is a type of fetter or shackle, attached to the lower legs that restrict movement and were used to train a horse to amble or walk slowly.

23. Evans, p. 1224.

24. Harbaugh, p. 249.

25. Harbaugh, p. 249, the marriage year for William-III and Barbara McDowell was possibly calculated based upon the birthdate of their first child in 1785.

26. William Ely, *The Big Sandy Valley* (Central Methodist: Catlettsburg, Ky, 1887), digital version, p. 13, *Internet Archive* (http://www.archive.org : accessed September 2013).

27. Ely, p. 14, food of the pioneers.

28. 1820 United States Census, population schedule, penned, Fayette Township, penned vertically in margin, Lawrence County, Ohio, unpaged, eighth entry for Barbara Davidson, digital image 2 of 3, *FamilySearch* (https://familysearch.org : accessed September 2012), citing NARA microfilm publication M33, (Washington D.C.: National Archives and Records Administration, n.d.).

29. 1830 United States Census, population schedule, penned, Fayette Township, Lawrence County, Ohio, p. 315, tenth entry for Barbary Davidson, digital image 3 of 8, *FamilySearch* (https://familysearch.org : accessed September 2012), citing NARA microfilm publication M19, (Washington D.C.: National Archives and Records Administration, n.d.).

30. National Archives and Records Administration, Suitland Reference Branch (WNRC), Credit Patent, Chillicothe Land Office, Tract Book, Fractional Section 5, Township 1N, Range 17W, Ohio River Survey, p. 586, entry for William Davidson, photocopy of penned document obtained December 2011 referencing final certificate 1003 (land entry number), NARA, 4205 Suitland Road, Suitland, Maryland 20746.

31. Evans (1903), p. 1224. Death date and burial location of Barbara Davidson.

32. Harbaugh (1949), p. 249, death date of Barbara Davidson.

33. Ferguson, Chapter 2.

34. Hardesty (1882), p. 27, death date of Barbara McDowell-Davidson.

35. This name would further serve to distinguish the *First Davidson Cemetery* established by William-III, from a second cemetery frequently referenced as the *Davidson Cemetery*, located at North Kenova Road and North Meadow Lane in South Point. A third cemetery nearby that may be of interest is the *White Cottage Cemetery* situated at the corner of North Kenova Road and Solida Road (at the northeast boundary of *Fractional Section 5*). All three cemeteries lie in *Fractional Section 5*.

– 12 –

Subsequent Events

In June 1832, a law suit was brought to the Court of Common Pleas, in Ironton, Lawrence County, Ohio, involving one of William-III and Barbara's daughters, Sarah Davidson. In 1803, Sarah had married another early resident of Lawrence County, a man named William McKee who apparently led the proceedings against his father-in-law's estate since he is first named in the suit.[1]

William-III had died in 1811, so the question immediately arises as to why the legal battle did not commence until more than twenty years after his death. According to William-III's last will, title to his land was to be given to Barbara until such time that she might marry again or until her death.[2] We know from the records that Barbara never remarried, so she enjoyed possession of the land until she died in

October 1831.[3-5] It was following the death of Barbara that William-III's land would be divided among their children.

The will further stipulated that each of William-III's five youngest sons were to receive one fifth part of the land. This did not occur because one them, Jesse, died in 1814 at the young age of eleven years.[6]

Not all the documents surrounding this legal battle were found, however the gist of the argument could be gleaned from one surviving instrument recorded in the form of a deed.[7] It seems the heirs felt that since Jesse had died prior to receiving his inheritance, and possibly because some of the land had already been sold, the remainder could no longer be divided fairly. Also, the land was appraised, but the heirs disagreed as to the value returned in the appraisal.

Although these outwardly seem to be arguable complaints, the will specifies that the land was to go to William-III's five sons, explicitly named in the will. However, Sarah, the party bringing suit, was obviously a daughter, not a son. This issue raises the question as to the legal basis for the argument. Unfortunately the rationale was not presented in the single surviving document describing these events.

In the end, the judge ordered the land to be auctioned to the highest bidder and the funds to be subsequently divided evenly among not just the surviving sons, but all the surviving heirs. The sheriff, Charles Wilgus, held the public auction on 21 April 1833.[8] One of the originally named heirs won the auction and paid $440 for the 52-acre tract of land which title went to William W. Davidson (William-IV).[9] Interestingly, through a clerical error on the part of the sheriff, William-IV did not receive his deed until October 1848, which finally brought the legal issues to a close.[10-15]

William-III died and was buried in Gallia County. His *Fractional Section 5* became a part of Fayette Township when Lawrence County was formed in December 1815. This means that Barbara died in Lawrence County, even though she didn't relocate.

Although many sources reference South Point when discussing William-III, in most cases, this is a matter of convenience. Actually, South Point wasn't formed until 1853 when William-III's son, William-

IV, divided the remainder of his father's land, some of which he purchased at the auction from the law suit. The parcels were carved into lots and were sold for about $170 each.[16-18] These were laid out to form the Village of South Point, 42 years after William-III was buried!

Ferguson recorded that "floods and erosion" washed away all traces of the "old pioneer cemetery" by 1941.[19] The severity of the flooding and erosion may be exemplified by the fact that South Point's streets, those that run parallel with the Ohio River, today begin with 2nd Street.[20] The old river bank, as William-III saw it, along with Front Street (called the Old River Road by Ferguson) have been washed away! In the flood of 1937, the river water rose as high as Highway 52, which covered the area in which William-III's cabin stood and also the cemetery in which he and Barbara and others were buried.[21]

A group of descendants of William-III gathered in South Point in 1941 and unveiled a monument commemorating his service as a "Ranger" in the Revolutionary War and as a pioneer of Lawrence County.[22,23] His monument is located at Old 52 (4th Street West) and Solida Road (County Road 18) at the north end of Ferry Street.

The rough stone monument stands upright in the ground, bearing a rectangular bronze plaque affixed by screws. According to Ferguson, the monument is located:

> ...on the corner of the First Baptist Church lot which overlooks the time-erased pioneer cemetery where the 'Ranger' was buried. The monument was purchased and dedicated by the captain James Lawrence Chapter of the Daughters of the American Revolution and was installed by Pearl G. and Dick Davidson, great-grandson and great-great-grandson respectively, of the Ranger. During the ceremonies, Mary (Molly) Davidson Ferguson, granddaughter of the Ranger, was honored as the last remaining grandchild of an American Revolutionary War veteran in Lawrence County.[24]

William "Ranger" Davidson

The plaque inscription reads as follows:

In remembrance of
William Davidson
1747 – 1811
Revolutionary Soldier
First Settler in Fayette Township
Erected by his Descendants
Dedicated by
Capt. James Lawrence Chapter, DAR

A second monument in honor of William-III was added in 1988 in the Village Park during the Village Government's Centennial celebration. This monument appears as a rectangular stone tablet, about six inches thick, and engraved. This stone is located beneath a flagpole in the park near the playground. It is akin to a replacement gravestone and reads:

IN MEMORY OF OUR FOUNDER
WILLIAM RANGER DAVIDSON
1747 ——— 1811
REVOLUTIONARY WAR VETERAN

The well intentioned and noble effort on the part of the local historians to memorialize William-III in this way is touching and only praise should be offered for this generous donation. However, it should be remembered that the nickname "Ranger" was coined by Harbaugh nearly 130 years after William Davidson died.

Subsequent Events

1. Elizabeth Davidson Harbaugh, *The Davidson Genealogy* (Ironton, Ohio: self-published, 1948; Ann Arbor, Michigan : Lithoprinted, Edwards Brothers, Inc., 1949), p. 258, print, OCLC: 23167553.

2. William Davidson, "William Davidson's Estate," Register of Wills, Will books 1 and 2, Volume A, pp. 232-238, 295, dated 20 June 1810, proved 8 September 1812, recorded 5 April 1813, Gallipolis, Gallia County, Ohio.

3. 1820 United States Federal Census, population schedule, penned, Fayette Township, penned vertically in margin, Lawrence County, Ohio, unpaged, 8th entry for Barbara Davidson, digital image 2 of 3, *FamilySearch* (https://familysearch.org : accessed September 2012), citing NARA microfilm publication M33, (Washington D.C.: National Archives and Records Administration, n.d.).

4. 1830 United States Census, population schedule, penned, Fayette Township, Lawrence County, Ohio, p. 315, tenth entry for Barbary Davidson, digital image 3 of 8, *FamilySearch* (https://familysearch.org : accessed September 2012), citing NARA microfilm publication M19, (Washington D.C.: National Archives and Records Administration, n.d.).

5. Harbaugh, p. 249, death and burial of Barbara McDowell at South Point, Fayette Township, Lawrence County, Ohio, on 18 October 1831.

6. Harbaugh, p. 284, death of Jesse Davidson at South Point, Fayette Township, Lawrence County, Ohio, on 14 February 1814.

7. Lawrence County, Ohio, Recorder's Office, Deed Book 14: 302, Deed "Heirs of Jesse Davidson, Joshua Hambleton, Sheriff to William W. Davidson," 30 October 1848, recorded 26 April 1853, digital copy obtained August 2013, Lawrence County Courthouse, Ironton, Ohio. William McKee and Sarah (Davidson) his wife brought suit against the heirs of Jesse Davidson, deceased.

8. Ibid.

9. Ibid.

10. Ibid.

William "Ranger" Davidson

11. Ruth Bowers and Anita Short, *Gateway to the West*, Volume I (Baltimore, MD: Genealogical Publishing Co., 1989), p. 486, Library of Congress No. 88-82636; ISBN 0-8063-1237-8, located at the Genealogical and Historical Library, Bartow, FL in 2007. This record was abstracted from what is now known as Will Estate and Guardianship Book 1 & 2 as found in the Probate Court of Gallia County, the period of 1803-1815. This entry corresponds to the date of the will (20 June 1810) and lists the names of the fourteen surviving children of William Davidson (Rose was deceased).

12. William Davidson, "William Davidson's Estate," p. 295. The inventory of William-III's possessions was conducted 2 May 1813. On 5 September 1814, Barbara Davidson, Abraham Davidson (son), and Joseph Davidson (nephew) acknowledged their probate surety bond of $800 and they were recognized by the court as the official executrix and executors of the estate. Presumably, shortly afterward they began administering their duties by distributing the bequests recorded in the will.

13. Karen Mauer Green, *Pioneer Ohio Newspapers 1802 – 1818 Genealogical and Historical Abstracts* (Galveston: The Frontier Press, 1988), article transcribed from *The Scioto Gazette*, Volume XIII, No. 725, Monday, January 30, 1815, ISBN 0-932231-04-7, located at the Genealogical and Historical Library, Bartow, Florida in 2006. This source references a law suit in the venue of Gallipolis, Gallia County, Court of Common Pleas, entitled "Abraham A. M. Davidson vs. Thomas Davidson, Wm. Davidson, Joseph Davidson, John Davidson, David Davidson, Lewis Davidson, Cynthia Davidson, Alexander Courtney [*sic*] and Comfort his wife, Mordecai Williams and Mary his wife, John Francis and Peggy his wife, Wm. Lynn and Betsey [*sic*] his wife, and William M'Kee [*sic*] and Sarah his wife. All are heirs of William Davidson, late of Gallia County, dec'd." Only thirteen of the children were named because both Rose and Jesse were deceased. The nature of this case was not discovered; the Gallia County Genealogical Society indicated that the records could not be found at the courthouse. Given the timing, this may have been a settlement hearing in which the executrix and executors reported completion of their duties and were likely released from their administrative responsibilities by the court.

14. The deed, dated 30 October 1848, listed the parties to a law suit dated 30 June 1832, brought by William and Sarah [Davidson] McKee. Listed are "Abraham D. Davidson, William W. Davidson, Morris Davidson, Joseph Davidson, Peggy, wife of John R. Francis, Cynthia wife Jonathan Croly, Betty, wife of William Lynd, William Davidson, James Davidson, John Davidson, Joseph Davidson, Jeremiah Davidson, Jane, wife of Thomas Ker, Cynthia or Polly wife of Jacob

Subsequent Events

Synoch, Polly wife of Mordicai Williams, Comfort wife of Alexander McCartney, Lewis Davidson, and the heirs of David Davidson number and names unknown." So it appears that William McKee had to wait more than 20 years following the death of William-III to engage in a legal battle over the estate, yet still did so. If the $440 received from the auction was divided among at least the 18 persons named, then they each would have received only about $24 from which any legal, court, and auction fees would also be subtracted. It seems the squabble was hardly worth the time and effort that was put into it.

15. It appears the remaining land consisted of two separate parcels, neither of which were legally described. However, reference is made to "lot number 2" which must have contained about 10 acres since it is designated as the "fifth part included in the same" 52 acres owned by the estate. All the property fell inside William-III's original *Fractional Section 5* (S5-T1N-R17W).

16. "South Point," Ironton Register, 31 March 1853, Volume 3, No. 36, page 2, printed from microfilm, Hamner Room, Briggs Lawrence County Public Library, Ohio. This article announced the "new town" of South Point being "laid out" by Rev. William W. Davidson.

17. "Great Sale of Lots at South Point," Ironton Register, 31 March 1853, Volume 3, No. 36, page 3, printed from microfilm, Hamner Room, Briggs Lawrence County Public Library, Ohio. This article advertised the sale at public auction of "a large number of building lots" in the "newly laid out town on the Ohio River" to take place on 5 May 1853.

18. "South Point," Ironton Register, 12 May 1853, Volume 3, No. 42, page 2, printed from microfilm, Hamner Room, Briggs Lawrence County Public Library, Ohio. This article stated that the "first sale of lots at the new town of South Point…was well attended." Eighteen lots were sold for an average of just over $170 each. This means that William W. Davidson made more than $3,000 on this auction alone. He paid only $440 for the 52 acres of land from his father's estate auction held fifteen years earlier.

19. Arthur Ferguson, *The History of South Point Village*, not published, (printed by South Point Centennial Committee, Ohio, 1988), spiral bound, Chapter 2, (http://www.villageofsouthpoint.com : accessed 2007).

20. Even though "2nd Street" infers there was once a "1st Street," no evidence for the existence of a "1st Street" was found, even on the earliest available maps of South Point.

21. Ferguson, *The History of South Point Village*.

22. Harbaugh, p. 129.

23. Ferguson, *The History of South Point Village*.

24. Ibid.

The End

Appendix

A. Map of Sussex County, Delaware 260

B. Hannah Davidson's Delaware Survey 262

C. Pennsylvania Geopolitical Boundaries 263

D. Lewis-I's Pennsylvania Survey 264

E. William-III's Pennsylvania Survey 265

F. Officers and Companies of the 4th Battalion 266

G. Captain Conwell's Company 267

H. Company Pay Roll 268

I. Militia Loan Counterpart 269

J. Militia Loan Certificate 270

K. Return of Company Elections 272

L. Ohio Geopolitical Boundaries 273

M. Boundaries of *Fractional Section 5*, Ohio 274

N. William Davidson's Estate 275

Appendix A

Map of Sussex County, Delaware

Hannah Davidson's 179-acre parcel was on the north side of Bracey Branch, a small creek, shown on this 1804 Delaware map which has been cropped to show the details of Sussex County. This tract was in the family until 1753. Given that William-III was about six years of age when his grandmother's home was sold, he would likely have had an early memory of this area.

Lewis owned a 234-acre parcel adjacent to Marsh Island on Rehoboth Bay where William-III spent his first eight years. Marsh Island is represented by one of the small circles next to the words Rehoboth Bay. Another map from the same era mentions that the bay "abounds with oysters" which leads us to speculate that William-III collected them to supplement their diet.

The Head of Broad Kill Creek is where William-III lived from about age nine until age 20 and where Lewis-I owned eight acres of land, a house, and a farm that included an orchard. The town of Broad Kill, also once known as Conwell's Landing, later became the town of Milton. It is likely that the Davidsons and Conwells hauled their produce from their farms to the nearby shores of Broad Kill Creek in, or near, the town of Broad Kill, where it was loaded onto ships for distribution elsewhere. The family departed from this area when they left for southwestern Pennsylvania in 1767.

Lewis-I made several journeys to the town of Lewes where many of his land transactions were recorded. On some of these short trips he may have taken William-III with him. A road or path is shown leading from Bracey Branch to Lewes, likely the route they travelled.

The names of four principal creeks flowing into Rehoboth Bay include Burton Creek, Bracey Branch, Herring Creek, and Goldsmith Creek. However, over the decades their names were changed, and for unknown reasons, Bracey Branch has vanished from modern-day maps.

Map of Sussex County, Delaware

Comparison of the map shown to modern-day maps is easily accomplished to achieve a good frame of reference for the locations where William Davidson spent his childhood and formative years.

Delaware Public Archives, Dover.

Appendix B

Hannah Davidson's Delaware Survey

R. Shankland's survey of Hannah Davidson's 179-acre parcel of land on the north side of Bracey Branch, in Angola Neck, Sussex County, Delaware is pictured. The purchase of this parcel was arranged by William Davidson (William-II) in partnership with Joshua Stockley whose adjoining 82-acre parcel is also shown. Hannah lived here until her death about 1747. Her children sold the tract in 1753, when William-III was about six years of age.

Hannah's tract was bounded by four white oak trees (W:O), a red oak (R:O) and Bracey Branch, the thick creek marked on the left. The thick black rectangle marks the location of "an old stump." A small creek called Green Branch also flows through her property. Hannah's neighbors included Thomas gray, William Reed, and Joshua Stockley. North is to the right.

Delaware Public Archives, Dover.

Appendix C

Pennsylvania Geopolitical Boundaries

This table outlines the changing boundaries that describe the location of William-III's 303.5-acre *Dispute Ended* parcel and Lewis-I's 170-acre *Fortune* tract over the decades. Included are the dates these changes took place and some of the records found confirming the locations.

Beginning	Event	Location	Records
27 Jan 1750	Cumberland County Formed	-n/a-	-n/a-
Jun 1767	Davidsons arrived in Pennsylvania	Cumberland (Valley) Township	1768, 1769, 1770 Cumberland Taxes
9 Mar 1771	Bedford County Formed	Springhill Township	1771 Delaware land sale; 1773 Supply Tax, Bedford County
26 Feb 1773	Westmoreland County Formed	Manallen/ Menallen Township	1783 Supply Tax; Indenture of 1781
11 Oct 1773	Virginia Claimed land Overlapping Pennsylvania	West Augusta District	Determined by maps
30 Sep 1780	County Formed By Virginia	Monongalia County	Determined by maps
26 Sep 1783	Fayette County Formed	Luzerne Township	Warrantee Township Map; 1785 & 1786 Supply Tax Indentures of 1799, 1804

Appendix D

Lewis-I's Pennsylvania Survey

Survey from June 1786 of Lewis-I's 170-acre tract called *Fortune* on the east side of the Monongahela River, opposite Muddy Creek. This parcel was bounded by posts, stones, black oak trees, a white oak tree, a dogwood tree and the Monongahela River. His neighbors included son Thomas, stepson William Conwell, and Thomas Stokely. North is at the bottom. Lewis-I's ferry was attached to this parcel.

Pennsylvania State Archives, Harrisburg.

Appendix E

William-III's Pennsylvania Survey

Survey from November 1786 of William-III's 303.5-acre tract of land on the east side of the Monongahela River, opposite the modern-day town of Crucible. *Dispute Ended* was situated where today's Log Cabin Road intersects Arsenburg Road Ext. William settled on this claim by 1768, purchased this tract from his father, and later obtained a patent. His parcel was bounded by stones, posts, a maple, sugar, white oak, black oak, and ash trees, and the Monongahela River. His southern neighbor was William Conwell.

Pennsylvania State Archives, Harrisburg.

Appendix F

Officers and Companies of the 4th Battalion in 1778

William-III likely served under one or more of these officers, in addition to Captain William Conwell. These represent the permanent companies and Battalion assignment. If subject to the rotation rules and called to active duty, these officers would form new companies based on their assigned classes.

Field Officers
Benjamin Davis, Colonel
John McClelland, Lieutenant Colonel
Samuel Wilson, Major

1st Company
William Sparks, Captain
John Allen, 1st Lieutenant
Andrew Arnal, 2nd Lieutenant
James Cravin, Ensign

2nd Company
William Conwell, Captain
Jesse Rude, 1st Lieutenant
John Armstrong, 2nd Lieutenant
Samuel Adams, Ensign

3rd Company
John Vanmeter, Captain
John Reed, 1st Lieutenant
William Morgan, 2nd Lieutenant
William Albion, Ensign

4th Company
John Kyle, Captain
Peter Wedel, 1st Lieutenant
Joseph Pierce, 2nd Lieutenant
Lewes Pierce, Ensign

5th Company
Andrew Robb, Captain
Hugh Gilmore, 1st Lieutenant
Thomas McKibbens, 2nd Lieutenant
William Frame, Ensign

6th Company
Edward Morton, Captain
William Moore, 1st Lieutenant
William Banker, 2nd Lieutenant
Philip Howel, Ensign

7th Company
Philip Rogers, Captain
Robert Richey, 1st Lieutenant
William Downard, 2nd Lieutenant
Abraham Westfall, Ensign

8th Company
James Marshall, Captain
Samuel Clark, 1st Lieutenant
John Castleman, 2nd Lieutenant
Robert Forsyth, Ensign

Pennsylvania State Archives Series 6, Volume II, page 285.

Appendix G

Captain Conwell's Company

The following is a list of the men who served on active duty in Captain William Conwell's Company, in Westmoreland County in 1778. This list was reproduced using the same order as given in the source. The spelling of the names were taken from the County Distribution Ledger. These men served with William-III in the same company and on the same tour of duty.

This doesn't necessarily mean they served together more than once; some of the men could have been substitutes, from other units, recruited to fill one or more vacancies. William-III himself may have served as a substitute.

1. William Conwell, Capt.

2.	Samuel Adams	14.	George Hill
3.	William Davidson	15.	John McConnel
4.	Samuel Scott	16.	Ephraim January
5.	John Adams	17.	Adam McConnel
6.	John Adams, Jr.	18.	John Hall
7.	Alexander Hinds	19.	Henry Hookman
8.	Thomas Major	20.	Joseph McClean
9.	Samuel Lynch	21.	Alexander Stewart
10.	Michael Flud	22.	Samuel Birnes
11.	John Brand	23.	David Allen
12.	James Linsey	24.	Elijah Barclay
13.	Robert Walker, Ju^r	25.	Robert Walker

Pennsylvania State Archives, Series 3, Volume XXIII, page 316.

Appendix H

Company Pay Roll

This pay roll, created about 1785, indicates that William Conwell collected an interest payment for himself and on behalf of Samuel McGibben, Samuel Adams, John Adams, and Wm Davison. William-III was owed one pound, five pence for which he received a Militia Loan Certificate.

Pennsylvania State Archives, Harrisburg.

Appendix I

Militia Loan Counterpart

William-III received a Militia Loan Certificate for active duty service in Captain William Conwell's Company in 1778. The certificate was torn off and given to William-III or his agent while the issuer retained the counterpart (pictured). When redeemed, the uneven edge of William-III's certificate was matched to this counterpart for authentication. The certificate counterpart for Samuel Scott, who served in the same unit, is beneath William-III's.

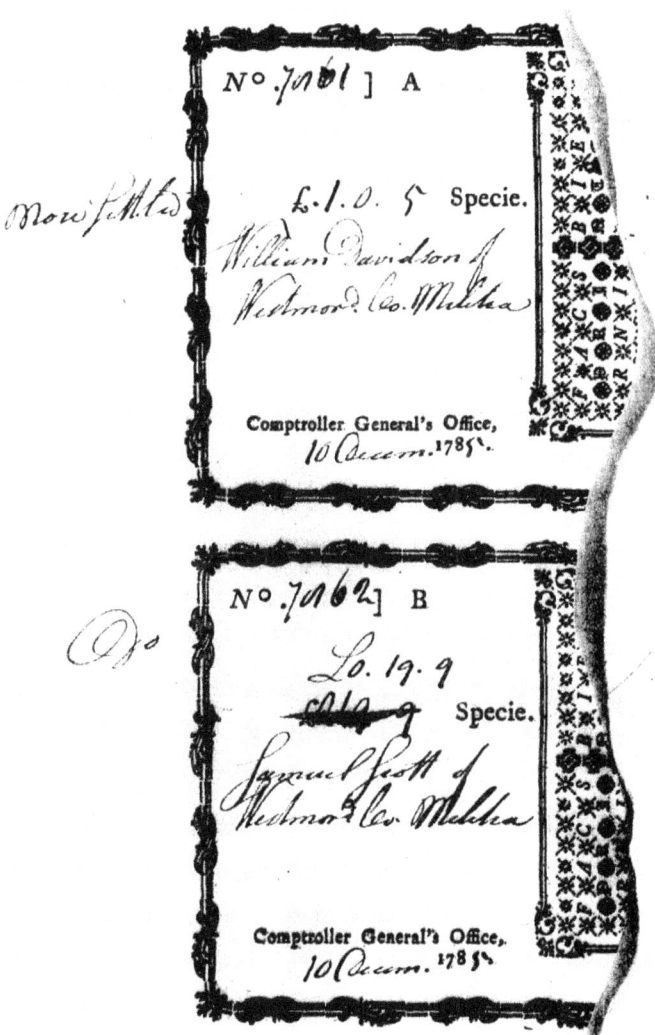

Pennsylvania State Archives, Harrisburg.

Appendix J

Militia Loan Certificate

William-III was issued the militia loan certificate, pictured, for his active duty service in Captain William Conwell's Company in 1778. The certificate (right side) was torn off and handed to William-III, or his agent. The certificate was prepared 10 December 1785 and earned 6% interest beginning 1 July 1783. William's certificate was fully redeemed in 1790. The jagged authentication edge of the certificate still matches its counterpart.

The font used in the certificate provides several good examples of the use of the old English long-s which appears as ʃ. The long-s was typically used in the middle of a word and sometimes at the beginning of a word.

When the certificate and its counterpart are placed together, letters printed in the tear area, when read in alternating order vertically, spell the name Francis Bailey, the printer of the certificates. He was a well-known Revolutionary Era printer, working in Philadelphia in 1785, but the specific date this certificate was printed is unknown.

```
F   A   C   S   B   I   E
  R   N   I       A   L   Y
```

Transcript of the certificate:

No. *7861*] A   £ *1.0.5*   Specie

I DO hereby Certify, that the State of Pennsylvania is indebted to *William Davidson of Westmor^d. Co. Militia* in the Sum of

one pound five pence

Specie, with lawful Interest from the first day of July, one thousand seven hundred and eighty three ; the same being due upon an Account settled in this Office. Pursuant to an Act of Assembly, passed the first Day of April 1784.

> Comptroller-General's Office   }
>
>   *10 December 1785*   }   *M. Nicholson*

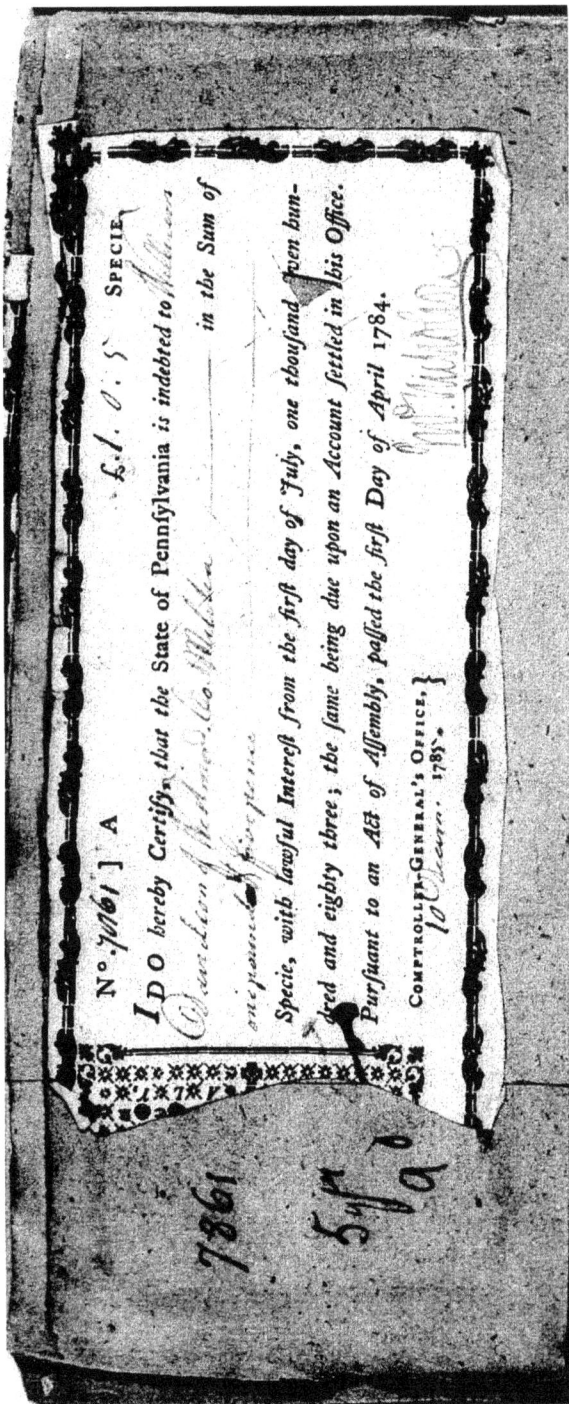

Pennsylvania State Archives, Harrisburg.

Appendix K

Return of Company Elections

William-III was elected ensign of the 4th Battalion, 4th Company, Westmoreland County Militia on 24 September 1783, just twenty-four days after the Revolutionary War ended. By accepting this commission, William obligated himself to serve another three year term of service. The "Line" is a reference to the Mason-Dixon line settling the Virginia/Pennsylvania boundary dispute. The text reads:

> A Return of Election of Companys in the
> 4th and 5th Batalions in Consequence of
> Resignations Removals &c the others were Commiss[ion]
> =ed the last year when the Line was Run and those
> Who Claimed under Virginia fell in ---

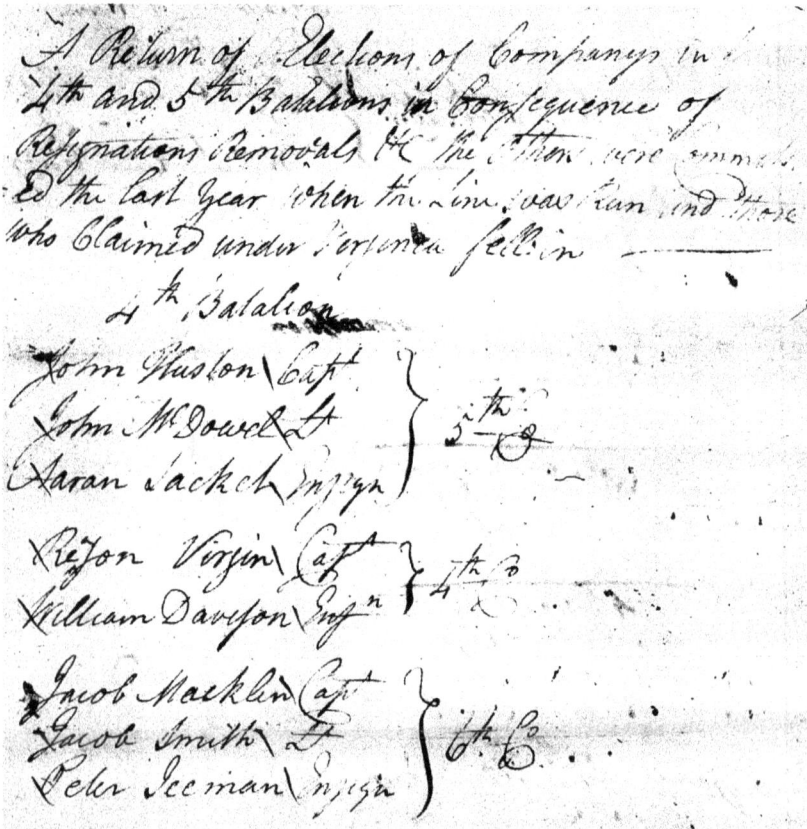

Pennsylvania State Archives, Harrisburg.

Appendix L

Ohio Geopolitical Boundaries

The parcel of land settled by William-III in Ohio consisted of all of *Fractional Section 5*. As in Pennsylvania, the geopolitical boundaries in Ohio changed over time. *Fractional Section 5* was found in the following areas:

Beginning	**Location**
Before 1784	Indian Territory
3 Jan 1784	Unorganized Federal Territory
13 Jul 1787	Northwest Territory
27 Jul 1788	Washington County, Northwest Territory
Nov 1798	Levi Whipple surveyed *Fractional Section 5*
Apr 1799	William Davidson arrived and settled in Gallipolis Township, Washington County, Northwest Territory
1 Mar 1803	Gallipolis Township, Washington County, Ohio (statehood achieved)
30 Apr 1803	Union Township, Gallia County, Ohio
21 Dec 1815	Fayette Township, Lawrence County, Ohio
Mar 1853	Village of South Point formed in *Fractional Section 5*

Appendix M

Boundaries of Fractional Section 5, Ohio

The parcel of land settled by William-III in Ohio consisted of all *Fractional Section 5*, the triangular area shown on the map. His parcel enclosed 242.99 acres in Fayette Township, Lawrence County. When he arrived, this area was unbroken frontier, absent of any improvements, but had already been surveyed. His boundaries included a white oak, a buckeye tree, and the Ohio River. His land was subdivided by William-IV in 1853 to create the Village of South Point.

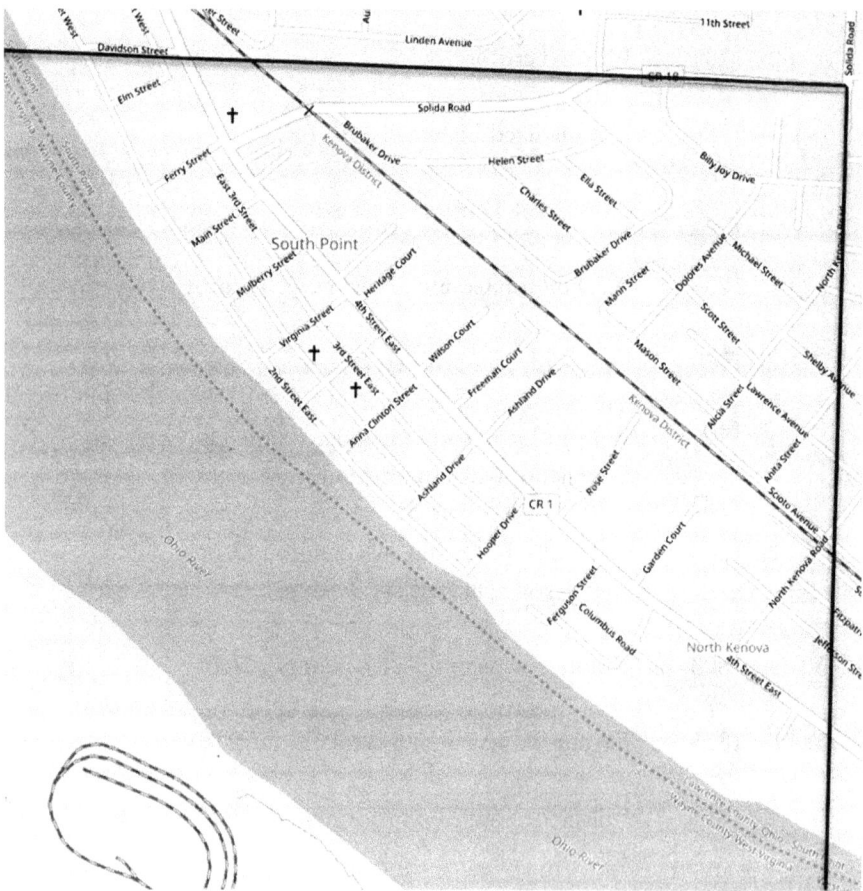

© OpenStreetMap contributors (http://www.openstreetmap.org/)

Appendix N

William Davidson's Estate

Gallia County ss }   Be it Remembered that heretofore to wit at a Court of Common pleas Continued & held at the court House in the Town of Gallipolis County of Gallia and State of Ohio Before the Honorable John Thompson esquire president Judge, Joseph Fletcher and Fuller Elliot esquires associate Judges of the Court of Common pleas for the County of Gallia aforesaid, on tuesday the eighth Day of September in the year of our Lord one thousand eight hundred and twelve. The last will and Testament of William Davidson late of this County Deceased was presented for probate. Whereupon David McCoy one of the subscribed witnesses thereto came before the Court and after being duly Sworn declared that he was present when the Testator signed and acknowledged the Same and that he believed he was of sound mind memory and Judgment at the time of his signing & acknowledging the same as his last will and Testament and that he witnessed the same in the presence of the other witnesses at the request of the Said Testator and Thereupon on motion a Dedimus is awarded to take the Deposition of Richard Sharp another of the Subscribed witnesses the Said Dedimus to be directed to James Holderby and George Ward Esquires of the State of Virginia or either of them

and afterwards to wit at another day to wit as a Court of common pleas continued and Held at the Court House aforesaid on tuesday the twenty Second day of December then next Ensuing the Dedimus Directed to James Holderby and George Ward Esquires of Cabell County Virginia to take the Testimony of the said Richard Sharp Subscribed witness to the last will and Testament of the said William Davidson, is returned, and the same being not Sufficiently full to embrace the requisitions of the Statute. Therefore ordered by the court that Dedimus be renewed and will attached and that said Justice propound to said witness the following interogations –

First, whether he was present when the Testator signed and acknowledged this Instrument as his last will (presenting the Same).

Secondly, whether David McCoy and himself subscribed the same in presence of Testator at his request and in presence of Each other.

William "Ranger" Davidson

Thirdly - whether he believes the Testator to be of Sound mind, memory and judgment at the time of Signing and acknowledging this last will.

And now at this day to wit at a Court of Common pleas Begun and Held at the Court House aforesaid on monday the fifth Day of april in the year of our Lord one thousand eight hundred and thirteen. The Dedimus directed to James Holderby and John Ward esquires is returned and Thereupon the Said Richard Sharp personally came before this Court and after being duly Sworn Declared he was present when William Davidson the Testator Signed and acknowledged the Same as his last will and Testament and that he believed he was of Sound mind, memory, and Judgment at the time of his Signing and acknowledging the Same and that he witnessed the Same at the request of the Testator and in the presence of the other witnesses.

Whereupon the Said will Having also been proven by the oath of David McCoy (another of the Subscribed witnesses) at the last September Term of this Court. Therefore the Same is proved, approved, and allowed as the Last will and Testament of the Said William Davidson Deceased, and ordered to be Recorded.

On motion ordered That David McCoy, Edward Simmons and Mashac Collier* are appointed appraisers of the personal property of Said Deceased.

Ordered also that the Executors named in Said will Execute their Bond with Security in the Sum of Eight hundred Dollars Conditioned for the faithful Discharge of the Trust reposed in them as Executors aforesaid.

Hence follows a copy of the last will and Testament of the Said William Davidson late of this County Deceased and the Same is in the words and figures following to wit -

I William Davidson citizen of the State of Ohio Do Declare this my last will and Testament revoking all others.

First all my Just Debts are to be punctually and Speedily paid and the Legacies Herein bequeathed are to be Discharged in the manner hereafter Directed. To my Beloved wife Barbara Davidson I Bequeath all my moveable property and kitchen furniture, my debts being first paid out of the Said moveable property, also all Legacies hereafter Bequeathed to be Discharged

William Davidson's Estate

out of the aforesaid moveable property and further I Do Bequeath to my Beloved wife the whole benefit or income of my fractional Section No. 5 on which we now live for her use and the use of children that belong to her and me that are under age or Such as chuses to remain under her Jurisdiction During her widowhood, and at her Decease I Do Direct all the property that She, my wife, may have of the before mentioned moveable property may fall into the hand of my Daughter Cinthia if living, if not to whom of our Children She chuses.

I Do Bequeath To my Eldest Son John Davidson thirty Dollars to be paid out of the above mentioned moveable property in fifteen months after my Decease if not paid in my Life.

To my Second Son Lewis Davidson I Do Bequeath the Sum of one Dollar.

To my Eldest Daughter Comfort McCourtney I Do Bequeath the Sum of one Dollar.

To my Son David Davidson I Do Bequeath one Dollar.

To my Daughter Mary Williams I Do Bequeath the Sum of one Dollar.

To my Daughter Peggy Francis I Do Bequeath one horse beast to be worth forty Dollars.

To my Daughter Betty Lynd I Do Bequeath the Sum of thirteen Dollars.

To my Daughter Sarrah McKee I Do Bequeath one horse beast to be worth forty Dollars.

To my Daughter Cinthia I Do will and Bequeath one horse beast worth forty Dollars, one good cow and calf, one Bed & Bedding. I further Direct that the Legacy left to my daughter Cinthia be paid to her at her marriage if She be married before She be twenty years of age, if not married to be paid to her at that age.

To my Son Abraham A. M. Davidson I Do Bequeath one fifth part of my fractional Section No. 5 the place on which we Now live.

William "Ranger" Davidson

Likewise to my Son Thomas one other fifth part of the Same also to my Son William one other fifth part of the Same.

To my Son Jesse one other fifth equal part and To my Son Joseph one other fifth Equal part To fall into their hands at the Death or marriage of their mother, my Beloved wife, if of age, if not of age the Same I Direct to be put to their use by Suitable Guardians of their own or the Court's Chusing by rent until they Do become of full age according to Law and I further Desire that I may be intombed in a Decent and orderly manner with Such of my family as are intombed on my Home place.

I Do Constitute and appoint my Dearly Beloved wife Barbara Davidson, my Son Abraham A. M. Davidson and my nephew Joseph Davidson Executrix and Executors of this my will.

This twentieth Day of June Eighteen hundred and ten I William Davidson being in sound mind and memory Do Execute this my Last will & Testament.

In the presence of Joseph Davidson   }   William Davidson
David McCoy - Richard Sharp   }

and afterwards to wit on the Seventh day of June then next ensuing to wit in the Year one thousand Eight hundred and thirteen, was filed in the Clerk's office of our Said Court the following Inventory and appraisement of the personal Estate of Said Deceased and the Same is in the words and figures following to wit:

In Compliance with an appointment to us Directed from the last april Term, We David McCoy, Edward Simmons & Mashac Coylier* Have assembled on the premises of Willm Davidson Deceased on the 2nd Day of may 1813 & after being duly Sworn as the Law Directs has appraised the following property to wit:

15	heads of Hogs valued at	$18.75
1	young Sorrel Stud horse 3 years old @	51.66
1	Bright bay horse named Fox @	41.66
1	brown filly 2 years old	26.66
2	two years old Heifers & one Stear	20.00

William Davidson's Estate

3	years olds @	14.00
1	luting box & Dung fork	2.33
1	Shovel and fire Shovel @ 75 each	1.50
1	Graning Knife $1 - & dung fork 75	1.75
2	augers and 4 Chisels	2.25
1	hand Saw $1.75 1 broad ax @ 3 Dollars	4.75
1	Iron Square 50 cts 1 foot adze $1.00 cooper adze 75 cts	2.25
1	pair compasses 75 cts 1 mattock $1.50	2.25
1	frow $1 one Drawing knife 50 cts	1.50
2	Iron Wedges $1 to 1 Gig 75 cts	1.75
1	Iron Ladle 50 cts 1 Iron bail link & fetters $1	1.50
1	mill pick & Stone Hammer at 75 cts ps.	1.50
2	falling axes @ $2 ps	4.00
2	axes @ 75 cts ps	1.50
1	waggon & Bulet Bands	36.00
1	flat Iron 33 cts	.33
1	pair of Horse Gears @ $3.75 & 1 do. @ $3	6.75
2	old Blind Bridles @ 25 cts ps	.50
1	Gun & accoutrement 19.33	19.33
1	Loom tackling & great wheel	9.00
1	pot & Bail	2.00
1	Single tree, tea kettle & frying pan	1.00
1	Large kettle & bail	4.00
1	kettle and bail	2.50
1	trammel	2.00
1	bake oven	1.25
1	Spider	1.00
1	tea kettle	1.50
1	flax Hackle	2.00
1	pair warping Barrs	.75
1	big wheel	1.25
1	pair boots	1.00
1	box Shoemaker's tools	.75
2	deer Skins	.75
2	boxes of old Irons	2.50
3	Sickles	1.25
1	Bedstead Bed & Beddings	9.50
1	Bell	.37 ½

William "Ranger" Davidson

3	Barrels & 1 Gun	1.00
1	kegg	.25
	Bed Stead & Bedding	16.00
1	old box of tools	1.00
1	razor & box	.50
1	candle Stick and candle moulds	.50
1	funnel	.25
1	Coffee mill	.50
1	pair Saddle bags & Lock	2.25
1	cow & calf	14.00
1	do.	12.00
1	do.	14.00
1	do.	11.00
1	Dresser & ware belonging to S^d	23.00
20	Books	7.25
1	Table, Knives & forks	3.75
1	pair Steelyards	4.00
1	Jug & Pitcher @ 37 ½ ps	0.75
1	Tramel & Hook	1.12 ½
1	Sheep @	2.50
1	Spinning wheel	3.00
1	chuk Reel	0.75
1	Log chain	2.50
1	Churn	0.62 ½
8	pannels of Glass	1.00
1	pocket Book	0.25
	Great coat, Straight Coat & Waist Coat @	4.25
1	Chest & Box	2.75
1	Basket Spools @	1.25
½	Doz. chairs	2.50
1	Woman's Saddle	4.00
1	old Saddle	1.00
13	barrels & tubs @	3.75
1	half bushel & horse Shoes	0.37 ½
	Wood Screws tacks & fish hooks	1.50
2	Weeding hoes @	.66
1	Brush @	.25
1	plough & Double trees	6.50

William Davidson's Estate

1	do.	12.00
2	pairs of Harns & Collars & 1 pair of Chains	4.00
1	man's Saddle @	7.50
3	barrels & 1 tub	1.75
1	paddle lock & hatter Chain	1.00
	Harrow @	6.50
3	bells 1 @ 75 and 2 @ 50 ps	1.75
1	Hoe @	37 ½

N. B. – amount $497.50 ½ See below $ 496.25 ½

We the above named subscribers each of union Township, Gallia County & State of Ohio the date above mentioned, Certify the above appraisement & Inventory to be just and true. Given under our hands and Seals the Date above Written.

David McCoy
Edward Simmons
Mashac Colyer*

one [year] old Sheep was produced after we Signed our names in our presence
valued at $1.25
which adds to   496.25 ½
                      Total $497.50 ½

Notes:

Do.   Ditto or same as above.

ps.   Apiece.

cts.   Cents.

S^d   Said (referring to William Davidson).

*This name should be Meshach Collier. He is found in the 1820 Census in Fayette Township, Lawrence County. Meshach is a biblical name found in the Book of Daniel.

Illustrations

Cover:

> Lossing, Benson John. *Our Country*, Vol. 1. New York: Johnson and Bailey, 1895. 746. Wood engraving of a farmer with a rifle, plowing a field. *Internet Archive* (http://archive.org : November 2015).

Introduction:

> Howe, Henry. *Historical Collections of Ohio*. Cincinnati: Bradley & Anthony, 1850. 261. Wood engraving of a colonial era blockhouse. *Internet Archive* (http://archive.org : May 2016).

Ancestry:

> *One Hundred Years' Progress of the United States*. Hartford, Conn: L. Stebbins, 1870. 27. Wood engraving of a pioneer family building a cabin. *Internet Archive* (http://archive.org : November 2015).

William's Parents:

> *One Hundred Years' Progress of the United States*. Hartford, Conn: L. Stebbins, 1870. 214. Wood engraving of a man and woman on horseback. *Internet Archive* (http://archive.org: November 2015).

Delaware:

> Coffin, Charles Carleton. *The Boys of '61*. Boston: Estes and Lauriat, 1886. 121. Wood engraving of a fruit harvest. *Internet Archive* (http://archive.org : May 2016).

Pennsylvania:

> Lossing, Benson John, ed. *Harper's Encyclopedia of United States History*, Vol. X. New York, NY: Harper & Brothers, 1905. 82. Wood engraving of a log cabin by a river. *Internet Archive* (http://archive.org : October 2014).

Illustrations

Revolutionary War:

> Lossing, Benson John. *Our Country*, Vol. 1. New York: Johnson and Bailey, 1895. 775. Wood engraving of a farmer called up for soldier duty. *Internet Archive* (http://archive.org : November 2015).

Other Pennsylvania Records:

> Lossing, Benson John, ed. *Harper's Encyclopedia of United States History*, Vol. X. New York, NY: Harper & Brothers, 1905. 85. Wood engraving of a pioneer aiming a flintlock rifle. *Internet Archive* (http://archive.org : October 2014).

Families:

> Taylor, Edward. *The Model History*. Chicago: Scott, Foresman & Co., 1897. 72. Wood engraving of a view inside a pioneer cabin. *Internet Archive* (http://archive.org : October 2014).

Ohio:

> Mason, Augustus Lynch. *The Romance and Tragedy of Pioneer Life*. Cincinnati, O: Jones Brothers and Company, 1883. 600. Wood engraving of a flatboat by Alfred Rudolph Waud. *Internet Archive* (http://archive.org : September 2014).

Final Years:

> *One Hundred Years' Progress of the United States*. Hartford, Conn: L. Stebbins, 1870. 103. Wood engraving of pioneer women working in a garden. *Internet Archive* (http://archive.org: November 2015).

Subsequent Events:

> *One Hundred Years' Progress of the United States*. Hartford, Conn: L. Stebbins, 1870. 26. Wood engraving of several American Indians. *Internet Archive* (http://archive.org: November 2015).

The End:

> Howe, Henry. *Historical Collections of Ohio*. Cincinnati: Bradley & Anthony, 1850. 542. Wood engraving of a cabin and a man on horseback. *Internet Archive* (http://archive.org : May 2016).

Bibliography

BOOKS & HISTORICAL REFERENCES:

Adams, Richard C. *A Brief History of the Delaware Indians*. U. S. Government Printing Office, 1906. Digital version. *Google Books*. http://books.google .com : accessed March 2010.

Albert, George Dallas. *History of the County of Westmoreland Pennsylvania*. Philadelphia: L. H. Everts & Co., 1882. Digital version. *Google Books*. http://books.google.com : accessed August 2011.

Albert, George Dallas. See *Report of the Commission to Locate the Site of the Frontier Forts of Pennsylvania*.

Atlas of Lawrence County, Ohio, Hardesty 1882 and Lake 1887 (Combined), 1st edition. Reprint. Ironton, Ohio: Lawrence County Historical Society, 1985.

Bausman, Joseph Henderson and John Samuel Duss. *The History of Beaver County Pennsylvania*, Volume I. New York: The Knickerbocker Press, 1904. Digital version. *Google Books*. http://books.google.com : accessed June 2011.

Blackstone, William. *Commentaries on the Laws of England*, Twelfth Edition. Book I of IV. London: A. Strahan and W. Woodfall, 1793. Digital version. *Google Books*. http://books.google.com : accessed June 2016.

Boucher, John N. *History of Westmoreland County Pennsylvania*, Volume I. New York: The Lewis Publishing Company, 1906. Digital version. *Google Books*. http://books. google.com : accessed June 2011.

Butterfield, Consul Willshire. *An Historical Account of the Expedition Against the Sandusky*. Cincinnati : Robert Clarke & Co, 1873. Digital version. *Internet Archive*. http://www.archive.org : accessed March 2011.

Callahan, James Morton. *Genealogical and Personal History of the Upper Monongahela Valley West Virginia*, Volume III. New York: Lewis Historical Publishing Company, 1912. Digital version. *Google Books*. http://books.google.com : accessed April 2011.

Bibliography

Commemorative Biographical Record of the Counties of Harrison and Carroll, Ohio. Chicago: J. H. Beers & Co., 1891. "Lewis H. Davidson." Digital version. *Internet Archive.* http://www.archive.org : accessed April 2011.

Conrad, Henry Clay. *History of the State of Delaware*, Volume II. Wilmington, Delaware: Henry Clay Conrad, 1908. Digital version. *Google Books.* http://books.google.com : accessed 2012.

Conwell, T. C. *The Conwell's of Dyer's Delight.* Not published. Dated 1984. 91 typewritten pages. Digital version. *Ancestry.* http://www.ancestry.com : accessed October 2013.

Conyngham, David Hayfield. *Reminiscences of David Hayfield Conyngham.* Wilkes-Barr, PA: Wyoming Historical and Genealogical Society, 1904. Digital version. *Google Books.* http://books.google.com : accessed April 2011.

Crawford, Michael H. *The Origins of Native Americans: Evidence from Anthropological Genetics.* Cambridge, United Kingdom: Cambridge University Press, 1998.

Crumrine, Boyd. *History of Washington County, Pennsylvania.* Philadelphia: L. H. Everts & Co., 1882. Digital version. *Google Books.* http://books.google.com : accessed April 2011.

Davidson, Lewis H. See *Commemorative Biographical Record of the Counties of Harrison and Carroll, Ohio.*

Dorman, John Frederick, FASG. *Adventurers of Purse and Person, Virginia 1607-1624/5.* 4th ed. 4th printing. Volume 1. Families A-F. Baltimore, MD: Genealogical Publishing Company, 2004.

Ellet, Mrs. *Pioneer Women of the West.* New York: Charles Scribner, 1856. Digital version. *Internet Archive.* http://www.archive.org : accessed November 2013.

Ellis, Franklin. *History of Fayette County Pennsylvania with Biographical Sketches of many of its Pioneers and Prominent Men.* Philadelphia: L. H. Everts & Co., 1882. Digital version. *Internet Archive.* http://www.archive.org : accessed April 2011.

William "Ranger" Davidson

Ely, William. *The Big Sandy Valley*. Catlettsburg, KY : Central Methodist, 1887. Digital version. *Internet Archive*. http://www.archive.org : accessed March 2014.

Evans, Nelson W. *History of Scioto County, Ohio*. Portsmouth, Ohio: Self-published, 1903. Reprint. Markham, Virginia: The Apple Manor Press.

Fayette Township Cemeteries. Not published (hardbound black cover). Call number: REF 977.188 Fa. "FA-4," page untitled and undated. Entries created by Robert L. Bruce and Michael Stevens. Briggs-Lawrence County Public Library. Hamner Room. 321 S 4th St, Ironton, OH. This book is a compilation of headstone inscriptions created by many different volunteers. Included are inscriptions found in the *First Davidson Cemetery* in Lawrence County, Ohio. This is the only surviving document providing the inscription of William Davidson's headstone by eyewitnesses.

Fears, Rufus J. *A History of Freedom*, Part II, Lecture 20: "The Tyranny of George III." Chantilly, VA: Teaching Company, 2001. Great Courses, audio compact disc. ISBN 978-1565853553.

Ferguson, Arthur. *The History of South Point Village*. Not published. Ironton, Ohio: Printed by South Point Centennial Committee, 1988 (spiral bound). Chapter 2. Digital copy. http://www.villageofsouthpoint.com : accessed 2007.

Fraser-MacKintosh, Charles. *Antiquarian Notes a Series of Papers regarding Families and Places in the Highlands*. Inverness, Scotland: printed at the Advertiser Office, 1865. Digital version. *Google Books*. http://books.google.com : accessed April 2011.

Geiser, Karl Frederick. *Redemptioners and Indentured Servants in the Colony and the Commonwealth of Pennsylvania*. New Haven, Conn.: The Tuttle, Morehouse & Taylor Co., 1901. Digital version. *Google Books*. http://books.google.com : accessed November 15.

Glasgow, William Melancthon. *History of the Reformed Presbyterian Church in America*. Baltimore: Hill & Harvey, Publishers, 1888. Digital version. *Google Books*. http://books.google.com : accessed November 2011. This work includes a transcript of the baptismal record for Rosanna Hutchinson, first wife of William Davidson.

Bibliography

Hanna, Charles Augustus. *Historical Collections of Harrison County in the State of Ohio.* New York: privately printed, 1900. Digital version. *Internet Archive.* http://www.archive.org : accessed April 2011.

Harbaugh, Elizabeth Davidson. *The Davidson Genealogy.* Ironton, Ohio: self-published, 1948. Ann Arbor, Michigan: Lithoprinted, Edwards Brothers, Inc., 1949. 482 pages. Online Computer Library Center number (OCLC): 23167553.

Hardesty. See *Atlas of Lawrence County, Ohio, Hardesty 1882 and Lake 1887 (Combined).*

Hassler, Edgar W. *Old Westmoreland: A History of Western Pennsylvania During the Revolution.* Cleveland, Ohio: The Arthur H. Clark Company, 1900. Digital version. *Google Books.* http//books.google.com : accessed July 2011.

Hatcher, Patricia Law. *Abstract of Graves of Revolutionary Patriots*, Vol. 1 (A-D). Westminster, Maryland: Pioneer Heritage Press, 2007.

Heck, L. W., A. J. Wraight, D. J. Orth, J. R. Carter, L. G. Van Winkle, and Janet Hazen. *Delaware Place Names.* Geological Survey Bulletin 1245. Prepared by the Geological Survey, U.S. Department of the Interior and Geodetic Survey, U.S. Department of Commerce. Washington: United States Government Printing Office, 1966. *USGS Publications Warehouse.* https://pubs.usgs.gov/bul/ 1245/report.pdf : accessed June 2016.

Holland, W. J., Editor. *Annals of the Carnegie Museum, Volume I, 1901 – 1902.* Published by the authority of the Board of Trustees of the Carnegie Institute: September 1902. Digital version. *Internet Archive.* http://www.archive.org : accessed April 2011.

Hulbert, Archer Butler. *The Ohio River.* New York and London: G. P. Putnam's Sons, The Knickerbocker Press, 1906. Digital version. *Google Books.* http://books.google .com : accessed June 2011.

Johnson, Charles and Patricia Smith, and the WGBH Series Research Team. *Africans in America: America's Journey through Slavery.* Video. New York: Harcourt Brace, 1998.

Jordan, John W. and James Hadden. *Genealogical and Personal History of Fayette County, Pennsylvania*, Volume II. New York: Lewis Historical Publishing

William "Ranger" Davidson

Company, 1912. Digital version. *Internet Archive.* http://www.archive.org : accessed October 2013.

Knepper, Dr. George. *The Official Ohio Lands Book*, first paperback edition. Ohio: Publication of the Auditor of State, 2002. Digital version. *Auditor of the State of Ohio.* http://ohioauditor.gov : accessed July 2011.

Lawyer, James Patterson. *History of Ohio*, Second Edition. Columbus, Ohio : Union Publishing Co, 1905. Digital version. *Google Books.* http://google.books.com : accessed April 2011.

Leckey, Howard L. *The Tenmile Country and Its Pioneer Families: A Genealogical History of the Upper Monongahela Valley.* Baltimore, MD: Genealogical Publishing Co, 2001.

Mason, Elaine Hastings and F. Edward Wright. *Land Records of Sussex County, Delaware 1782-1789, Deed Book N No. 13.* Westminster, Maryland: Willow Bend Books, 2002.

Nelson, S. B. *Nelson's Biographical Dictionary and Historical Reference Book of Fayette County Pennsylvania.* Uniontown, PA: S. B. Nelson Publisher, 1900. Digital version. *Google Books.* http://google.books.com : accessed May 2011.

Powell, Bob. *The Walking Plow.* Not published. Not dated. Illustrated. 3 pages. Digital version. *ALHFAM.org.* http://www.alhfam.org/pdfs/FARM_PIG_Info_sheet-1.pdf : accessed June 2013.

Report of the Commission to Locate the Site of the Frontier Forts of Pennsylvania, Volume Two. "The Frontier Forts of Western Pennsylvania." George Dallas Albert. Clarence M. Busch, State Printer of Pennsylvania, 1896. Digital version. *Google Books.* http://books.google.com : accessed August 2011.

Runk, J. M. & Co. *Biographical & Genealogical History of the State of Delaware*, Vol. 1. Chambersburg, PA: J. M. Runk & Co., 1899. Digital version. *Google Books.* http://books.google.com : accessed April 2016.

Schaumann, Merri Lou Scribner. *Tax Lists - Cumberland County, Pennsylvania, 1768, 1769, 1770.* Carlisle, Pennsylvania: 1972.

288

Bibliography

Scharf, John Thomas. *History of Delaware: 1609 – 1888: General History*, Vol. I. Philadelphia: L. J. Richards & Co., 1888. Digital version. *Google Books*. http://google.books.com : accessed 2012.

Scharf, John Thomas. *History of Delaware: 1609 – 1888*, Vol. II. Philadelphia: L. J. Richards & Co., 1888. Digital version. *Google Books*. http://google.books .com : accessed 2012.

Sipe, C. Hale. *The Indian Wars of Pennsylvania*. Harrisburg, PA: The Telegraph Press, 1929. Digital version. *Internet Archive*. http://www.archive.org : accessed April 2011.

Steinberg, Jennifer. "Last Voyage of the Slave Ship Henrietta Marie." *National Geographic Magazine*. August 2002.

The Official roster of the soldiers of the American Revolution buried in the state of Ohio, Vol 1. Columbus, Ohio: F. J. Heer Printing Co., 1929. Bartow Genealogical and Historical Library, Bartow, Florida.

Thomas, Hugh. *The Slave Trade*. Simon and Schuster, 1997.

Trussell, John B. B. *The Pennsylvania Line Regimental Organization and Operations, 1776-1773*. Harrisburg: Pennsylvania Historical and Museum Commission, 1977.

Van Voorhis, John S. *The Old and New Monongahela*. Pittsburgh, PA: Nicholson, Printer and Binder, 1893. Digital version. *Internet Archive*. http://www.archive.org : accessed July 2011.

Vastine, Roy E. *Scioto – A County History*. Portsmouth, OH.: Knuaff Graphics, 1986.

Veech, James. *The Monongahela of Old*. Pittsburg, PA.: 1858-1892. Digital version. *Google Books*. http://books.google.com : accessed April 2011.

White, C. Albert. *A History of the Rectangular Survey System*. Washington, D.C.: U.S. Government Printing Office, 1983. Digital version. *Google Books*. http://books.google.com : accessed November 2016.

William "Ranger" Davidson

Wright, F. Edward. *Land Records of Sussex County Delaware 1769-1782, Deed Books L No. 11 & M No. 12.* Westminster, Maryland: Family Line Publications, 1994.

CEMETERY MARKERS:

Find A Grave. http://www.findagrave.com. Ann (Alexander) Davidson (1772-1848). Memorial 7409008. Pennsylvania. Fayette County. Redstone Township. Dunlap Creek Presbyterian Cemetery.

———. David (Hutchinson) Davidson (1777-1828). Memorial 85119785. Pennsylvania. Fayette County. Luzerne Township. Williams Cemetery.

———. Jane (Bryson) Davidson (1809-1889). Memorial 43987439. Pennsylvania. Fayette County. Fayette Township. Davidson Cemetery.

———. Jeremiah Davidson (1768-1851). Memorial 7409004. Pennsylvania. Fayette County. Redstone Township. Dunlap Creek Presbyterian Cemetery.

———. Joseph W. Davidson (1806-1872). Memorial 43987316. Pennsylvania. Fayette County. Fayette Township. Davidson Cemetery.

———. Lavina (Yingling) Davidson (1815-1898). Memorial 55664424. Ohio. Lawrence County. Fayette Township. South Point. White Cottage Cemetery.

———. Rev. William W. Davidson (1798-1883). Memorial 40072966. Ohio. Lawrence County. South Point. White Cottage Cemetery.

CENSUS RECORDS (FEDERAL & STATE):

Kentucky. Carter County. 1840 U.S. census, population schedule. Digital images. *FamilySearch.* https://familysearch.org.

Kentucky. Carter County. 1850 U.S. census, population schedule. Digital images. *FamilySearch.* https://familysearch.org.

Maryland. Allegany County. 1800 U.S. census, population schedule. Digital images. *FamilySearch.* https://familysearch.org.

Maryland. Allegany County. 1810 U.S. census, population schedule. Digital images. *FamilySearch.* https://familysearch.org.

Bibliography

Ohio. Auglaize County. 1850 U.S. census, population schedule. Digital images. *FamilySearch*. https://familysearch.org.

Ohio. Lawrence County. 1820 U.S. census, population schedule. Digital images. *FamilySearch*. https://familysearch.org.

Ohio. Lawrence County. 1830 U.S. census, population schedule. Digital images. *FamilySearch*. https://familysearch.org.

Ohio. Lawrence County. 1840 U.S. census, population schedule. Digital images. *FamilySearch*. https://familysearch.org.

Ohio. Lawrence County. 1850 U.S. census, mortality schedule. Digital images. *FamilySearch*. https://familysearch.org.

Ohio. Lawrence County. 1850 U.S. census, population schedule. Digital images. *FamilySearch*. https://familysearch.org.

Ohio. Lawrence County. 1860 U.S. census, population schedule. Digital images. *FamilySearch*. https://familysearch.org.

Pennsylvania. Fayette County. 1786 Septennial Census. Digital images. *Ancestry*. http://www.ancestry.com.

Pennsylvania. Fayette County. 1800 Septennial Census. Digital images. *Ancestry*. http://www.ancestry.com.

Pennsylvania. Fayette County. 1790 U.S. census, population schedule. Digital images. *FamilySearch*. https://familysearch.org.

Pennsylvania. Fayette County. 1800 U.S. census, population schedule. Digital images. *FamilySearch*. https://familysearch.org.

Pennsylvania. Fayette County. 1810 U.S. census, population schedule. Digital images. *FamilySearch*. https://familysearch.org.

Pennsylvania. Fayette County. 1820 U.S. census, population schedule. Digital images. *FamilySearch*. https://familysearch.org.

William "Ranger" Davidson

Pennsylvania. Fayette County. 1830 U.S. census, population schedule. Digital images. *FamilySearch*. https://familysearch.org.

Territory Northwest of the River Ohio. Washington County. 1800 U.S. census, population schedule. Digital images. *Ancestry*. http://www.ancestry.com.

LAND & SURVEY RECORDS IN DELAWARE:

Delaware. Sussex County. Deed Book I. Record Group 4555. Digital images of penned documents. Delaware Public Archives. Dover.

Delaware. Sussex County. Deed Book L. Record Group 4555. Digital images of penned documents. Delaware Public Archives. Dover.

Delaware. Sussex County. Deed Book Q. Record Group 4555.031. Digital images of penned documents. Delaware Public Archives. Dover.

Delaware. Sussex County. Shankland Survey. Book 2. Record Group 4555. Digital images of penned documents. Delaware Public Archives. Dover.

Delaware. Sussex County. Court of Chancery. Case File C, Number 25. Record Group 1225.026. Digital images of penned documents. Delaware Public Archives. Dover.

LAND RECORDS IN OHIO:

Bureau of Land Management. "Land Patent Search." Database and digital images. *General Land Office Records*. http://www.glorecords.blm.gov/default.aspx.

Ohio. Official Title Resolution Case. Opened by the Bureau of Land Management with the National Archives and Records Administration, Washington, D.C. Resulting from an inquiry about the missing land entry file for fractional Section 5, Township 1 North, Range 17 West. December 2011. NARA replied that the land entry file, which should exist for William Davidson, was either damaged or destroyed before it could be archived.

Ohio. Chillicothe Land Office. Tract Book, p. 586. Fractional Section 5, Township 1 North, Range 17 West. Entry 1003 for William Davidson. Photocopy of penned document. National Archives and Records Administration. Suitland Reference Branch (WNRC). Maryland.

Ohio. Lawrence County. Recorder's Office. Deed Books. Lawrence County Courthouse. Ironton, Ohio.

Whipple, Levi [surveyor]. *Township Survey Plat Map of 1798.* Twp. Plats - OH, Ohio River Survey, R. 17, T. 1 & 2. Record group 49. Digital copy on compact disc, 2012. National Archives and Records Administration. Special Media Archive Services Division (NWCS). Cartographic and Architectural Branch (NNSC), College Park, Maryland.

LAND RECORDS IN PENNSYLVANIA:

Pennsylvania. Fayette County. Records of the Land Office. Record Group 17. Patent Books, Volume P. Photocopies of penned documents. Pennsylvania State Archives, Harrisburg.

Pennsylvania. Fayette County. Records of the Land Office. Record Group 17. Ledgers and Journals. Photocopies of penned documents. Pennsylvania State Archives, Harrisburg.

Pennsylvania. Fayette County. Records of the Land Office. Record Group 17. Survey Books. Photocopies of penned documents. Pennsylvania State Archives, Harrisburg.

Pennsylvania. Fayette County. Recorder of Deeds. Deed Books. Photocopies of penned documents. Uniontown, Pennsylvania.

Pennsylvania. Westmoreland County. Recorder of Deeds. Deed Books. Photocopies of penned documents. Greensburg, Pennsylvania.

Pennsylvania State Archives. Harrisburg. Series 3. Volume I. "Minutes of Board of Property." William Davidson v. John Stokely. Digital copy of transcript. *Fold3.com.* http://www.fold3 .com : October 2012.

MAPS:

Arrowsmith & Lewis. *Seventh American Map of Delaware.* Engraved by Lawson. Boston: Thomas and Andrews, 1804. State Map Collection. Resource Identifier 325-003-203-0023. Digital copy. *Delaware Public Archives, Dover.* http://archives.delaware.gov : accessed November 2015.

William "Ranger" Davidson

Atlas of the County of Fayette and the State of Pennsylvania. Philadelphia: G.M. Hopkins & Co., 1872. Digital copy. *USGenWeb Archives.* http://www .usgwarchives.net/maps/pa/county/fayett/1872/luzerne.jpg : accessed 2015.

Atlas of Lawrence County, Ohio, Hardesty 1882 and Lake 1887 (Combined), 1st edition. Reprint. Ironton, Ohio: Lawrence County Historical Society, 1985.

Cade, Douglas E., PE, PS (Lawrence County Engineer), *Highway Map of Lawrence County, Ohio,* 2012.

Campbell, John H., Chief Draftsman. *Warrantee Township Map.* Harrisburg, Pennsylvania: Records of the Land Office, 1920. Pennsylvania State Archives, Record Group 17, Series 17.522. Digital copy. *Commonwealth of Pennsylvania's Enterprise Portal.* http://www.portal.state.pa.us.

Genealogical Map of the Counties, Eleventh edition, 1999. Harrisburg, Pennsylvania: Compiled and prepared in the Land Office, 1933. Pennsylvania State Archives. Digital copy. *Commonwealth of Pennsylvania's Enterprise Portal.* http://www.portal .state.pa.us/ : accessed January 2011.

Long, John H., ed. *Atlas of Historical Counties: Delaware.* Chicago, Illinois: The Newberry Library, 2010. Digital images. *The Newberry Library.* http://publications.newberry .org/ahcbp/index.html.

Long, John H., ed. *Atlas of Historical Counties: Ohio.* Chicago, Illinois: The Newberry Library, 2010. Digital copy. *The Newberry Library.* http://publications.newberry.org/ahcbp/index.html.

Long, John H., ed. *Atlas of Historical Counties: Pennsylvania.* Chicago, Illinois: The Newberry Library, 2010. Digital images. *The Newberry Library.* http://publications.newberry.org/ahcbp/index.html.

OpenStreetMap. http://www.openstreetmap.org/. Available under the Open Database License. See also, https://www.openstreetmap.org/copyright.

Whipple, Levi [surveyor]. *Township Survey Plat Map of 1798.* Twp. Plats - OH, Ohio River Survey, R. 17, T. 1 & 2. Record group 49. Digital copy on compact disc, 2012. National Archives and Records Administration. Special Media Archive Services Division (NWCS). Cartographic and Architectural Branch (NNSC), College Park, Maryland.

Bibliography

NEWSPAPER ARTICLES & OBITUARIES:

"South Point." *Ironton Register.* 31 March 1853, Volume 3, No. 36, p. 2. Photocopied from microfilm. Hamner Room, Briggs Lawrence County Public Library, Ohio. This article announced the "new town" of South Point being "laid out" by Rev. William W. Davidson.

"Great Sale of Lots at South Point." *Ironton Register.* 31 March 1853, Volume 3, No. 36, p. 3. Photocopied from microfilm. Hamner Room, Briggs Lawrence County Public Library, Ohio. This article advertised the sale at public auction of "a large number of building lots" in the "newly laid out town on the Ohio River" to take place on 5 May 1853.

"South Point." *Ironton Register.* 12 May 1853, Volume 3, No. 42, p. 2. Photocopied from microfilm. Hamner Room, Briggs Lawrence County Public Library, Ohio. This article stated that the "first sale of lots at the new town of South Point...was well attended." Eighteen lots were sold for an average of just over $170 each.

"Obituary. Davidson. James Davidson." *Ironton Register.* 10 January 1895, Volume 46, No. 26, p. 5. Photocopied from microfilm. Hamner Room, Briggs Lawrence County Public Library, Ironton, Ohio.

REVOLUTIONARY WAR:

Pennsylvania State Archives. Harrisburg. Series 1. Volume IV.
———. Series 1. Volume VI.
———. Series 1. Volume VIII.
———. Series 2. Volume IV.
———. Series 3. Volume I.
———. Series 3. Volume II.
———. Series 3. Volume VII.
———. Series 3. Volume XXIII.
———. Series 4. Volume III.
———. Series 5. Volume IV.
———. Series 6. Volume II.
———. Series 6. Volume V.

Pennsylvania State Archives. Website: Pennsylvania Historic and Museum Commission. http://www.phmc.state.pa.us/ also http://www.phmc.pa.gov/. Various pages.

Roach, Hanna Benner, FGSP, FASG. "The Pennsylvania Militia in 1777." Reprint from *The Pennsylvania Genealogical Magazine*. Volume XXIII, Number 3, 1964. The reprint retains the page numbers as they appeared in the original article, pp. 161-230.

"United States Revolutionary War Pension and Bounty Land Warrant Applications, 1800-1900." *FamilySearch*. http://familysearch.org : accessed 7 July 2015. File for Joseph Pyles. Pension number S. 5169, service Penn. From "Revolutionary War Pension and Bounty-Land Warrant Application Files." Database and digital images. *Fold3.com*. http://www.fold3.com : n.d. Citing NARA microfilm publication M804, (Washington, D.C.: National Archives and Records Administration, 1974).

Wehmann, Howard H. "Revolutionary War Pension and Bounty – Land – Warrant Application Files: National Archives Microfilm Publications Pamphlet Describing M804." Washington: National Archives and Records Service. General Services Administration, 1974. Digital copy. *National Archives*. http://www.archives.gov/ : accessed 2011.

Westmoreland County. Militia Loan Accounts. Militia Loan Certificate Books. Certificate Registers. County Lieutenant Ledgers. State Ledger and Receipt Rolls. Records of the Office of the Comptroller General. Record Group 4. Pennsylvania State Archives. Harrisburg.

Westmoreland County. Return of Elections of Officers, 24 September 1783. Entry for William Davison. General Returns of the Militia (Continental Line), Not Arranged. Military Returns, 1777-1790, Series 27.33. Supreme Executive Council, 1770 to 1790. Records of Pennsylvania's Revolutionary Governments, Record Group 27. Photocopy of penned document obtained July 2011. Pennsylvania State Archives, Harrisburg.

Westmoreland Militia. *Revolutionary War Military Abstract Card*, Number 2569. Revolutionary War Military Abstract Card File, 1785-1893. Series 13.50, Record Group 13. Pennsylvania State Archives, Harrisburg. Online database and digital images. *fold3.com*. http://www.fold3.com : accessed 2008.

TAX RECORDS IN OHIO:

Tax Duplicate 1801. "Ohio Tax Records, 1800-1850." Digital images of penned documents. *FamilySearch*. https://familysearch.org/ : accessed November

2012. Citing Auditor, Gallipolis Township, Washington County, Ohio Historical Society Library, Columbus.

Tax Duplicate 1802. "Ohio Tax Records, 1800-1850," Digital images of penned documents. *FamilySearch*. https://familysearch.org/ : accessed November 2012. Citing Gallipolis Township, Washington County, Ohio Historical Society Library, Columbus.

TAX RECORDS IN PENNSYLVANIA:

Pennsylvania. Bedford County, *1773-1775, 16th, 17th, 18th of the 18 Penny Tax*. Tax and Exoneration Lists, 1762-1794, Series 4.61. Records of the Office of the Comptroller General, Record Group 4. *Springhill Township, 1773*. Pennsylvania State Archives, Harrisburg.

Pennsylvania. Cumberland County. *Tax Rates. 1768, 1769, 1770* [Book 004]. Cumberland Township. Digital copy of penned documents online, *Tax Rates Book, 1768-1770*. Commissioners Record Series. *Cumberland County Archives*. http://records.ccpa.net : accessed January 2016. Carlisle, Pennsylvania.

Pennsylvania. Cumberland County. *Tax Rates. 1771-1772* [Book 005]. "Cumberland rates 1771." Digital copy of penned document online. *Tax Rates Book, 1736-1930*. Commissioners Record Series. *Cumberland County Archives*. http://records.ccpa.net : accessed January 2016. Carlisle, Pennsylvania.

Pennsylvania. Fayette County. Luzerne Township. *1785 Supply Tax*. Digital images of penned documents. Pennsylvania, Tax and Exoneration, 1768-1801. Digital images of penned documents. *Ancestry*. http://www .ancestry.com : accessed 2011. Citing Microfilm Roll: 327, Tax & Exoneration Lists, 1762–1794, Series 4.61; Records of the Office of the Comptroller General, Record Group 4. Pennsylvania State Archives, Harrisburg.

Pennsylvania. Fayette County. Luzerne Township. *Pennsylvania, U.S. Direct Tax Lists, 1798*. Schedules *A, B, D,* and *E*. Digital images of penned documents. *Ancestry*. http://www.ancestry.com : accessed 2011. Citing microfilm M372, Tax Lists for the State of Pennsylvania, Records of the Internal Revenue Service, 1791-2006, Record Group 58. National Archives and Records Administration, Washington, D.C.

William "Ranger" Davidson

Pennsylvania. Westmoreland County. Menallen Township. *1783 Supply Tax.* Digital images of penned documents. Pennsylvania, Tax and Exoneration, 1768-1801. Digital images of penned documents. *Ancestry.* http://www .ancestry.com : accessed 2011. Citing Microfilm Roll: 341, Tax & Exoneration Lists, 1762–1794, Series 4.61. Records of the Office of the Comptroller General, Record Group 4. Pennsylvania State Archives, Harrisburg.

Schaumann, Merri Lou Scribner. *Tax Lists - Cumberland County, Pennsylvania, 1768, 1769, 1770.* Carlisle, Pennsylvania: 1972.

WILLS:

Delaware. Sussex County. Sussex County Probate. Record Group 4545.009: 1755-1796. Delaware Public Archives. Dover. Digital images of typewritten and penned documents.

Indiana. Vermillion County. District and Probate Courts. "Vermillion County, Indiana, Will Records, 1829-1929." Digital images of penned documents. *Ancestry.* https://www.ancestry.com.

Maryland. Allegany County. County Courts. "Maryland Probate Estate and Guardianship Files." Digital images of penned documents. *FamilySearch.* https://familysearch.org.

Maryland. Allegany County. Cumberland Courthouse. "Maryland Register of Wills Records, 1629-1999." Digital images of penned documents. *FamilySearch.* https://familysearch.org.

Ohio. Franklin County. Columbus. Probate Court. "Estate Accounts, 1803-1879, 1977." Digital images of penned documents. *Ohio History Connection.* http://catalog.ohiohistory.org.

Ohio. Gallia County. Gallipolis. Register of Wills. Will Books. Photocopies of penned documents.

Ohio. Harrison County. Cadiz. Probate Court. "Ohio, Wills and Probate Records, 1786-1998." Digital images of penned documents. *Ancestry.* https://www.ancestry.com.

Bibliography

Ohio. Lawrence County. Record of Wills. "Ohio Probate Records, 1789-1996." Digital images of Penned documents. *FamilySearch*. https://familysearch.org.

Pennsylvania. Fayette County. Orphans' Court Records. "Pennsylvania Probate Records, 1683-1994." Digital images of penned documents. *FamilySearch*. https://familysearch.org.

Pennsylvania. Fayette County. Uniontown. Register of Wills. Will Books. Photocopies of penned documents.

Pennsylvania. Greene County. "Will Books, 1796-1918; Index to Wills and Estates, 1796-1967." Digital images of penned documents. *Ancestry*. https://www.ancestry.com.

West Virginia. Ohio County. "West Virginia Will Books, 1756-1971." Digital images of penned documents. *FamilySearch*. https://familysearch.org.

SOME OTHER SOURCES NOT ELSEWHERE CITED:

Bowers, Ruth and Anita Short. *Gateway to the West*, Volume I. Legal notice recorded 8 September 1812 from the probate of the estate of William Davidson. Baltimore, MD: Genealogical Publishing Company, 1989. Citing "Will Estate and Guardianship Book 1 & 2" as found in the Probate Court of Gallia County, Ohio, the period of 1803-1815. Bartow Genealogical and Historical Library, Bartow, Florida, 2007.

Brewer, Mary Marshall. *Land Records of Sussex County Delaware (1753-1763)*. Westminster, Maryland: Heritage Press, 2008.

Commonwealth of Pennsylvania 1909, Official Documents, Vol. III. Harrisburg, PA.: C. E. Aughinbaugh, Printer to the State of Pennsylvania, 1910. Digital version from print, pp. 32a-34a. *Google Books*. http://books.google.com : accessed 2011. Includes a map of the various land purchases made by Pennsylvania. Also, discusses a boundary dispute in 1909 affecting the land entries of both Lewis and son Thomas Davidson and includes a portion of the Warrantee Township Map showing the tracts involved. Although the case is unrelated genealogically, the information is of interest as it discusses some of the details of the Davidson surveys.

William "Ranger" Davidson

Creigh, Alfred. *History of Washington County*, 2nd Edition. Harrisburg, PA: B. Singerly, Printer, 1871. Digital version. *Books Google*. http://books .google.com : accessed April 2011.

Drescher, Seymour and Stanley Engerman. *A Historical Guide to World Slavery*, 1st ed. New York: Oxford University Press, 1998.

Fields, Helen S. *Register of Marriages and Baptisms Performed by John Cuthbertson.* 1934, Reprint. Baltimore, Maryland: Clearfield Company by Genealogical Publishing Company, 2009. Particularly pages 70-71; includes a transcript of the baptism of Rosanna Hutchinson, first wife of William Davidson.

Green, Karen Mauer. *Pioneer Ohio Newspapers, 1802-1818: Genealogical and Historical Abstracts*. Galveston: Frontier Press, 1988. Citing "The Scioto Gazette," Volume XIII, No. 725, Monday, January 30, 1815. Bartow Genealogical and Historical Library, Bartow, FL. This legal notice lists the surviving children of William Davidson who engaged in legal proceedings relating to William Davidson's estate.

Malone, Johnita P. *Land Records of Sussex County, Delaware, Deed Book G No. 7 (1732-1743)*. Westminster, Maryland: Heritage Books, 2008.

Merriam-Webster Online Dictionary. http://www.merriam-webster.com : accessed 2015, "presentism."

Powell, Esther Weygandt. Early Ohio Tax Records: Reprinted with "The Index to Early Ohio Tax Records." 1971.

Riegel, Mayburt Stephenson. *Early Ohioans' residences from the land grant records.* 1976, Republished, Provo, UT: The Generations Network, Inc., 2005. *Ancestry*. http://www.ancestry.com : accessed March 2013. Particularly page 36, which lists William Davidson as a patent holder in Lawrence County, Ohio.

www.ingramcontent.com/pod-product-compliance
Lightning Source LLC
Chambersburg PA
CBHW062200270326
41930CB00009B/1602